# Voices of the Civil War

# Voices of the Civil War · Chattanooga

*By the Editors of Time-Life Books, Alexandria, Virginia*

# Contents

8 Bitter Fruits of Defeat . . . and of Victory

*Opening the Cracker Line*

48 Bloody Sideshow at Knoxville

70 The Battles for Chattanooga

*Lookout Mountain*

*Missionary Ridge*

142 Tennessee in Union Hands

160 *Glossary*

161 *Acknowledgments*

162 *Picture Credits*

163 *Bibliography*

165 *Index*

# THE FIELD AT CHATTANOOGA

*For two months after the Battle of Chickamauga, the victorious Confederates besieged the vanquished Federals, who had holed up in Chattanooga. In late November 1863 the Yankees, now under Grant, drove Bragg's army from its positions atop Lookout Mountain and Missionary Ridge, breaking the siege and pushing the Rebels into Georgia. This artist's rendering depicts the rugged setting of the struggle.*

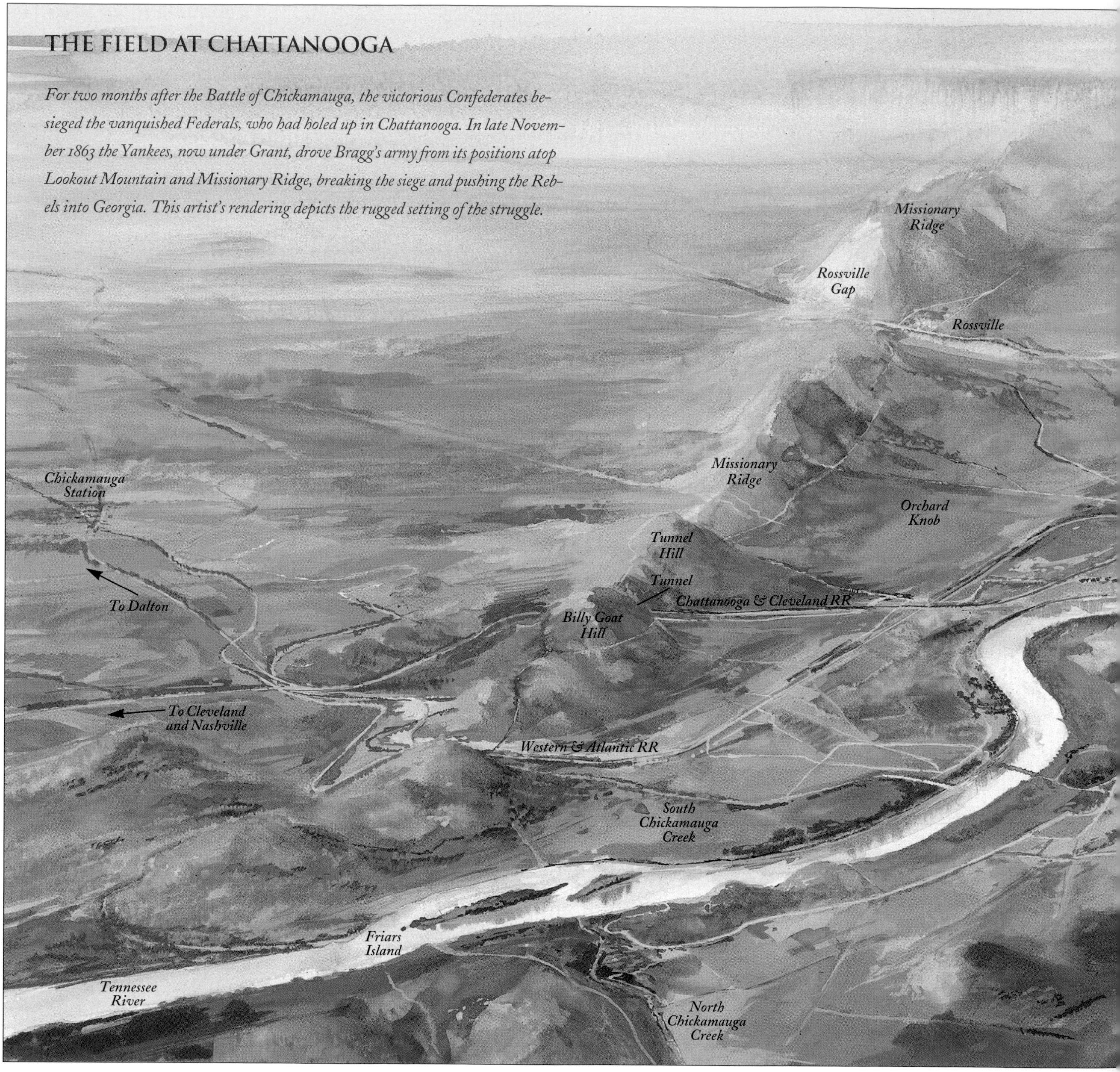

S
N
The Palisades
Chattanooga Valley
Lookout Valley
To Bridgeport
Lookout Mountain
Wauhatchie
Chattanooga Creek
Nashville & Chattanooga RR
Lookout Creek
Ross Tow Head
Moccasin Point
Kelley's Ferry
Chattanooga
Cameron Hill
Raccoon Mountain
Brown's Ferry
hattanooga Island
Tennessee River
Williams Island
Walden's Ridge

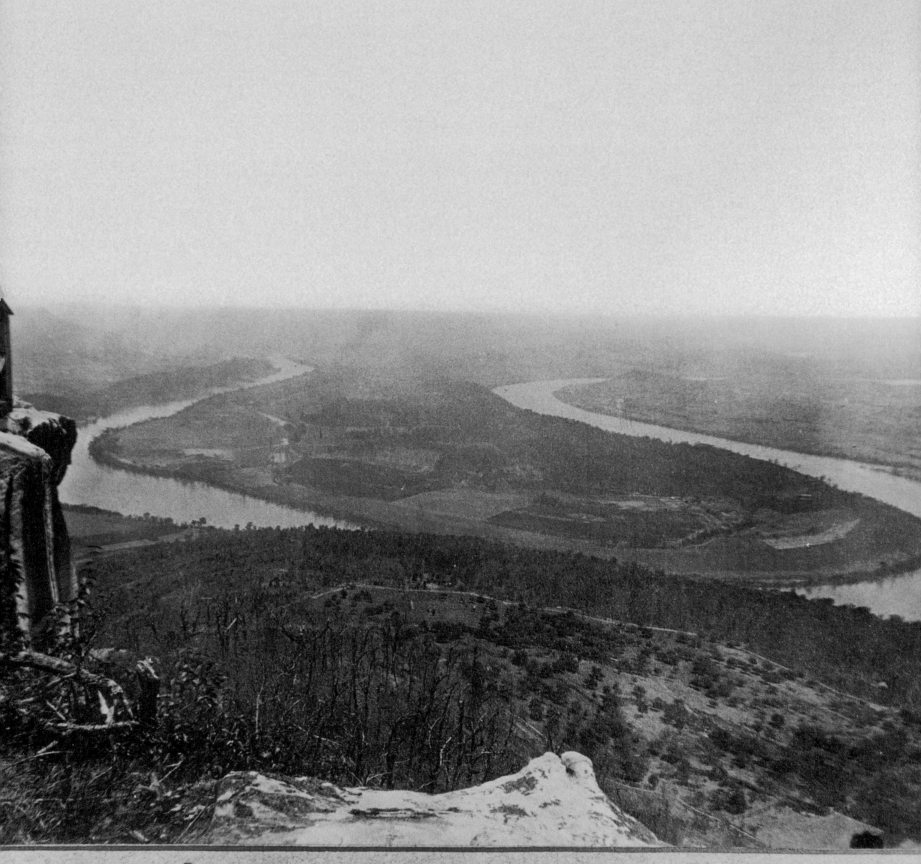

Moccasin Point, Tennessee River; looking down from Lookout Mountain

# Bitter Fruits of Defeat ... and of Victory

When Major General William S. Rosecrans, commander of the Federal Army of the Cumberland, maneuvered General Braxton Bragg and his Confederate Army of Tennessee out of Chattanooga without firing a shot in early September 1863, it marked the third time in nine months that Rosecrans had outgeneraled his adversary. Coming on the heels of Union victories at Vicksburg and Gettysburg, the seizure of the strategic little city on the east bank of the Tennessee River in southeastern Tennessee—the junction point of several of the South's most important railroads—sparked elation in the North and anxiety in the South. Chattanooga was popularly known as the Gateway to the South. President Abraham Lincoln, with little exaggeration, had termed its capture "fully as important as the taking and holding of Richmond."

Rosecrans' feat, combined with the seizure of Knoxville by Major General Ambrose E. Burnside's Army of the Ohio on September 2, provided the Army of the Cumberland with an ideal staging base to carry the Union fight deep into the heart of Dixie. "With Rosecrans to lead," one of his junior officers exulted, "we think we can go anywhere in the Confederacy."

But this pronouncement would soon prove wildly inaccurate. The real struggle for Chattanooga had scarcely begun.

Less than two weeks after Rosecrans' coup, Southern hopes rebounded, as General Bragg and his Army of Tennessee struck back with a vengeance. Reinforced by troops of Lieutenant General James Longstreet, who had been transported through the Carolinas and Georgia by rail from Robert E. Lee's Army of Northern Virginia, Bragg confronted Rosecrans yet again. This time the setting was a little creek tucked into the corner of northwest Georgia, about 12 miles southeast of Chattanooga. The Cherokee had named it Chickamauga, often translated as River of Blood.

On the morning of September 19, a brigade of Rebel cavalry led by General Nathan Bedford Forrest splashed across the Chickamauga and unexpectedly collided with a brigade of infantry on the extreme left of the Federal

*From heights such as this Lookout Mountain perch over Moccasin Point on the Tennessee River, General Braxton Bragg's Rebels controlled nearly all routes to Chattanooga (right center), thus throttling the flow of supplies to the Union army in the town.*

line. The battle began and with each passing hour increased in fury. Both generals fed division after division into the fray until 120,000 men were engaged—the Confederates having a slight numerical advantage. All day long, Yankee and Rebel lines surged bloodily back and forth in an area less than five miles wide and so densely wooded that it was often nearly impossible to distinguish friend from foe. A Union officer described the fighting as a "mad, irregular battle, very much resembling guerrilla warfare on a vast scale, in which one army was bushwhacking the other."

On the second day, Sunday, September 20, fortune smiled on the Confederates. At 11:30 that morning, General Longstreet launched 16,000 men against the Federal right. Just as the Rebel attack was about to begin, Rosecrans made one of the most disastrous battlefield errors of the war. Mistakenly thinking that a gap existed on his left, he ordered the division of Brigadier General Thomas J. Wood, which happened to be directly in the path of the imminent onslaught, to shift to the north. Wood pulled his men out of the line, and in a matter of minutes Longstreet's juggernaut smashed through the hole thus opened. "On they rushed," recalled one Confederate officer, "shouting, yelling, running over batteries, capturing trains, taking prisoners."

The Federal right was quickly rolled up. Thousands of Yankees began a panic-stricken flight back toward Chattanooga through a gap in the hills to the north. With them went Rosecrans himself. Only a heroic stand by an assortment of units from three different corps organized by Major General George H. Thomas—who would ever after be known as the Rock of Chickamauga—prevented a total rout.

That night, after fighting off assault after assault—Longstreet alone estimated that he launched 25 attacks—Thomas executed a skillful withdrawal. Bragg declined to pursue his beaten enemy, and by September 22 the entire Army of the Cumberland was safely back inside the Chattanooga defenses.

Bragg's failure to follow up his victory frustrated and enraged many of his officers, who held that precious time had been wasted and a golden opportunity thrown away. "What does he fight battles for?" snarled the ferociously combative Forrest. Longstreet, for one, had made preparations for more action. "I ordered my line to remain as it was," he later recalled, "ammunition boxes to be filled, stragglers to be collected, and everything in readiness for the pursuit in the morning."

But Bragg seemed to have good reasons for not continuing the fight. His men were exhausted, his ammunition and supplies low. And his losses had been horrific. Casualties on both sides numbered about 34,500, more than 18,000 of them Confederate, including nine brigade and two division commanders. Indeed, in terms of days of combat and numbers of troops engaged, no battle of the Civil War was bloodier than Chickamauga. When an officer pressed Bragg to drive on Chattanooga, the irascible North Carolinian shot back: "How can I? Here is two-fifths of my army left on the field, and my artillery is without horses."

Instead, Bragg decided to take Rosecrans under siege. He ordered his troops to occupy the steep and spiny heights looming above Chattanooga to the south—Raccoon Mountain, Lookout Mountain, and Missionary Ridge. All of them overlooked the Tennessee River and the main roads and the railroads leading to the city. By clamping a stranglehold on Federal supply lines, Bragg hoped to wait out Rosecrans and starve him into either withdrawal or submission.

Until Chickamauga, Rosecrans had been getting his supplies by rail from Nashville. The trains ran southeast to Stevenson, Alabama, on the Nashville & Chattanooga Railroad, and thence northeast through Bridgeport, Alabama, for a distance of 35 miles to Chattanooga on the Memphis & Charleston line, passing beneath Lookout Mountain. But now that the Confederates occupied the high ground overlooking the city, Federal supplies could be transported directly only as far as Bridgeport, 27 miles to the southwest. Bragg's men had destroyed the railroad bridge that crossed the river there, and his artillery and sharpshooters were zeroed in on the roads leading eastward.

The only safe route from Bridgeport was a roundabout dirt path that led some 40 miles up the wet and muddy Sequatchie Valley to Anderson's Crossroads, 20 miles northwest of Chattanooga. From there the route turned southeast and followed a steep, rocky, winding trail over Walden's Ridge and down to the north bank of the Tennessee opposite Chattanooga. There the Federals laid down a pontoon bridge to carry the goods over the river and into the city.

Before the siege the rail journey had taken about an hour; now the wagon road over Walden's Ridge took from eight to 20 backbreaking days, depending upon the weather. It was, one Union officer recalled, "the muddiest and the roughest and steepest ascent and descent ever crossed by army wagons and mules." Despite herculean efforts by scores of teamsters and thousands of mules, only a trickle of food, ammunition, medicine, new shoes, and warm clothing could get through to the city.

The route was also exposed to Confederate cavalry raids. Early in October, Major General Joseph Wheeler led a force of 5,000 riders behind the Federal lines. Over a nine-day period his troopers destroyed several railroad bridges, about 300 wagons, and more than 1,000 mules before finally being driven back across the Tennessee River.

As the siege continued, the Yankees went on starvation rations. Food grew so scarce that men stole corn from the horses and mules or hunted for it on the ground where the animals had eaten. "I have often seen hundreds of soldiers following behind the wagon trains which had just arrived," said correspondent W. F. G. Shanks of the *New York Herald,* "picking out of the mud the crumbs of bread, coffee, rice etc., which were wasted from the boxes and sacks by the rattling of the wagons over the stones."

The 3,500 civilian residents of Chattanooga suffered even more than the soldiers. They were not only hungry but living in squalor. Their once pretty and prosperous town had been turned into an army camp of 35,000 men jammed together in a tiny area of no more than one square mile. The soldiers, to obtain fuel for their campfires, tore down many of the town's frame houses, forcing the locals to live in makeshift huts. These, Shanks wrote, "surpassed in filth, number of occupants and general destitution the worst tenements in New York City."

Amid all the hardship—and with worse threatening—Rosecrans seemed almost paralyzed. Although he had ordered steamboats built and railroads repaired and begun discussing ways to improve his supply lines, he had no real plan to regain the initiative and break out of the beleaguered city. Much of his en-ergy seemed to be spent on seeking scapegoats for his failure at Chickamauga. Eventually two corps commanders, Generals Alexander M. McCook and Thomas L. Crittenden, were singled out and removed from their commands for allegedly abandoning the field after Longstreet's attack. A court of inquiry later cleared both men of any responsibility for the Federal defeat.

Only a few weeks earlier, Rosecrans had been riding high, having baffled and frustrated Bragg with a series of bold flanking moves. Now, bottled up in Chattanooga, he had become unnerved and unsure of himself. Assistant U.S. Secretary of War Charles A. Dana, who had been sent west by Secretary of War Edwin M. Stanton to keep an eye on the Army of the Cumberland, described the commanding general in a letter to Washington as "dazed and mazy" and "insensible to the impending danger."

President Lincoln did what he could to buck up his general. The very night that news of the Chickamauga debacle reached Washington, Lincoln had wired back words of encouragement, saying: "We have unabated confidence in you and in your soldiers and officers."

And Lincoln backed up his words with action, promptly ordering that heavy reinforcements be sent to the area. On September 25 Major General Joseph Hooker, who had been inactive since his shattering defeat at Chancellorsville five months before, left Manassas, Virginia, bound for Bridgeport, Alabama, with a 20,000-man command from the Army of the Potomac, consisting of Major General Henry W. Slocum's XII Corps and Major General Oliver O. Howard's XI Corps. And an additional four divisions totaling 17,000 men, under Major General William Tecumseh Sherman, were already on the march from Memphis and Vicksburg, with orders to repair the Memphis & Charleston Railroad as they came.

Through a series of telegrams, Lincoln tried to talk grand strategy with Rosecrans and convince him that the Army of the Cumberland still held the upper hand. After two years of failures at places like Bull Run, Fredericksburg, and Chancellorsville, the Union army had seen the war finally turn in its favor. By the fall of 1863, Union warships had clamped an ever tightening blockade around the major Southern ports, and Union armies controlled huge stretches of the South, including western Virginia, much of Tennessee, and parts of Arkansas and Louisiana, as well as most of the contested border states of Missouri and Kentucky.

Southern hopes of intervention from abroad were fast fading. The Emancipation Proclamation, which took effect on January 1, 1863, gave the Union the moral high ground with European governments, and the Union triumphs at Gettysburg and Vicksburg had convinced many that the Confederacy could no longer win the contest of arms. What was important strategically, Lincoln argued to Rosecrans, was not that the Army of the Cumberland had lost at Chickamauga but that Chattanooga and Knoxville remained firmly in the Union grasp. "If we can hold Chattanooga and East Tennessee," Lincoln told him, "I think the rebellion must dwindle and die."

But nothing could rouse the demoralized general, and he continued to move sluggishly. On October 12 the president sent yet another telegraph of encouragement: "You and Burnside now have the enemy by the throat, and he must break your hold or perish." But again Rosecrans' reply was one of tired resignation: "We must put our trust in God," he wired back, "who never fails those who truly trust." Sage words, perhaps, but completely lacking in the fighting spirit that the president so desperately wanted to see in Rosecrans. The commander of the Army of the Cumberland seemed incapable of coming to grips with the crisis. Chickamauga, Lincoln at last concluded, had left Rosecrans "stunned and confused, like a duck hit on the head."

Things were not markedly better on the Confederate side. Despite Bragg's great triumph, his command was in as much turmoil as Rosecrans', if not more. The top Rebel generals were in a state of open revolt against their commander. Almost to a man, they held him accountable for failing to exploit the victory at Chickamauga.

Like Rosecrans, Bragg had followed the battle with a purge of supposedly errant officers. Blaming General Leonidas Polk for a crucial delay on the morning of the battle's second day, Bragg relieved him and sent him to Atlanta to await orders. Bragg also sacked Major General Thomas C. Hindman.

Partly in self-defense, Bragg's subordinates mounted a campaign to have him replaced as commander of the Army of Tennessee. Arrayed against him was a formidable roster of generals, headed by Longstreet, Polk, Daniel Harvey Hill, and Simon Bolivar Buckner —all corps commanders. On October 4 these officers, as well as eight other generals commanding divisions or brigades, sent a joint letter to Jefferson Davis urging Bragg's removal.

"Two weeks ago this army, elated by a great victory, . . . was in readiness to pursue its defeated enemy," it read. "Today . . . it is certain that the fruits of the victory of the Chickamauga have now escaped our grasp. The Army of Tennessee, stricken with a complete paralysis, may deem itself fortunate if it escapes from its present position without disaster." The petitioners attributed this situation to the poor state of Bragg's health, which they said "unfits him for the command of an army in the field."

President Davis' initial reaction to the discord was to intercede on behalf of Polk, whom he liked. But Bragg not only refused to reinstate Polk, he preferred formal charges against him. These were dropped by the war department, and Polk was restored to his command, but he was unwilling to serve any longer under Bragg. As the uproar grew, Davis boarded a train in Richmond for the long journey to Bragg's headquarters in northwest Georgia.

Davis arrived on October 9. That night he presided over a most peculiar and awkward council of the war. Except for Polk, whose place was taken by Major General Benjamin F. Cheatham, all the corps commanders were present—as was Bragg. After a discussion of the military situation, Davis asked for comment on Bragg's fitness to command. Since Bragg himself was there, staring stonily at the wall, the situation was extremely uncomfortable. When Davis insisted on a response, Longstreet declared, as he later recalled, "that our commander could be of greater service elsewhere." The other corps commanders concurred.

On this note the meeting ended. Bragg must have been profoundly humiliated, but his feelings were assuaged by a piece of information that the other officers did not have: Before the session Davis had assured Bragg that he would not be relieved of command. Davis was one of the few people who genuinely liked the harsh-tempered general. Besides, the president could not come up with anyone to replace Bragg as commander of the Army of Tennessee. Even before leaving Richmond, Davis had concluded that there was no one else to whom he could entrust the command.

Having made that decision, Davis dealt with the command problems simply by demoting or replacing all those opposed to Bragg. The Army of Tennessee was reorganized into three corps. Polk was assigned to General Joseph E. Johnston's Alabama-Mississippi department in exchange for Lieutenant General William J. Hardee, who returned to the Army of Tennessee as a corps commander. Simon Buckner was reduced from corps commander to division commander and was soon after granted a leave of absence. Daniel Harvey Hill was suspended and sent home, and his corps turned over to Major General John C. Breckinridge, who, although an implacable foe of Bragg's, had not signed the petition that sought his removal. Bragg then relented in one case, returning Thomas Hindman to command under Breckinridge.

It was obviously impossible to dispose so easily of Longstreet, one of the most able and respected generals in the entire Confederate army. Longstreet was stripped of several divisions—he kept only his two from Virginia—but neither Davis nor Bragg could have demoted the general without setting off a furor throughout the Confederacy.

While the wrangling among brother generals continued for most of October, little action took place between the Yankees and the Rebels. "The two armies are lying face to face," wrote Union brigadier general John Beatty. "The Federal and Confederate sentinels walk their beats in sight of each other. The tents of the troops dot the hillsides. We see their signal lights on the summit of Lookout Mountain and on the knobs of Mission Ridge." Now and again Confederate artillerymen lobbed a shell or two into Chattanooga, and a sharpshooter or two took an occasional potshot, but most of the time the soldiers did little except watch each other. Some fraternized, swapping Rebel tobacco for Yankee coffee, trading newspapers and friendly insults, and exchanging gossip.

But soon all that would change and the war resume in earnest. On October 19 President Lincoln and Secretary of War Stanton abruptly revamped the entire command structure in the West, creating a unified new command known as the Military Division of the Mississippi. But more significant than the reorganization was Lincoln's decision about who would lead the new command—the one Union general who had proved he could win battles, Major General Ulysses S. Grant. Grant's forces would consist of his own Army of the Tennessee, the Army of the Cumberland, and Burnside's Army of the Ohio. In making this choice, Lincoln set in motion a chain of events that would, by turns, break the Confederate siege of Chattanooga, drive the Rebels clean out of Tennessee, and set the stage for a scourging Yankee progression through Georgia to the Atlantic Ocean.

Grant learned of his new assignment from Stanton in Louisville, where he had been summoned from his command at Vicksburg. Told that he could keep Rosecrans at the head of the Army of the Cumberland or replace him with George H. Thomas, Grant didn't hesitate. He immediately fired off a telegraph to Chattanooga, relieving Rosecrans and ordering Thomas to "hold Chattanooga at all hazards." The Rock of Chickamauga replied: "We will hold the town until we starve."

When Grant reached Chattanooga on October 23 he personally toured the tortuous supply route. He then declared that his first order of business would be to organize a better system to feed the starving troops. Grant called the task "opening up the cracker line."

## CHRONOLOGY

| | |
|---|---|
| 1863 | |
| September 2 | *Burnside occupies Knoxville* |
| September 19-20 | *Battle of Chickamauga* |
| September 21-22 | *Rosecrans' defeated army falls back to Chattanooga* |
| September 23 | *Bragg begins siege of Chattanooga* |
| October 3 | *Hooker, with part of the Army of the Potomac, joins Rosecrans' forces* |
| October 16 | *Grant takes command of Military Division of the Mississippi, replaces Rosecrans with Thomas* |
| October 23 | *Grant assumes personal command at Chattanooga* |
| October 27 | *Federals capture Brown's Ferry* |
| October 28-29 | *Federals capture Wauhatchie in night attack* |
| October 30 | *Cracker Line opened* |
| November 4 | *Bragg orders Longstreet to Knoxville* |
| November 13 | *Sherman's Army of the Tennessee begins arriving at Bridgeport* |
| November 23 | *Thomas captures Orchard Knob* |
| November 24 | *Hooker captures Lookout Mountain* |
| November 25 | *Battle of Missionary Ridge* |
| November 27 | *Cleburne's stand at Ringgold Gap* |
| November 28 | *Confederates retreat to Dalton, Georgia* |
| November 29 | *Longstreet attacks Fort Sanders at Knoxville* |
| December 3 | *Sherman's relief force nears Knoxville; Longstreet withdraws* |

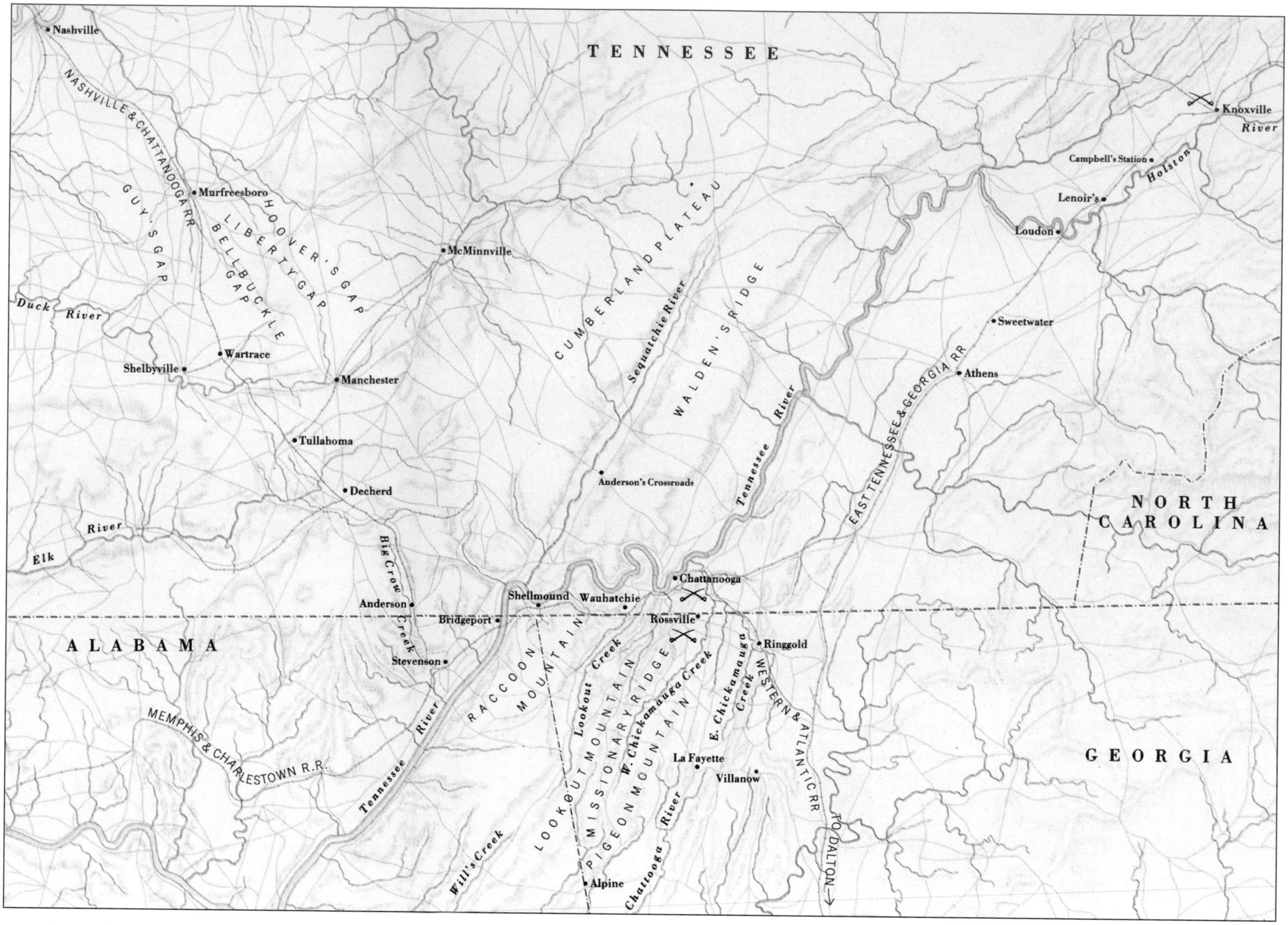


*By early October 1863 all of Tennessee but its extreme eastern part was in Federal hands. Ambrose Burnside held Knoxville, guarding the Cumberland Gap. William S. Rosecrans held Chattanooga, although under siege from Bragg's Confederates following the Federal defeat at Chickamauga. To break the stalemate at Chattanooga, President Lincoln placed Ulysses S. Grant in overall command and authorized Joseph Hooker, in Virginia, and William Tecumseh Sherman, on the Mississippi, to converge on Chattanooga. With Grant, Hooker, and Sherman in place, and Rosecrans replaced by George H. Thomas, the stage was set for a series of battles around Chattanooga, the so-called Gateway to the South.*

# ORDER OF BATTLE

## MILITARY DIVISION OF THE MISSISSIPPI (Federal)

Grant 86,000 men

### ARMY OF THE CUMBERLAND Thomas

**IV Corps Granger**

1st Division Cruft
*Whitaker's Brigade*
*Grose's Brigade*

2d Division Sheridan
*F. T. Sherman's Brigade*
*Wagner's Brigade*
*Harker's Brigade*

3d Division T. J. Wood
*Willich's Brigade*
*Hazen's Brigade*
*S. Beatty's Brigade*

**XIV Corps Palmer**

1st Division R. W. Johnson
*Carlin's Brigade*
*M. F. Moore's Brigade*
*Starkweather's Brigade*

2d Division J. C. Davis
*Morgan's Brigade*
*J. Beatty's Brigade*
*D. McCook's Brigade*

3d Division Baird
*Turchin's Brigade*
*Van Derveer's Brigade*
*Phelps' Brigade*

**XI Corps Howard**

2d Division von Steinwehr
*Buschbeck's Brigade*
*O. Smith's Brigade*

3d Division Schurz
*Tyndale's Brigade*
*Kryzanowski's Brigade*
*Hecker's Brigade*

**Engineer Troops W. F. Smith**

*Engineers*
*Pioneer Brigade*

**XII Corps**

2d Division Geary
*Candy's Brigade*
*Cobham's Brigade*
*Ireland's Brigade*

**Post of Chattanooga Parkhurst**

### ARMY OF THE TENNESSEE W. T. Sherman

**XV Corps Blair**

1st Division Osterhaus
*C. R. Woods' Brigade*
*Williamson's Brigade*

2d Division M. L. Smith
*G. A. Smith's Brigade*
*Lightburn's Brigade*

4th Division Ewing
*Loomis' Brigade*
*Corse's Brigade*
*Cockerill's Brigade*

**XVII Corps**

2d Division J. E. Smith
*Alexander's Brigade*
*Raum's Brigade*
*Matthies' Brigade*

## ARMY OF TENNESSEE (Confederate)

Bragg 49,000 men

**Longstreet's Corps (16,000 men—Detached November 4 for Knoxville)**

McLaws' Division
*Kershaw's Brigade*
*Humphreys' Brigade*
*Ruff's Brigade*
*Bryan's Brigade*

Jenkins' Division
*Bratton's Brigade*
*Robertson's Brigade*
*Law's Brigade*
*G. T. Anderson's Brigade*
*Benning's Brigade*

**Breckinridge's Corps**

Cleburne's Division
*Govan's Brigade*
*J. A. Smith's Brigade*
*Polk's Brigade*
*Lowrey's Brigade*

Stewart's Division
*Gibson's Brigade*
*Strahl's Brigade*
*Holtzclaw's Brigade*
*Stovall's Brigade*

Bate's Division
*Lewis' Brigade*
*Tyler's Brigade*
*Florida Brigade*

Stevenson's Division
*Brown's Brigade*
*Cumming's Brigade*
*Pettus' Brigade*
*Vaughn's Brigade*

**Hardee's Corps**

Cheatham's Division
*J. K. Jackson's Brigade*
*J. C. Moore's Brigade*
*Walthall's Brigade*
*Wright's Brigade*

P. Anderson's Division
*Tucker's Brigade*
*Manigault's Brigade*
*Deas' Brigade*
*Vaughan's Brigade*

B. R. Johnson's Division
*Fulton's Brigade*
*Gracie's Brigade*
*Reynolds' Brigade*

Gist's Division
*Maney's Brigade*
*McCullough's Brigade*
*Wilson's Brigade*

# "Morning after morning, our skirmish line advanced, hoping to find the enemy gone during the night, but no, there he was still ready to receive us."

## BRIGADIER GENERAL ARTHUR M. MANIGAULT

Brigade Commander, Army of Tennessee

*The urbane Manigault was born into a wealthy South Carolina planter family in 1824. Like many men of his class, he served in a militia company in his youth and saw extensive action during the Mexican War—as a lieutenant in the Palmetto Regiment. At Chattanooga, Manigault's brigade and the rest of the Army of Tennessee could find no weak points in the Union defenses, and the Confederates soon resigned themselves to the slow work of laying siege to the city.*

Our lines were soon extended around the place, pickets and videttes thrown out, and the investment of Chattanooga was begun, our forces reaching from the river west of the town to the same stream east and above it, the enemy having the river at their rear and the country opposite in their possession. We were not strong enough to encircle it completely, or to divide our army by sending a portion of it across the river, a wide, deep, and rapid one. For many days it was confidently expected that the enemy would be forced to evacuate the place, and it was not believed that he could possibly supply and sustain himself there, as he had no railroad, that being in our possession, and the difficulty of hauling provisions a distance of eighty miles over a miserable road, forty miles of which was through the mountains and over them, was deemed impracticable, but still they held on. On several occasions, strong reconnoitring parties felt their position, but found their works fully manned and very complete. Unfortunately, we had done most of it for them. Morning after morning, our skirmish line advanced, hoping to find the enemy gone during the night, but no, there he was still ready to receive us. After a week or two, our pickets ceased firing at each other. Occasionally artillery on either side would open, but the sharpshooters sat down or walked their posts within three or four hundred yards of each other, perfectly exposed to view and offering a most tempting target; but the understanding between them was that as the siege, investment, or whatever it may be termed, promised to be a long one, and as no really active operations were going on on either side, there was no use to make themselves uncomfortable, and it would be more agreeable to watch each other without trying to kill, than to be necessarily engaged in that disagreeable duty, where one invariably ran a great risk of never getting back to his messmates again; so that for very nearly two months, an officer might inspect his lines and discharge his regular duty on the outposts without any misgivings or disagreeable apprehensions.

*Although marred by several stains, this Adolph Metzner watercolor of the Chattanooga region dramatically illustrates the commanding, cloud-ringed heights of Lookout Mountain and the sharp sweep of Missionary Ridge, seen on the horizon to the left. Both promontories were soon dotted with Confederate entrenchments and gun positions that frowned ominously down upon the Army of the Cumberland. The domination of the heights over the Union position at Chattanooga is further symbolized by the diminutive rows of Yankee tents the artist scattered about in the foreground and middle distance.*

## PRIVATE ALEXANDER R. THAIN

### 96th Illinois Infantry, Whitaker's Brigade

*In this account Thain describes the layout of Moccasin Point, a peninsula formed by a loop of the Tennessee River directly opposite Lookout Mountain. Though the sporadic long-range artillery exchanges described here caused few casualties, the mere idea of a cannonball traveling from the summit of Lookout Mountain into one's tent had a demoralizing effect on the Yankees camped in the mountain's shadow.*

Our brigade withdrew from Missionary Ridge on the night of September 21, and on the 22d we marched through Chattanooga, crossed to the north bank of the river and encamped on Moccasin Point. This memorable piece of ground lies within a loop of the Tennessee at the northern extremity of Lookout Mountain, its shape bearing some resemblance to an Indian moccasin, the tow being thrust between Lookout and Chattanooga and the heel lying down toward Brown's Ferry.

The side of the point which lies next to the mountain is low and fertile, and prior to our occupancy had been covered with a fine crop of corn and beans which, fortunately for us, had been somewhat carelessly harvested. Our camp was situated several hundred yards from the river, nearly opposite the northern base of the mountain, and a little distance behind the camp rose a considerable ridge—the instep of the moccasined foot—on which was posted the 18th Ohio Battery. This loud-mouthed neighbor occasioned us a good deal of anxiety during our stay on the point. As soon as it was securely sheltered by strong works it began to talk to the mountain in a very emphatic way, and Lookout wrinkled its rocky brows and began to talk back. These occasional dialogues would not have troubled us in the least if the principal parties had kept the conversation exclusively to themselves, but the Boanerges who held forth from behind Pulpit Rock on the crest of Lookout had an inconvenient way at times of talking at large to the whole camp. At such times he had many listeners who paid very close attention to his remarks, but who fervently wished that he would bring his fire-and-brimstone preaching to a speedy close. The northeast side of a tree was the favorite point for listening, and a puff of smoke on the point of the mountain was the signal that a monosyllabic remark, in the shape of a shell, would, in a few seconds, utter itself somewhere on the point, and the question was—*where!*

*A lone Yankee surveys a small section of the bombproofs and shelters constructed by the Rebels on Lookout Mountain. This photograph was taken sometime after the mountain had fallen into the hands of Major General Joseph Hooker's Federals.*

## CAPTAIN GEORGE T. TODD

1ST TEXAS INFANTRY, ROBERTSON'S BRIGADE

*The soldiers of the Army of Northern Virginia's Texas Brigade were renowned for their fighting prowess, but two and a half years of hard campaigning had greatly reduced this proud unit's strength. On October 18, 1863, about midway through the siege, Todd resigned his commission because only four men remained fit for duty in his company and he saw no prospect of obtaining new recruits.*

We staid there besieging the town two months. The federals erected a battery across the river on Moccasin Point, made by a bend in the Tennessee River, and every night, when they knew we had left the trenches and were asleep in our dog tents exposed to their fire, opened on some portion of our lines which formed a crescent around the city. In this way they killed and crippled some confederates before they could get under cover of the works. We became so accustomed to this nightly serenade that we only opened one ear to see what part of the line was selected, and if not near us went to sleep again.

One night, however, this scribe has cause never to forget. As Captain of Company A, with one of the men, J. L. Allen, I was in sound sleep in my little tent 20 feet from the "bomb-proof," when a shell from the federal battery burst in Company K adjoining us. The cries of a wounded man aroused Allen, and he woke me and said we had better "git" to cover. I answered that we had better wait for the next shot before getting up, but he insisted, and I rose to a sitting position, and was pulling on my boots when the next shot came striking the tent at my side, and passing across my knapsack where my head was resting the minute before, struck the ground between Allen's feet as he stepped from the tent, and without exploding entered the earth. We didn't wait any longer before rushing for our "bomb-proof." Next morning the boys dug up a ten-pound steel-pointed parrott shell at a depth of 8 feet. This was only one instance of many narrow escapes from sudden death.

## LIEUTENANT SPILLARD F. HORRALL

42D INDIANA INFANTRY, CARLIN'S BRIGADE

*Horrall describes the trading that was common during the siege of Chattanooga even though the high commands of both sides officially prohibited fraternization. Bartering of foodstuffs slackened as Rebels and Yankees alike ran short of rations, but a lively exchange of tobacco, coffee, and newspapers continued.*

As brigade inspector, [I] always had charge of the picket line in our brigade front. For days and days the pickets of the two armies were exactly on opposite banks of Chattanooga creek; and not fifty yards apart for at least one-half of the brigade line.

On visiting the pickets for inspection one day, and on approaching a sentinel on one of the posts, it was observed that he had no gun in hand, and was unarmed at the edge of the water in the creek. It was likewise noticed that the rebel sentinel on the opposite side of the stream was unarmed, and in the same way was busy at something at the water's edge. Surprised beyond measure at such hazardous business while on duty by a sentinel, in the face of the enemy, this writer quickened his steps, and by all the authority at command demanded of the sentry;

"Well, you see this small piece of plank? This is our ship. We have named her 'Peace.' "

"What in thunder are you doing or daring to try to do?"

*Sentry* (very coolly): "Opening up trade and commerce with a foreign country."

"But I don't understand you, sir."

*Sentry* (composedly): "Well, you see this small piece of plank? This is our ship. We have named her 'Peace.' Now 'we'uns' on this side, as 'they all' say on that side, discovered that 'they all' on the other side had plenty of tobacco. Now 'we all' on this side have plenty of coffee, but 'they all' have none; and 'we all' no tobacco. Now we declared an armistice, established this line of communication, and, Lieutenant, see how it works?"

Saying this the comrade's ship was given the necessary propelling power, and the ship touched port on the other side, its cargo of coffee was unloaded, the ship reloaded with tobacco, and safely landed in port whence it started. The sentinel as he unloaded the tobacco triumphantly said:

"You see, Lieutenant, it is the simplest thing in the world. *'Reciprocity.'* See? Take a chew?"

Then shouldering his gun and bringing it to a "present," he resumed his duty, as the corporal of the guard bore away the tobacco to the "reserve."

## LIEUTENANT ROBERT M. COLLINS

### 15TH TEXAS CAVALRY (DISMOUNTED), J. A. SMITH'S BRIGADE

*Enlisting in February 1862, Collins was captured at the Battle of Arkansas Post on January 1, 1863. He was exchanged in the spring, fought at Chickamauga and Chattanooga, and was wounded in the battle at Peachtree Creek in 1864, although he recuperated in time to participate in the final months of the war. Collins considered the Rebel defeat at Chattanooga the "death-knell of the Confederacy."*

Being in the immediate presence of the enemy, we beat the Confederacy out of about six weeks' drilling. We put in a part of September, October and a part of November in guard duty. The writer's brigade was near the center of the line. Guard duty was pretty trying; our line of pickets was about two hundred yards from the Federal line; we could see their pickets plainly, and when no big officer on either side was near, we would sometimes get up a temporary armistice, lay down our arms and meet on half way grounds and have a nice friendly chat, swapping our flat tobacco for Lincoln coffee, our little 8x10 newspaper, "The Chattanooga Rebel," for their big blanket-sheet dailies, such as the New York Herald, Tribune, Cincinnati Times and Louisville Journal. Sometimes we would strike Federals on duty who would have none of us; these were generally Pennsylvania troops. We could always get along with Ohio and other western troops, but those first named and all other eastern troops always seemed to have a big red mad on.

Our bill of fare was pretty tough; corn-bread and poor beef was about all we had as a rule, and when the rule was suspended, it was generally by a day's rations of bacon. The writer's mess consisted of Capt. J. A. Farmwalt of Hood County, Texas, and Lieut. Jerry Johnson of Johnston County; Lieut. John Willingham belonged to it but he was generally at regimental headquarters acting as adjutant; we kept a cook hired, by the name of Ad Huffstuttler, at $30.00 per month in Confederate money; guess he was a Dutchman by his name, anyway he could forage and cook like one; he would prowl around the butcher pen, get beef heads, feet, liver, brains, sweet-breads, marrow, gut and other parts that we had always seen thrown away and make up messes nice enough for a king. He also done our washing and mending. When the day for the draw of old Ned came around as the boys called it, Capt. Farmwalt would be our head cook; he would fry the grease out of the bacon, and with our cornbread, water and the grease, make a dish he called "cush"; this with some of the cornbread burned to a black crisp, out of which we made coffee, was fine living; however we "reckon" the hard exercises each day and the total absence of anything like dyspepsia or indigestion was what made it all go down so well.

Der Krieg in Tennessee.— Einige mit Cedern-Zweigen bedeckte Rebellen versuchen die föderalen Vorposten bei Chattanooga zu überraschen. (Nach einer Skizze des Herrn C. E. F. Hillen.)

*This engraving depicts Rebels camouflaged with shrubbery advancing upon two Yankee pickets, who are less than fooled by the ruse and await the intruders with muskets at the ready. Although many soldiers passed their time on the picket line in friendly trading sessions with the enemy, relations could quickly turn hostile between the vedettes, as each side was continually probing the other's defenses for weak points during the siege. These sorties often provoked small but deadly exchanges of gunfire.*

## LIEUTENANT ALBION W. TOURGEE

105TH OHIO INFANTRY, VAN DERVEER'S BRIGADE

*Tourgée (above, right) had a military career that would have overcome most men. Confederate gunfire cost him his left eye at First Manassas, and after he recovered in his native state of Ohio, he joined the 105th in 1862. He survived spinal injury, capture, major battles, near starvation at Chattanooga, and arrests for insubordination before resigning in December 1863. During Reconstruction, Tourgée was a carpetbagger judge in North Carolina; he wrote several novels based on this experience.*

But if the bombardment was of little moment, an insidious foe which made much less noise, threatened us with something worse than mere defeat. On its arrival at Chattanooga the Army of the Cumberland had hardly ten days' rations. These, with very slight additions, were all that it had to subsist on for nearly forty days. A long and devious road, over sixty miles of mud and hill, exposed to frequent attacks of the enemy's cavalry, lay between Chattanooga and the line of supply, the railway from Nashville to Bridgeport. Over this only a meager and uncertain supply of food could be obtained. From the first we were on what was termed "half-rations"; soon these grew less until one or two hard-tack a day were all that were obtainable and by and by, the time came, when the good-natured quartermaster could make no farther excuse and the conscientious commissary sergeant in making a last issue, broke the fifth cracker in twain, as he issued his own ration—a little less than five for eight days! The whole five were hardly enough for a day—especially to men who for two weeks or more had not once had enough. Men picked up the kernels of corn scattered upon the ground where the few horses still left in the city were fed, and ate them. Officers who drew no rations, fared even worse, since there was nothing to buy. The hides and tails of the few cattle brought in to be slaughtered across the river were gladly pressed into service for food. A cow's tail found a ready market at $10. One mess of officers bought a fresh hide; removed the hair by some process before unknown and now forgotten, and by cooking it a long time made what is still declared by its partakers to have been a "savory mess." Duty and disease made heavy inroads upon men thus weakened. Starvation did not come, but his foot was at the opening of every tent. An officer . . . was detailed with his company to go with the train that brought in the first loads of corn. As the lean mules dragged them up the slippery slope from the bridge, crowds of gaunt men eyed the yellow ears hungrily. At length there was a rush—the wagons were overturned and every man caught what he could carry of the precious stuff and ran. Several wagonloads were thus "distributed" before one was allowed to pass. It was a terribly mutinous way of satisfying hunger, and the officer was put under arrest for not preventing it. There is no record of his punishment, and it is probable that his superiors regarded the offense, under the circumstances, as creditable rather than discreditable to him. The grim soldier, who was in command of the train, shouted for the men to fire upon their hungry comrades, but no one of his command heard the order.

## PRIVATE ESAU BEAUMONT

3D BATTERY, WISCONSIN LIGHT ARTILLERY

*Beaumont and his batterymates were still recovering from the mauling they took at Chickamauga, where they lost 26 men and five of six guns, when they were forced to confront near starvation at Chattanooga. Sergeant John D. Galloway, another member of the 3d, later recalled picking through boxes of wet, mushy, rancid hardtack, trying to find "an inch of sound cracker" to eat. Galloway described this time as the "darkest period" of the battery's service.*

Immediately our horse feed became scarce and grazing was soon used up. Some of the boys would crawl through the lines and pull grass for feed while they would be in the shelter of anything to screen them from sharpshooters. They would put the grass in corn sacks and drag them in behind themselves to our own lines. The rebels were within short range but never shot anyone, undoubtedly thinking it was surrender or starvation in a short time. The little corn soon disappeared and the horses in the best condition were sent to Bridgeport to save their lives. Many had already died tied to trees or posts, which they gnawed as long as they had strength. During the siege 10,000 horses and mules died of starvation.

All this time the besieged were throwing up entrenchments and continually strengthening the lines, heavier guns were placed in position and we were drawn into the outskirts of the town. The great problem now was how little a man could subsist on. It was really pitiful to see the men scratch over the ground where the mules had been fed to find a kernel of corn that might be trod in the mud (a horse does not look over ground closer or make cleaner work of a dirt pile). Many of the mules had to be sent to bring crackers over the mountains by packing. Others were being used to carry the wounded over the same mountains from the camp across the Tennessee, opposite Chattanooga, where the poor fellows were without food. Those who survived the trip were landed at Stevenson, Ala., only to receive a handful of cracker dust—not a very satisfying amount of food after riding in an army wagon over sixty miles of all sized stones.

We suffered with cold as the weather became severe. All stumps and shade trees to be found were dug up to burn. A large raft of logs was sent down the Tennessee river to destroy our pontoon bridge but our boys captured it, saved the bridge and made firewood of the logs.

Our rations kept diminishing, and we received but a pint of corn for three days' rations. We parched the corn, ground it in coffee mills and made a porridge of it. Frequently while preparing this dish, children of the miserably poor and destitute natives would drift into our camp and after wistfully gazing upon it would say, "I like cohn." Such pathetic appeals always resulted in their receiving a portion of the coarse and scant supply. A corn loaf of unsifted meal, baked in a common sized bake kettle, would be cut into 26 parts, and would sell for 50 cents a piece. Cow's heads divested of meat would bring $1. For soup purposes, animal tripes were eagerly eaten after a homely preparation.

*A muleteer leads a train of gaunt mules carrying Union supplies over the Anderson road, a rough trace across the barren, forbidding prominence west of Chattanooga known as Walden's Ridge. Pack animals, broken down by privation and harsh labor, died by the hundreds on this route, and their carcasses lined the roadway. Such conditions greatly reduced the flow of rations into the suffering city.*

# "It was really pitiful to see the men scratch over the ground where the mules had been fed to find a kernel of corn that might be trod in the mud."

## CAPTAIN IRVING A. BUCK

STAFF, MAJOR GENERAL PATRICK R. CLEBURNE

*Buck recounts Cleburne's polite but unalloyed view, expressed to President Jefferson Davis, that despite General Bragg's many merits as a soldier, his entire command had lost all confidence in him. Most of the generals who were transferred from Bragg's command later performed valuable service elsewhere in the army.*

The lack of confidence in General Bragg started with the close of the Kentucky campaign, grew with the retreat from Murfreesboro and evacuation of Middle Tennessee, and was intensified after Chickamauga to an extent that on October 4 a petition couched in respectful but firm language was addressed to President Davis, asking that another commander than General Bragg be assigned to the army. This was signed by a number of officers of high rank. On October 10 President Davis visited Missionary Ridge, and soon after called a meeting at General Bragg's headquarters, of these officers, and of each one in turn asked if he had signed such a petition, and, if so, to give his reasons therefor. This was a curious meeting: the president calling to the presence of the commanding general subordinates who had asked his removal; but none flinched or denied his own signature or hesitated to state reasons frankly. The most pronounced in opinion and expression were the two ranking officers present, and of the army. As there were no written minutes of this meeting it is difficult to give the exact language of each one's opinion, so that memory of the hearsay at the time has to be relied upon, and inference drawn from communications afterwards exchanged between some of those who were present. Therefore the details may not be absolutely stated, but the concensus of or rather the unanimous opinion as expressed, and here given, can be depended upon as substantially correct, viz.: that a change of commander was absolutely essential. The recollection as to Cleburne's reply is distinct—that, while he esteemed General Bragg a good organizer, disciplinarian, and a skillful soldier, the non-success attending the Kentucky, Tennessee, and Chickamauga campaigns had totally lost him the confidence of the army, and that no matter what his real ability as a general might be, this fact alone destroyed his usefulness, and his conviction was that a change was absolutely necessary. Some others of the signers did not handle the matter with the same delicacy of expression.

Meanwhile, Lieutenant-General Polk and Major-General Buckner had been suspended from command, and on the 15th of October, a few days after this meeting, Lieutenant-General Hill was relieved from duty with the army, and subsequently General Longstreet detached and sent to East Tennessee. Thus the four ranking officers of the army—with the exception of Cheatham—were removed or elsewhere assigned. Despite these petitions and protests, General Bragg was kept in command. This retention may be likened to the opening of the fourth seal in Revelations, "and all hell followed him"—at Missionary Ridge.

## BRIGADIER GENERAL WILLIAM W. MACKALL

CHIEF OF STAFF,
ARMY OF TENNESSEE

*These excerpts from Mackall's diary give an insider's view of the tense atmosphere at army headquarters and reveal Mackall's own disenchantment and indecision regarding Bragg's abilities. Three days after Davis left, Mackall resigned, another competent soldier no longer willing to serve under Bragg.*

October 5, 1863.

We opened our guns on the enemy this morning about ten. It is nearly three now and as I expected made a big noise and nothing more. Last night we found out that there was a petition to the President to relieve General Bragg, circulating among the General Officers. It gave Bragg much distress and mortification. I do believe he thought himself popular. I feel sincerely sorry for him. He has labored with great industry and great zeal. I do not see any good to result from relieving him, as the President won't use the only useful man—Johnston. They have telegraphed the President to come on. I suppose we will hear tonight.

October 9, 1863.

Mr. D. comes this evening. . . . Bragg thinks now that he will triumph, but he was very despondent yesterday, and is as blind as a bat to the circumstances surrounding him. He ought not to command this army unless his enemies are taken away, for he is vindictive and cannot do justice.

October 10, 1863.

The President, three aides including Custus Lee, Colonel Preston Johnston and General Pemberton arrived last evening. . . . I heard yesterday that Longstreet had signed the petition for the removal of Bragg, and if he has not, at all events he is talking about him in a way to destroy all his usefulness. Bragg is in fine humor today, evidently thinking he has the President on his side, but Mr. Davis is as wily as a serpent and Bragg has yet to discover whether he is as harmless as a dove. . . .

The President is riding around the lines this morning and the troops are hurrahing, which I am glad of for the common good. I am satisfied that Bragg cannot usefully command this army and that I can do no good, for if Mr. D. sustains him, he will be too elated to listen to reason. I do not know a single contented general in this army; a very sad fact in the presence of the enemy. I do not believe that Mr. Davis could do as much good by sending ten thousand men to this army as by putting Lee or Johnston here, and I do not think he can do anything but mischief by putting any other. If Longstreet, this will be very acceptable to the corps, but all the others will say: "We don't know him, and we know that Bragg is careful of us, doesn't fight unless he has a good chance, and he has never been beaten exactly, and this time has beaten Rosencrantz badly."

Octotber 12, 1863.

. . . In his speech this evening, the President told the audience that he had ridden over the battlefield and that the General who could drive a foe from such a field, the hardest he had ever seen, was worthy of all confidence and the shafts of malice had been hurled harmlessly against him. The mob shouted, of course, and they would have shouted just as loud if he had told them that their comrades' lives had been uselessly sacrificed and he would send them a better General. Poor man, he is an enigma to himself.

The President has now been here two days and I believe has decided to sustain Bragg. Under the circumstances of the troubles in the army, I am in doubt what to do. Should I quit my position now, it might look as though I were wanting to add to the troubles, and to stay is very disagreeable. I will take time and reflect earnestly, and if God assists decide rightly. I want success, by whom it comes I care not, but I don't want for my children's sake to lose all reward of labor. I do not want them sneering at me in future years.

## SERGEANT MAJOR JOHN W. GREEN

9TH KENTUCKY (C.S.) INFANTRY, LEWIS' BRIGADE

*Most of the Rebels at Chattanooga were ill-clothed and ill-fed during the siege, contributing to their low morale and dislike of Bragg. Meanwhile, stocks of supplies remained piled up at railheads due to administrative bungling and neglect, benefiting only a lucky few like Green, a member of Kentucky's famous Orphan Brigade.*

Our army was accumulating large Commissary & Quartermaster supplies at Tyners Station & also at Chicamauga station & we had heavy guard duty to protect them & to keep watch in our rear to see that no raiding Yankees threatened our base of supplies. Some Alabama troops shared this duty with us. They were almost daily cheered & comforted by boxes received from their homes; but every body was not so fortunate as to receive these marks of loving remembrance & the pangs of hunger & want caused some to develope a willingness to help themselves to whatever they could find not closely guarded.

One night some of our Kentucky boys who permitted their desires to obscure their moral perception slipped through the guards & stole a box of very munificent appearance which they found in tempting position at the RR. depot; but they were perplexed as to how they could carry it off as it was too heavy for the two of them to carry it further. The Alabama boys were on guard & our fellows bargained with one of these boys who had just been relieved from duty that if he would help carry it down into the woods they would divide it with him. It proved to be a rich haul indeed, three hams, delicious pickels & preserves, nice warm wollen socks, two coats, a pair of shoes, & various other good things. The Ky boys each took a coat & as the shoes just fit Alabama they said, "Here Yellowhammer you may have the shoes."

The socks & other things were pretty fairly divided but finally they came to a letter at the bottom of the box & Kentucky said, "Yellow hammer as we sort of got you in the division of coats & socks you may have the letter."

He threw some fresh wood on the fire to make a good light to read the letter by while the other two stretched themselves to rest awhile. Alabama soon grew serious & he turned to the end of the letter to read the name when he exclaimed, "Look here boys, dern my fool skin! This box is from my mother, sent to me. Now look here, youens aint going to keep my things is you?"

But the Kentuckians told him they were surprised at him. "Did'nt we keep our bargain with you & divide fair? Surely you aint going to back out on your bargain when we acted so fair with you. Why look here, there are two of us to your one, [and] we need not have given you any of the things if we had not been gentlemen of our word."

He replied, "Now look here boys, these things all belong to me & youens aint got no right to em."

But the only compromise he could get out of them was to give him back the two coats. They said that after a Yellowhammer's trying to go back on a bargain like he had done they would not wear an old . . . Jeans coat for fear they would run away from the next battle they went into.

They do tell that the next night this same Yellowhammer tried his hand at stealing a box. He had to get some help to carry off his prize but when the box was opened it proved to be a dead soldier who was to be Shipped home for burial.

## B. L. T.

QUARTERMASTER CORPS, WILLICH'S BRIGADE

*Known only by his initials, this army teamster recounts in detail how the mule teams were hitched to the wagons and how the trains of supplies for the troops starving in Chattanooga were conducted. Even the agonizingly long, tortuous overland route they followed did not secure the caravans completely from the hazard of fire from Confederate sharpshooters, and they always ran the risk of Rebel cavalry raids.*

The regulation team for each wagon was three span of mules hitched tandem; the span in front the smallest, the middle span larger, while the largest or wheel span was next the wagon, with the stiff tongue between them. On the left wheel mule was a plain saddle, on which the teamster rode, and drove the six mules by a single line.

He had to aid him a long whip and a good supply of oaths, which he

*Lookout Mountain looms in the background as a Union officer reports to Brigadier General August Willich at the latter's headquarters. The balding Willich, depicted with a pet raccoon perched upon his shoulder, was a Prussian native who had fled Germany after the failed revolutions of 1848. A brave soldier who was solicitous of his troops' welfare, Willich was liked and respected by his men, although they could not resist imitating his thick German accent. He served in the Army of the Cumberland until wounded at Resaca, Georgia, in 1864.*

could sing out in true teamster style and never miss a note. In traveling, the rule was for the wagons to be kept one immediately behind the other and as close together as possible, and thus economize space and protection.

If you can now imagine a long line of the teams and canvas-covered wagons, lumbering along on a fairly good road, with an occasional wagon-master on horseback, riding the line to keep everything in order, you will have an ideal wagon train.

But in getting such heavy wagons up steep hills, over mountains where no road has been prepared, or through a wet valley where the mud is deep, then the real work of life hits the teamster hard, and I am sorry to say he is apt to hit his mules the same way. . . .

We crossed the bridge north of the town and went the short route that crosses a spur or two of Waldron's Ridge, some five and eight miles out of town. This road in some places runs close to the bank of the Tennessee River, which is a wide, swift stream, though only deep enough for small steamboats. This trip we made without special danger, but hard, heavy pulling for the teams, arriving in Chattanooga the night of the third or fourth day out.

Next day we unloaded, made necessary repairs, rested some, and the following morning started again for Bridgeport with empty wagons. We had word as soon as we crossed the river that the "Johnnies" had some sharpshooters in the bushes on their side of the stream, where the hills on our side crowded the road close to the bank, and our teams were being killed. Well, there was no fun in reports of that kind, especially if they turn out true, which they did.

There was a train ahead of ours, and in a short time it would halt, then move ahead a few rods, and we followed in like manner. It was reported the Johnnies had one or two extra heavy rifles that did some fine shooting for them, but bad for us. No shots were heard for a half hour, and the trains moved along nicely until the head of our train had almost reached the particular spot where we might expect some compliments from the Confederacy; and they came without more delay.

The big rifle rang out, and in a few minutes two of our men came back carrying a teamster who had been shot while in the saddle, the ball having gone through both his limbs and the body of the mule he rode. Well, we had to run the gauntlet by holding the train back of the point, getting the front team in snug order, then the driver and others lashing the mules into a good run and getting them over that place in as short a time as possible.

We managed to get our train through without a wound, although some shots were fired. With loaded wagons we knew it would never do to try that passage, and we were forced to return by the long route on the north side of the mountain.

## LIEUTENANT ROBERT T. COLES

4TH ALABAMA INFANTRY, LAW'S BRIGADE

*Coles' regiment had journeyed west from the Army of Northern Virginia the preceding September as part of Longstreet's First Corps. In early October, Brigadier General Evander M. Law sent the 4th far to the Rebel left, onto the slopes of Raccoon Mountain, to gun down mules pulling Federal supply wagons alongside the Tennessee River. Coles describes how his men used Whitworth rifles, heavy-barreled sharpshooter weapons imported from England, with dire effect.*

We were perfectly aware that we were inflicting great damage on the enemy, and that we would not be permitted to remain there much longer without an effort on the part of the enemy to dispossess us.

We had brought our Whitworth rifles from Virginia with us. These were placed down the River on our extreme left to shoot down the front teams, which after being done, the road was entirely blocked and we then proceeded in a leisurely manner to use our English rifles. The road was too narrow between the bluff and River for the teams to turn around or escape in any manner, and were compelled to stand until all were shot down. I saw one of the Whitworth rifles, an English gun with globe sight carrying a large ball, a few of which ran the blockade, in the hands of one of our sharpshooters, kill two mules at one shot—the heavy missile passing through their necks. . . .

The position of the 4th Alabama was different from that of the 15th Alabama. Being up among the bluffs on Raccoon Mountain, no direct attack could be made upon it from the River. The only way to get us out was by a flank movement of the enemy. Our duties, summed up in a few words by Colonel Oates, were: "Law sent the 4th Alabama to do this perilous and all-important work down to the point of Raccoon Mountain, to act as sharpshooters, and prevent the use of the River and the wagon road on the other side of the River, and the 15th Alabama to picket the River from the right of the 4th Alabama, up to Brown's Ferry." . . .

The transportation of [our regiment] consisted of one poor old pack mule, which we kept busy packing up supplies up the mountain. We surrounded ourselves with a strong picket line day and night. Sampey of E Company fired his gun one night and called the Corporal of the guard and created thereby, among the few of us not on duty, no little consternation and uneasiness. When the Corporal reached the post he was informed by Sampey that, hearing someone approaching, and not obeying his challenge, he fired, and was positive he had killed a "Yankee," for he heard him struggling in the dry leaves. He and the Corporal then made an examination and found that Sampey had shot a large coon squarely through the head.

*This illustration dramatically depicts riflemen of the 4th Alabama firing upon a Union supply train. Turner Vaughan, a soldier in the 4th, reported that amid the pounding hoofbeats of stampeding mules and the crack of rifle fire echoing off the cliffs bordering the Tennessee River near Chattanooga, the mule drivers often "left their teams and took to the woods," leaving the Rebels to pick off the harnessed animals at their leisure.*

## COLONEL ADIN B. UNDERWOOD

33D MASSACHUSETTS INFANTRY, O. SMITH'S BRIGADE

*In describing the Federal change of command at Chattanooga, Underwood showed sympathy for Rosecrans. In the arrival of Grant, however, he acknowledged that a no-nonsense man of action had been placed in charge and that there were going to be changes. For Underwood, these changes had a personal consequence; he was wounded at Wauhatchie, during Grant's drive to restore the Union supply line.*

One day Gen. Rosecrans stopped here on his way to St. Louis, and the band gave him a serenade. "Old Rosey," as his men loved to call him, looked a noble officer, proud of his Army. . . . Well, he had won Murfreesboro and two or three other battles; had as good as a lost one, Chickamauga, but it was the last one, so exit "Rosey." Who was in his place? The old hero of the rear guard at that battle, Thomas, and over them all, the Cumberland, Tennessee and Ohio Armies as one military division, the silent man of Donelson, of Shiloh and Vicksburg. In two days came the order to march forward. The Vicksburg man meant business. . . .

The instant Gen. Grant was put in command of the military Division, (it was by Stanton in person) he telegraphed from Louisville, relieving Rosecrans, putting Thomas in command, and ordering him to hold Chattanooga at all hazards. "I will hold the town till we starve," was the response of the old veteran, and he at once ordered a concentration of our Corps at Bridgeport. While the band of the Thirty-Third was serenading Rosecrans, Grant was on his way to the front. He looked over the ground there with Thomas, and before he finished one cigar, gave the order for Hooker to open the road south of the river, get possession of the railroad, and free the river for navigation. Another hand was at the helm, and the "soft thing" was all up.

*While famished Yankees at Chattanooga ate candles and soap to survive, tons of supplies lay neatly piled at the nearby Federal supply dump of Stevenson, Alabama (below). Federal mule trains could carry only a tiny fraction of what was amassed.*

# "I suppose, they looked upon the garrison of Chattanooga as prisoners of war, feeding or starving themselves, and thought it would be inhuman to kill any of them except in self-defence."

## MAJOR GENERAL ULYSSES S. GRANT

COMMANDER, MILITARY DIVISION OF THE MISSISSIPPI

*During his hurried but arduous journey to Chattanooga, Grant, who had been seriously hurt in a fall from a horse in September, often had to dismount and be carried by his aides over the roughest stretches of a trail that was sometimes knee deep in mud. After arriving in the city on October 23, he immediately turned his attention to opening the Cracker Line from Bridgeport, Alabama.*

I found General W. F. Smith occupying the position of chief engineer of the Army of the Cumberland. I had known Smith as a cadet at West Point, but had no recollection of having met him after my graduation, in 1843, up to this time. He explained the situation of the two armies and the topography of the country so plainly that I could see it without an inspection. I found that he had established a saw-mill on the banks of the river, by utilizing an old engine found in the neighborhood; and by rafting logs from the north side of the river above, had got out the lumber and completed pontoons and roadway plank for a second bridge, one flying bridge being there already. He was also rapidly getting out the materials and constructing the boats for a third bridge. In addition to this he had far under way a steamer for plying between Chattanooga and Bridgeport whenever we might get possession of the river. This boat consisted of a scow, made of the plank sawed out at the mill, housed in, and a stern wheel attached which was propelled by a second engine taken from some shop or factory. . . .

The next day, the 24th, I started out to make a personal inspection, taking Thomas and Smith with me, besides most of the members of my personal staff. We crossed to the north side of the river, and, moving to the north of detached spurs of hills, reached the Tennessee at Brown's Ferry, some three miles below Lookout Mountain, unobserved by the enemy. Here we left our horses back from the river and approached the water on foot. There was a picket station of the enemy on the opposite side, of about twenty men, in full view, and we were within easy range. They did not fire upon us nor seem to be disturbed by our presence. They must have seen that we were all commissioned officers. But, I suppose, they looked upon the garrison of Chattanooga as prisoners of war, feeding or starving themselves, and thought it would be inhuman to kill any of them except in self-defence.

That night I issued orders for opening the route to Bridgeport—*a cracker line,* as the soldiers appropriately termed it. They had been so long on short rations that my first thought was the establishment of a line over which food might reach them.

# Opening the Cracker Line

Mud splattered and wet from his 60-mile horseback ride over the treacherous supply road from Bridgeport, Grant arrived at Thomas' headquarters in Chattanooga as darkness was falling on October 23. The new commanding general refused an offer of dry clothes and got right down to business, asking each of Thomas' staff officers to give his own appraisal of the military situation.

As the men spoke, Grant listened—"immovable as a rock and as silent as a sphinx," one officer recalled. The reports were so grim, Grant later wrote, that it "looked, indeed, as if but two courses were open; one to starve, the other to surrender or be captured." He had no intention of doing either. When Brigadier General William F. "Baldy" Smith proposed a way to open a new supply line, Grant perked up and peppered him with questions.

As chief engineer for the Army of the Cumberland, Smith had studied the area's geography, with special attention to the terrain between the army's position in Chattanooga and its supply base at Bridgeport and the serpentine meanderings of the Tennessee River between those two points.

Two and a half miles downstream from the city, the river interrupted its southwestward course and looped to the northwest around a tongue of land called Moccasin Point. From the pontoon bridge already in place at Chattanooga a road led across Moccasin Point for two miles until it hit the river again at Brown's Ferry. From Brown's Ferry the river flowed northwestward for five miles toward Walden's Ridge, then created another peninsula by looping around Raccoon Mountain—which was in Confederate hands. The road from Brown's Ferry continued west over Raccoon Mountain to another ferry, Kelley's, which, if the mountain could be cleared of Rebels, was reachable from Bridgeport by steamboat.

The road from Chattanooga to Kelley's Ferry was out of the range of the Rebel artillery on Lookout Mountain. If the Federals could drive the Confederates from Brown's Ferry and the heights of Raccoon Mountain, thus opening the road, they could get their supplies into Chattanooga with an overland haul of only eight miles.

Smith suggested that two forces move on Brown's Ferry—one marching across Moccasin Point while the other drifted down the river from Chattanooga in pontoon boats. After the waterborne force overpowered the pickets on the Confederate side of the river, the combined forces would build a bridge with the pontoons and move on to occupy the road to Kelley's Ferry.

Meanwhile, Hooker would send a third force across the Tennessee on pontoons at Bridgeport. Oliver O. Howard would lead the way with two divisions totaling 5,000 men, under Generals Carl Schurz and Adolph von Steinwehr. Brigadier General John W. Geary's division of 1,500 men would form a rear guard. These reinforcements would march eastward along the railroad that crossed the peninsula, around the flanks of the lightly held Raccoon Mountain to Wauhatchie, a hamlet just west of Lookout Mountain. They would thereby exert additional pressure on the Rebels from the west, helping to solidify the gains made by the Chattanooga force.

It was a daring plan that would also take advantage of the fact that many of the Confederates were as wet, cold, and hungry as the Federals. Grant endorsed it enthusiastically.

Preparations began in strictest secrecy, and at 3:00 a.m. on October 27 the Union troops left Chattanooga. While 3,500 infantrymen under Brigadier General John B. Turchin marched toward Brown's Ferry with three batteries of artillery, Brigadier General William B. Hazen and 1,500 men began floating down the river in 50 oar-equipped pontoons and two flatboats. After two tense hours of silent drifting, the lead boats spotted the signal fires lit on the Federal side of the river to mark the spot where they should row to the opposite shore. The surprise was total. Hazen's men sprang from the boats and scattered the Rebel pickets.

Colonel William C. Oates, commanding six companies of Alabamians on the ridge above Brown's Ferry, heard the gunfire and counterattacked. But Turchin's men had already begun to cross the river in the pontoon boats. The outnumbered Rebels soon withdrew.

By 4:30 p.m., the Federals had a pontoon bridge across the river. The operation had cost them just six lives among 38 total casualties. An exultant General Hazen strode along his lines, yelling to his men, "We've knocked the cover off the cracker box!"

The Confederate command on Lookout Mountain reacted slowly. Longstreet apparently regarded the action at Brown's Ferry as insignificant and did not even bother to inform Bragg. But although Bragg had not assigned enough troops to defend the landing, he realized its importance. When he heard the news of its loss on the morning of October 28, he angrily demanded that Longstreet regain it at once, using both of his divisions, with a third division borrowed from Breckinridge's corps in reserve.

For reasons never fully explained, Longstreet waited all day before acting. And while he hesitated, Hooker's eastbound forces advanced. On the evening of October 28, they halted for the night, Howard's contingent about a mile from Brown's Ferry and Geary's at Wauhatchie, three miles to the south.

Longstreet, apparently misunderstanding Bragg's intent, chose to ignore the strengthening Federal grip on Brown's Ferry to go after Geary's smaller force at Wauhatchie, employing a risky night assault by Colonel John Bratton's brigade of Brigadier General Micah Jenkins' division. Meanwhile, brigades led by Brigadier Generals Evander M. Law and Jerome B. Robertson were to block the Brown's Ferry-Wauhatchie road to prevent Howard from sending reinforcements to Geary.

About half past midnight on October 29, Bratton's troops attacked. Although surprised and outnumbered, the Federals had the advantage of knowing exactly where their own men were and thus could shoot in the dark without fear of hitting one another. Geary also had four cannons. For three hours the fighting raged around the railroad tracks. The Yankees were running low on ammunition when suddenly the Rebels broke off and retreated. Meanwhile, Howard's troops, moving toward the sound of the guns, had outflanked and driven Law's and Robertson's Confederates from the hills overlooking the Brown's Ferry-Wauhatchie road.

Later that same day, a makeshift steamboat pulling two barges of rations and forage docked at Kelley's Ferry. "Baldy" Smith's audacious plan had worked to perfection. Less than one week after his arrival in Chattanooga, Grant had opened up the Cracker Line—and none too soon. Only four boxes of hardtack remained in the warehouse. Soon that trickle of supplies would become a torrent of 30 railroad carloads daily. And with Sherman's corps approaching from the west, momentum in the struggle for Chattanooga had shifted to the Federals.

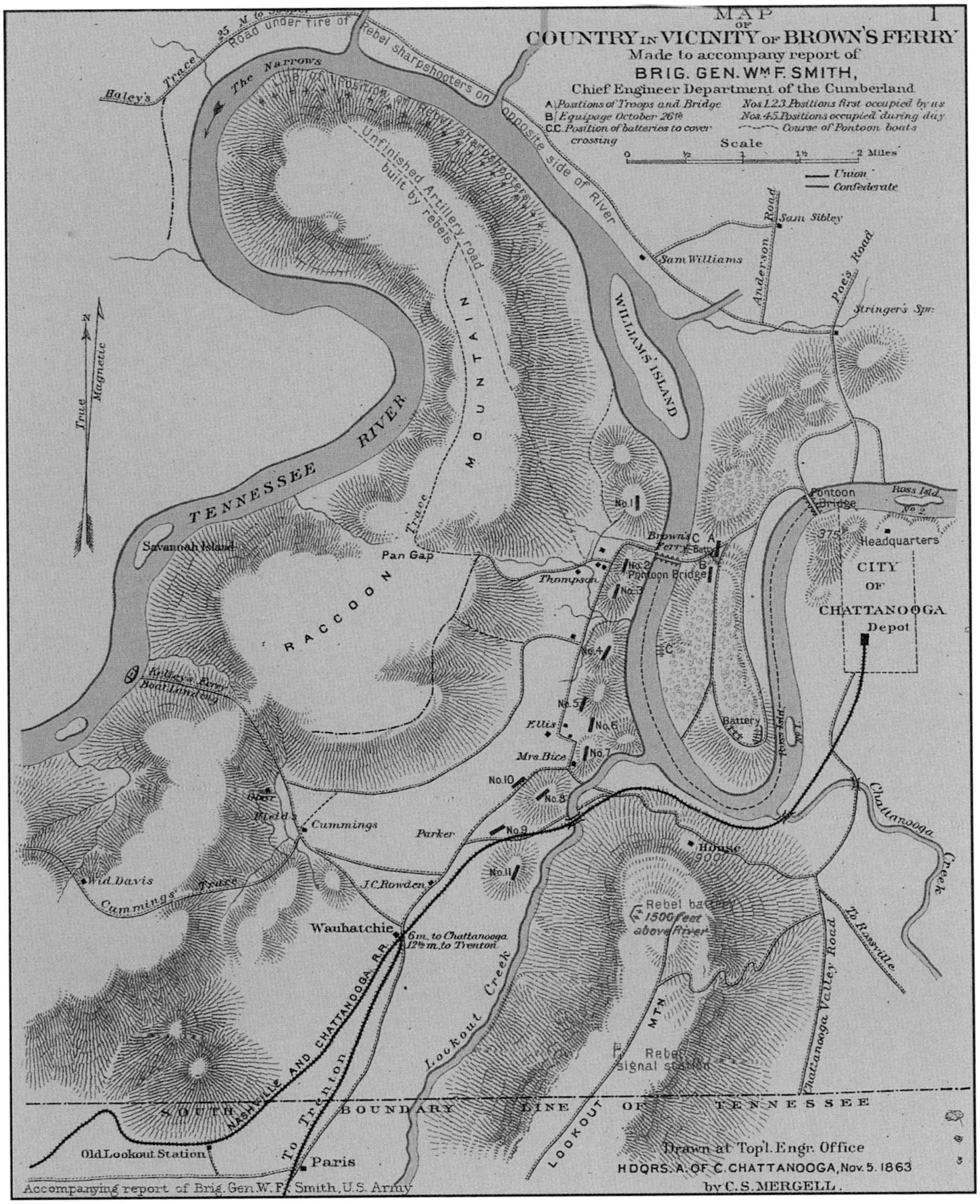


*On October 27, in an early morning waterborne attack, a Union force captured Brown's Ferry and cleared the Confederates from Raccoon Mountain. The next night, farther south, the Federals repulsed a Confederate counteroffensive at Wauhatchie. The two victories secured river lines to Kelley's Ford as well as the road from there to Brown's Ferry, allowing the Federals to begin resupplying Chattanooga.*

## BRIGADIER GENERAL WILLIAM B. HAZEN

### Brigade Commander, Army of the Cumberland

*Hazen had spent his adolescent years in Ohio, where he befriended future president James A. Garfield. Known for bravery and competency under fire during numerous battles in the West, Hazen was a good choice to lead the hazardous mission to capture Brown's Ferry, the first step in reopening the Cracker Line.*

Almost immediately after General Thomas assumed command, I was directed to report to General Baldy Smith. Smith told me his plan for opening the line of the river, and informed me that I had been selected for the delicate duty of carrying my brigade in boats at night down the river past the enemy's pickets to Brown's Ferry, nine miles from Chattanooga, there to effect a landing on the south bank, which would be fortified and held as a *tete de pont.* This would enable Hooker's command—the Eleventh and Twelfth Corps, then at Bridgeport—to come up on the south side of the river, make a junction there and hold Lookout Valley with a bridge secured across the river, without which it would not be safe to bring troops into that valley.

The river makes a long bend below Chattanooga so that, by marching directly across the neck from the town, Browns Ferry was only two miles away. We rode across that neck, and Smith pointed out the precise spot he had already chosen for the landing, made plain at night by a gap in the hills which lined the south bank of the river. I was to take thirteen hundred picked men of my brigade, in fifty-two parties in that number of boats, each under the command of a well-known and tried leader. The remainder of the brigade, about an equal number, under command of Colonel Bassett Langdon, First Ohio, joined by Turchin's brigade, were to march to Brown's Ferry across the neck, and as the boats unloaded, be ferried over in them as rapidly as possible.

It was desired that I should land and occupy the two hills to the left of [a nearby] house. There was a picket post at this point, and also one in the depression between the two hills. It was thought best to organize a party of seventy-five men who should be the first to land, and at once push out on the road that comes in at the house, clearing and holding it, while half the organized force should be landed simultaneously at each of two gorges, who should immediately push up the hills, inclining to the left, and following the crests until they were wholly occupied. Each party of twenty-five was to carry two axes; as soon as the crest should be reached, a strong line of skirmishers was to be pushed out, and all the axes put to work at once felling a thick abatis. Positions were also selected for building signal-fires to guide us in landing.

I afterward selected tried and distinguished officers to lead the four distinct commands, who, in addition to being fully instructed as to the part they were to take, were themselves taken to the spot, and every feature of the bank and landings made familiar to them. They, in turn, just before night [of October 26] called together the leaders of squads, and each was clearly instructed as to his duties; for they were of such a nature that each had in a great degree to act independently, but strictly in accordance with instructions. At twelve o'clock at night the command was awakened and marched to the landing, and quietly embarked under the superintendence of Colonel Stanley, of the Eighteenth Ohio Volunteer Infantry, each squad in its own boat.

*Brigadier General William F. Smith (left)—nicknamed Baldy by his peers—had an irascible nature that repeatedly placed him at odds with his superiors, often hurting his chances for advancement. But the West Pointer had an acknowledged genius for engineering, and Rosecrans, before he was relieved, appointed Smith chief engineer of the Army of the Cumberland. It was Smith who recognized the value of Brown's Ferry and planned the operation to seize the vital crossing point.*

*Infantrymen of the 18th Ohio, some of whom are shown here, literally held the success of the Brown's Ferry operation in their hands—as oarsmen for the boats that carried Hazen's troops. Recruited from southeastern counties of the Buckeye State that bordered the Ohio River, many soldiers of the 18th had worked as rivermen before the war and were a natural choice for this job. The regiment suffered 184 dead from combat or disease before it mustered out in November 1864.*

## PRIVATE PHILIP DINES

41st Ohio Infantry, Hazen's Brigade

*During the early hours of October 27, the plan to take Brown's Ferry was put into action. While Dines and his comrades in Hazen's brigade floated toward the Ferry, shivering in their overloaded skiffs, the men of Brigadier General John Turchin's brigade marched across Moccasin Point and readied themselves to be ferried over the Tennessee to join in the attack. Dines, still hampered by a wound received at Chickamauga, was wounded again on Missionary Ridge.*

Everything being in readiness, we were marched to the landing, just west of the town, where the boats were in waiting for our reception. I judge the time of starting to be about 1 o'clock in the morning of Oct. 27, 1863. Silently and swiftly the boats were filled as they came up, each containing about 25 men. As fast as filled the oarsmen pulled out one after another in close order, and like a great water-snake floated noiselessly down the silvery tide. When fairly under way our instructions were given; i.e., not a word was to be spoken above a whisper, no oars were to be used, no matches struck, and loud spitting was to be avoided. In fact, this move depended upon so much secresy that we almost held our breath; but what troubled us the most of all was the fact that we had no bait, so the chances for catching a 10-pound salmon each for breakfast was forever lost.

Soon all sights and sounds were lost to eye and ear in the camps we left behind us. Down, down, we floated, so close to Lookout Mountain that it seemed the rebs might have tossed the boys a plug of Virginia twist, which they would greatly have preferred to a plug of Virginia lead. The night was cold and damp, with a slight fog creeping up the stream, and we had great difficulty in keeping our teeth from striking up a tune, and thereby attracting the enemy's attention. After rounding the bend near Lookout Mountain, we still had about seven miles to go before reaching our destination, keeping all the time close to the right-hand shore, as the enemy was posted just over on the other shore. The writer being in the boat next to the lead had a good opportunity of seeing what took place at the front. At last we reached Brown's Ferry, and we heard the whispered command from the front boat, "Steer right for that light." Looking across the stream and some distance below could be seen a small picket fire glimmering like a star through the fog that still hung like a thin vail over the stream. This was the place selected for the attack, toward which the leading boat of our train headed. So silently did we approach that the two forward boats had almost touched the shore before the picket (who we could plainly see) gave the alarm by saying "Who comes thar?" but without waiting to be informed, discharged his gun and retreated on the reserve a few paces to the rear. And now that the alarm was sounded, our success depended upon unshipping in the most lively manner, which we did so quickly the 20 or 30 men were in line on the bank before the reserve pickets could resist the landing. Soon our rapidly-increasing force moved forward, when we met a force of the enemy at the gap, and a lively battle began and continued until the hills were ours. We could not see the foe during this battle, but fired at the flashes of their muskets and moved right up the hill. Our loss was six killed and 23 wounded.

## PRIVATE WILLIAM C. JORDAN

15TH ALABAMA INFANTRY, LAW'S BRIGADE

*Posted among the hillocks and ridges on the Confederate side of the river at Brown's Ferry were the tough soldiers of the 15th and 4th Alabama, survivors of the bloody attempt to take Little Round Top at Gettysburg. Jordan's account of his rude awakening vividly conveys how successful the Yankees were in keeping the operation a complete secret from the Rebel sentinels right up to the moment of attack during the quiet, dark night of October 27.*

*Brigadier General Evander M. Law (above) felt that Brown's Ferry could have been held if properly reinforced. He blamed its loss on what he viewed as the high command's inexplicable disinterest in the position.*

We were quite friendly and communicative with the Federals that evening. Our boys would tease them about hardtacks and they would guy us about corndodgers. I stepped out with a pan of eggs and told them to come over, that we had everything that a heart could wish. I took my empty bottle and handed it around to the boys, and all went through the blank motion of drinking. One Yank said, "I believe that fellow has got spirits." I heard what he said and told him to come over. He said he would the next morning and exchange papers and swap coffee for tobacco, if his colonel would let him and provided we would not take him prisoner. We told him that we would deal fairly and honorably with him.

There was a great deal of growth of bushes on the bank of the river. The moon was shining brightly which cast a shadow for some distance in the water on the south bank of the river. I stood vidette from 12 to 2 o'clock that night. Soon after I went on vidette post I heard a splash in the water, but heard it no more. I was very watchful and vigilant the entire time until I was relieved. I told Mr. Payne, the man that relieved me, about the splash in the water. I supposed that it was a large fish that had made the noise.

I went to the little cabin, smoked my pipe, pulled off my shoes and jacket, and went to bed as though all right. I don't know when I had made such preparations before for sleeping. My canteen was hung on a nail in the cabin and I put my pipe on the mantle.

About the time that Mr. Payne had stood watch about two hours he came running in about 4 a.m. saying, "Get up, boys! Get up! Yankees are coming!" Our Captain, N. B. Feagin, was also at this post. We had only three guns. I told one of the men to take my gun as there were several there without guns, and the two cavalrymen had no guns. I put on my shoes and jacket as quickly as I could, threw my bed spread into the basket helter skelter with the remnant of ham, turkey bones, eggs, biscuits, cake, etc. I ran to the bank of the river as quick as I could, took my gun and began firing as rapidly as I could reload.

About one dozen dugouts or batteaus containing about ten or twelve men apiece were landing at the old ferry. The Yanks were shooting as they were landing, saying, "Get out, boys! Get out, boys!" We had to get back up the pass. I ran into the cabin and got my basket, leaving my canteen and pipe. There was a little light in the cabin, and I saw the door darkened with blue jackets immediately after I retreated from the cabin up the pass. The cabin was repeatedly struck by their rifle balls.

*This rendering by William D. T. Travis shows Union pontoon boats reaching Brown's Ferry from the south, with the Confederate positions held by Law's men on the right. On the river's left bank is Moccasin Point and the foliage that sheltered Turchin's waiting bluecoats. Lookout Mountain rises in the background.*

## CORPORAL ARNOLD BRANDLEY

23D KENTUCKY (U.S.) INFANTRY, HAZEN'S BRIGADE

*Brandley was part of a small band of soldiers who manned the expedition's lead boat and were charged with the crucial responsibility of quickly securing the landing site. Though disaster threatened when their boat almost floated past Brown's Ferry, the Kentuckians were able to scramble ashore, climb the steep bank, and overwhelm the startled Rebel pickets in a matter of minutes. Their task accomplished, the Yanks then settled down to feast on captured meat.*

All went well until we passed under a tree that had fallen out from the bank and was still hanging by the roots just high enough to allow the boat to pass under; the order was whispered, "Everybody down." Sergt. Reeves (afterward Captain) of Co. G attempted to leap over the tree, but he was not quick enough and was caught by the branches and swept into the cold stream. We could not stop the boat

"One of the oarsmen, an 18th Ohio boy, dropped his oar with a rebel bullet in his arm. We were thoroughly aroused and anxious to fire back, but we remembered our orders."

or assist him, not daring to make a noise; neither did Reeves cry for help, and we passed on in doubt of whether we would ever again see our comrade.

On, on we floated until we observed a single picket-fire on the south bank. Col. Foy then hallooed to the boat in our rear, if he should land. Then Gen. Hazen sent the word to steer for that light, which we did hurriedly. We all raised to our feet. Gen. Hazen's order was heard by the rebel picket, who gave the alarm to "Fall in, the Yanks are coming!" I heard the officer of the guard give the command, "Ready, aim, fire!" One of the oarsmen, an 18th Ohio boy, dropped his oar with a rebel bullet in his arm. We were thoroughly aroused and anxious to fire back, but we remembered our orders. When the rebels fired their volley we were not more than 30 feet from shore. With one of our oars being gone, the boat swung around as if on a pivot. Capt. Tifft jumped to the front and luckily reached some willows, which he firmly grasped, thereby saving the boat from floating away. We leaped from the boat on to a pile of drift wood. Here we found the bank very high above us, but by the assistance of roots, brush, etc., we reached the top.

When I got up the bank I found four of our men ahead of me; one of them was Capt. Hardiman. I asked him what to do. He said lay down and wait for the balance of the boys. The rebs were in and about a log house at the edge of what is known as Brown's Gap; there was no chinking between the logs, and we could see their movements very plainly. They were trying to organize, but before they were able to do so we charged on them through the darkness, firing as we went. We followed them on through the Gap to an open field. Here Col. Foy ordered us to throw up a barricade of fence-rails, logs, etc. Before this could, however, be completed the rebels were re-inforced and charged us. Our squad was scattered hunting material for the barricade; thus it became an easy matter to force us back to the starting point—the Tennessee River. Capt. Tifft called loudly for us to rally on the reserve, hoping thereby to deceive the enemy in our numbers.

We halted but a few moments on the edge of the Gap, when Col. Foy gave the order to charge, which we did in good style, driving the enemy once more through the Gap to an opening where they were cooking a large kettle of beef. Daylight had made its appearance by this time, and right here at this kettle of beef, in an old log house, we halted. Grabbing for the beef—running hands and bayonets into the hot water, gobbling up the delicious pieces of half-done beef—and around this old kettle the battle of Brown's Ferry and the charge of the first boat's crew ended.

Out of our boat's 48 men, 17 were killed and wounded . . . Col. Foy was shot through his new hat. He lamented very much that he did not bring his old hat in place of this one.

## SERGEANT WILLIAM A. MCCLENDON

15TH ALABAMA INFANTRY, LAW'S BRIGADE

*Within moments after the attack began, the area around Brown's Ferry was swarming with Federal troops splashing out of flatboats and deploying into battle lines on the river's muddy shore. Although McClendon's company and another Rebel company rushed to aid their comrades, they were too few and too late to drive the Yankees back into the water. Nevertheless, they stubbornly kept the darkness punctuated with musket flashes as they engaged the enemy in a confused skirmish until they were forced to withdraw to the safety of Lookout Mountain's foothills.*

Our pickets increased their vigilance, so as not to be taken by surprise, but we felt sure that we could defeat any attempt to land that the Yankees would make, but preparations among them still went on and at early dawn of the 27th here they came. Co. "B" commanded by Capt. N. B. Feagan was on picket at what was afterwards ascertained to be Brown's Ferry, the place selected by the Yankees to make their landing. It was at early dawn when we felt secure in our warm beds, that the cracking of guns began in rapid succession. A runner from Capt. Feagan was dispatched to Col. Oates with the intelligence that the Yankees were crossing in large force, and that he could not maintain his position against such odds. Our company, commanded

*Colonel William C. Oates (left) of the 15th Alabama was in command at Brown's Ferry. After the Federal landing, Oates bravely led a futile counterattack, taking a bullet in the right leg. As his troops were helping him into the shelter of a cabin, Oates recalled later, the dwelling's female owner cried out, "Don't bring that nasty rebel into my house!" Oates' surgeon suggested she change her mind, or her home would soon be ashes. She blanched, and Oates was carried in forthwith.*

by Captain Waddell and Company "A," commanded by Captain Schaaff was formed, and hurried to the support of Co. "B" in double quick time. We left all our camp equipage, including our tents, oil cloths, blankets, cooking utensils and clothing, except what we had on, as prey for the Yankees. When we arrived at Co. "B," they were contending against great odds, and our two companys deployed and went at them firing volley after volley into their crowded ranks, but there was a whole brigade of them, eighteen hundred strong, commanded by Brigadier General Hazen, and they had landed and had gained a foothold so strong that we could not drive them back. We fought at close quarters for awhile. The left of my company were in the woods and advanced to the bluff and fired on them in their crowded condition on the sand-bar as they would get out of their boats. My position as first sargeant was the right guide of the company, and joined to the left of Co. "A." That part of our line was in an open field with no protection, the Yanks in the woods behind trees between us and the river. Two or three of our men were killed and several wounded, and among the wounded was our gallant Colonel Wm. C. Oates, and had to be toated from the field on a litter. Orders soon came for us to fall back as the Yankees were in force below us and our capture for a time seemed a certainty, but we made our way without any confusion, and recrossed Lookout Creek, and took position at the foot of Lookout Mountain.

## SURGEON ALBERT G. HART

### 41st Ohio Infantry, Hazen's Brigade

*Though 40-year-old Cleveland native Hart was often on sick leave with typhoid fever and was eventually rendered unfit for field service by the illness in June 1864, he was present at Brown's Ferry and gamely charged the Confederate positions with his regiment. Aquila Wiley, the colonel of the 41st mentioned by Hart in this account, lost his leg to Rebel fire within a month of Brown's Ferry while leading his men in a charge on Missionary Ridge.*

Stopping to dress a wounded man I get behind the regiment. I had not gone up more than two hundred yards, when I came upon a squad of sixty men of the 23d Kentucky holding the road, and although ten minutes had hardly elapsed since the landing, they were already cutting down trees to build a breastwork. I had only ascended a little distance when a fierce fight began at the point I had just left. I could not see it in the gloom, but I could hear the short, shrill yells of the rebs, so different from the cheer which our men use. Crack upon crack came the musketry. I could hear our men falling rapidly back; the rebels had got upon the opposite hill, and as our men retreated, the rebel shots crossed the road and came thick and fast around us. Our men threw out skirmishers to the right along the precipitous side of the hill to the right of the ravine, and the whole force pressed forward with furious cheers and moved up over the rocks, and up the almost perpendicular hill down which the rebels in the same order were advancing but a moment before. No man could guess what force the rebels had, or how soon we might run upon a line of battle which would sweep us down the hill like chaff. But the officers, who had been made fully aware of the ground to be gone over, pressed on the best speed they could make, and in a few minutes more they reached the top of the ridge on this hill.

Meanwhile our detachment of 600 men with which I had landed had moved up the precipitous path and reached the top of the hill on the left. The perpendicular ascent was not less than 300 feet. Great boulders, rocks, rubbish and underbrush were in their way. Along this ridge, or razor-back, a few feet wide, our men were posted when I reached them. Our regiment with Colonel Wiley is in the advance; the 6th and 124th O.V.I. and 5th Kentucky follow. The top is scarcely two yards wide, and in front again descends rapidly, but it is not so steep as on the river side. Our skirmishers form and push down the hill through the trees and underbrush. The rebels form rapidly, and, probably imagining our force to be small, make a furious effort to take back from us the ground we have gained. Our skirmishers fall back for a moment, but soon drive back the enemy, who, as the daylight advances, are to be plainly seen in the broad valley below, and can be heard giving orders for a rapid retreat. The day is won. But to secure ourselves in our position, our men throw up quickly a breastwork of small trees hastily cut down, loose stones and earth scratched up with their tin plates.

As soon as the position was secured, another act began. As I sat fronting the ferry, a crowd of men appeared on the opposite shore. At half-past 8 a.m. a pontoon bridge, made with the boats which carried us down, started from the bank. As it was pushed into the river, straight as an arrow, I thought how savage Indians of the olden time, watching its progress from the shore, would have thought it some wondrous animal, pushing itself across the water and bearing upon its broad back a thousand strange and unknown men, coming to drive them from their hunting-grounds. At 4 p.m. I crossed the river upon this bridge, capable of ferrying over a great army.

*As the sun rose over Brown's Ferry on October 27, its light fell upon the men of the 1st Michigan Engineers rapidly assembling the pontoon bridge across the Tennessee River. The Wolverines did their work heedless of the occasional shots fired by Confederate artillery on Lookout Mountain, and the bridge was completed by 4:00 p.m. The Rebel grip on Chattanooga's lifelines had begun to loosen.*

THE ARMY OF THE CUMBERLAND—BRIDGING THE TENNESSEE UNDER A REBEL FIRE FROM LOOKOUT MOUNTAIN.—Sketched by Mr. Theodore R. Davis.

[See Page 764.]

## LIEUTENANT GENERAL JAMES LONGSTREET

CORPS COMMANDER, ARMY OF TENNESSEE

*Longstreet and Bragg were meeting on Lookout Mountain on October 28 to determine how to minimize the effects of the loss of Brown's Ferry, when they learned that Hooker's column of Yankees was on the move. That night, Longstreet's men attacked Hooker's rear guard near the town of Wauhatchie.*

On the morning of the 28th I reported as ordered. The general complained of my party sending up false alarms. The only answer that I could make was that they had been about two years in that service, and had not made such mistakes before.

While laying his plans, sitting on the point of Lookout rock, the enemy threw some shells at us, and succeeded in bursting one about two hundred feet below us. That angered the general a little, and he ordered Alexander to drop some of his shells about their heads. As this little practice went on, a despatch messenger came bursting through the brushwood, asking for General Longstreet, and reported the enemy marching from Bridgeport along the base of the mountain,—artillery and infantry. General Bragg denied the report, and rebuked the soldier for sensational alarms, but the soldier said, "General, if you will ride to a point on the west side of the mountain I will show them to you." We rode and saw the Eleventh and Twelfth Corps under General Hooker, from the Army of the Potomac, marching quietly along the valley towards Brown's Ferry. The general was surprised. So was I. But my surprise was that he did not march along the mountain top, instead of the valley. It could have been occupied with as little loss as he afterwards had and less danger. He had marched by our line of cavalry without their knowing, and General Bragg had but a brigade of infantry to meet him if he had chosen to march down along the top of the mountain, and that was posted twenty miles from support.

My estimate of the force was five thousand. General Bragg thought it not so strong, and appearance from the elevation seemed to justify his estimate. Presently the rear-guard came in sight and made its bivouac immediately in front of the point upon which we stood. The latter force was estimated at fifteen hundred, and halted about three miles in rear of the main body.

A plan was laid to capture the rear-guard by night attack. He proposed to send me McLaws's and Jenkins's divisions for the work, and ordered that it should be done in time for the divisions to withdraw to the point of the mountain before daylight, left me to arrange details for attack, and rode to give orders for the divisions, but changed his mind without giving me notice, and only ordered Jenkins's division.

## LIEUTENANT RICHARD LEWIS

PALMETTO (SOUTH CAROLINA) SHARPSHOOTERS, BRATTON'S BRIGADE

*The heaviest fighting of the Battle of Wauhatchie—one of the war's rare major night actions—swirled about the camps of the 1,500 men of Union brigadier general John W. Geary's division. Here, Lewis describes his men's efforts to reach this enemy position, and their role in the chaotic battle. Lewis was shot in the leg and captured near Richmond in October 1864; the limb was later amputated.*

We had an awful time in climbing the mountain, it being so steep and rocky it looked frequently like an impossibility to clamber up it all. We kept pushing ahead though, until we got in the valley; all there came to a halt for a while, thinking our night's work was done, when came orders in a few minutes: "The enemy must be driven off the steep hills towering above you."

The brigade was drawn out in regular array of battle, and soon the loud and sonorous voice of Walker gave our regiment the command "*Forward!*" Then the whole line was seen moving with a steady and unwavering step, each soldier with a spirit of determination stamped on his brow. One hill after another in succession did we clamber over, still only a few flying Yankees to be found. At last though we began to come in sight of their campfires twinkling in the distance. All now began to realize that soon some Yankee picket would raise the battle cry. Sure enough, as we advanced nearer the camp a volley from them disputed our ground any further. After a very sharp contest between our line of skirmishers and the Yankees, the whole line raised a yell and moved up to within a few hundred yards of the enemy, and poured a tremendous volley into them, which was so terrific that everything was shroud-

*Union gunners of Knap's battery fire over the heads of Yankee infantry at Wauhatchie, punishing Rebel columns with their rapid, accurate salvos. While Geary exploited Knap's veteran Pennsylvania cannoneers in the battle, the attacking Rebels enjoyed no artillery support.*

ed in silence for a time. But ah! only for the time, for it soon raged with more fury than ever.

Coker, the gallant captain of the Sixth, acting adjutant, came around about now with orders for us to bear on the enemy's flank. So we accordingly advanced beyond the skirt of woods we were in, out into open field, and there halted in front of a battery which was belching forth its iron hail of destruction into the regiments on our right. Here the Colonel commanded us to concentrate our fire on it; and with one murderous volley the sheet of flame and smoke was no longer to be seen gushing forth. Moving back but a short distance the thundering voice was to be heard again. We then laid down and exchanged long and continuous volleys with them, until we were ordered to cease firing and shelter ourselves. After lying for some time with the minies pegging away at us, we were commanded to retire as the enemy, in very heavy force, was trying to get in our rear.

We were moving all night long over the mountain and did not get back until seven or eight o'clock in the morning, the most completely broken down set you ever saw.

## LIEUTENANT ALBERT R. GREENE

STAFF, BRIGADIER GENERAL GEORGE S. GREENE

*Expecting an attack, Geary's men had gone to sleep with loaded weapons and full cartridge boxes. Just after midnight on October 29, the Federals started awake at the pounding footsteps of Colonel John Bratton's attacking South Carolinians. Within moments both sides were casting garish silhouettes over the darkened fields with their opposing fire. Knap's battery alone lost 22 artillerymen during the engagement.*

We could distinctly hear the tramp of men at the double quick across the open field in front of us. It was so dark that they could not be seen, but they seemed to know our position perfectly. We distinctly heard the command to those men, "By the left flank!" But before the command of execution was uttered, on our line was, "Battery! Fire!" and the flash of the four guns lighted up our whole front, showing for an instant the line coming toward us. Then in the darkness the flash of the rebel muskets marked their line and the bullets began to come. Our men replied, but the delay of the One Hundred and Thirty-seventh was making bad work, and the men began to cluster around trees and to carry wounded to the rear. Finally the One Hundred and Thirty-seventh was got into position and the men made amends for the misconduct of their regimental commander.

While General Greene was riding at the very front, urging the men to stand and encouraging them by his example, and getting the formation of his brigade orderly and steady, he was struck in the face by a rifle ball, which entered at the lower left corner of his nose and passed diagonally across his mouth, badly breaking his upper jaw and tearing out through his right cheek. He was assisted to his tent, not more than seventy yards in the rear, and his servant got him again on horseback and went with him to a house some distance back, where a hospital had been established.

A considerable pioneer corps attached to the brigade had been deployed across the rear about the distance of the headquarters tent to check and drive back men carrying the wounded and any stragglers. Field, line and staff officers kept the men in their places, and soon the men began to shout back in reply to the rebel yells. Then we breathed easier; we knew the line was safe.

Knap's battery had done its share at Gettysburg, but the way that battery was worked this night was enough to immortalize it if it had never on any other occasion fired a gun. Its flashes lighted up its own position and half the rebel line. We could hear the devils shout, "Shoot the gunners! Shoot the gunners!" It was point-blank business. The lines were not over two hundred yards apart, and the air was literally loaded with death. After the canister was used up, shells were resorted to, and when an annoying fire came from men clustered around the log-house in the open, solid shot were put through that. With the infantry the officers stripped the dead and wounded of their cap and cartridge boxes and carried them to the line, for the brigade went into that wood with only sixty rounds and there was no reserve supply.

On the right the enemy got a line along the railroad embankment and opened a cross-fire. Rickard with some of his men dragged one of the guns up on to the embankment, doubled shotted it with canister, and ended that demonstration. On the left the rebels got around us in the swamp, but before they had done much their main line fell back, and some of the flanking party came in and surrendered. The firing lasted but a little over an hour, and at the close many of our men had but a single cartridge left. The attacking force went off, leaving their dead and all of their severely wounded.

This was the battle of Wauhatchie, and the first fighting in the west by troops from the Army of the Potomac. We had come to stay, and we stayed, but at a fearful cost.

*At the age of 62, Brigadier General George S. Greene (left), a former engineering instructor at West Point, was one of the oldest field officers in the Union army. Shortly after the fighting began at Wauhatchie, the well-respected Greene was knocked from his horse by a Rebel Minié ball that dealt him a grievous wound in the face and upper jaw. Amazingly, he managed to recover well enough to return to active duty in the Carolinas in the early spring of 1865, although the lingering effects of the wound plagued him until his death in 1899.*

## PRIVATE DAVID MONAT

### 29TH PENNSYLVANIA INFANTRY, COBHAM'S BRIGADE

*At one point, Bratton's hard-driving Rebel infantrymen nearly flanked the right of the Union line. Colonel William Rickards of the 29th Pennsylvania thwarted this effort by personally helping to drag a gun of Knap's battery across the bed of the Nashville & Chattanooga Railroad to a strategic spot, from where it repulsed the Rebels with terrifying point-blank blasts of canister. Monat's account also gives an idea of the verbal jousting that took place between the soldiers of the Army of the Potomac and their counterparts in the Army of the Cumberland.*

On the right a Reb Regiment came out of the woods into the open space and I heard their commander give the order "Halt! Front, ready, fire!" and then they dashed down to the Rail road bank and halted. If they had come on it would have been all up with us as we had no troops on our side of the track, only the 1 gun of the battery. This gun was in charge of Genl Geary's son, a Lieut. He had just raised from sighting the piece and had given the order to fire when the Rebs fired their volley and he fell shot on the right side of the forehead. Jack MacLauchlan and I stepped from behind the house and as we stooped to pick him up our Col. Rickards came along. I said, "Colonel, here's Geary's son." He said "My God, so it is; poor fellow, lay him down. We can't do anything for him now. I must get some of our fellows along the rail road." . . .

Pretty soon Capt. Millison came to the log shanty and ordered those of us who were there of Co. C & G of the 29th to drag the gun at which young Geary had been killed along the wagon road to where it crossed the Rail road track and ordered us to stay with the gun at all hazards. The Sergt. in charge said he would stay and if the Rebs took the gun they would take him dead. We all promised to stay along. Soon they had the gun charged and sighted down the embankment where the Johnnies lay and they did not stop for another shot.

On the left of our line the 137th and 78th New York were stationed and the Rebs got so close and on their rear that it was reported our men had to about face and fight. The mules in the wagon train got loose and broke in amongst the Rebs, creating a panic after 3 hours of hard fighting as ever we had experienced. The Johnnies left leaving about 150 prisoners and 175 dead. Our Company lost John Gilbert taken prisoner & who died at Andersonville, Ga. and Bobby Buchanan & Henry Fisher wounded. Company C had 2 killed and 3 wounded.

*Although brave and competent, Pennsylvania native John W. Geary (above, right) was also a politician who hoped martial glory would further his political ambitions. But his grief over the death at Wauhatchie of his son Edward (above, left), a lieutenant in Knap's battery, caused the general to lament, "I have gained a great victory. . . . But oh! How dear it has cost me . . . my dear beloved boy is the sacrifice. Could I but recall him to life, the bubble of military fame might be absorbed by those who wish it." In 1866 Geary became governor of the Keystone State.*

The first thing some of the prisoners asked us was if we did not belong to the Army of the Potomac. When we told them "Yes," they said we knew damn well you did, "for these western fellows wouldn't have staid like you'uns." We laid on our arms till morning.

Oct. 29, 1863—Genl Hooker came in early and we were relieved by some of the 11th & 4th corps troops. One of the western fellows said to me, "You fellows must have had a tough fight down here last night." I said, "Where?" He replied "Why here. Wasn't you in it?" I said "Oh, that was no fight, only a little kind of scrimmage." He says "Well, I don't know what you call a fight but it looks to me with all them dead Rebs as if one had been going on here and the shooting sounded as if all hell was loose."

I replied, "Oh, we're from the Potomac and we used to have those kind of rows nearly every morning to get up an appetite for breakfast."

## PRIVATE H. HOWARD STURGIS

44TH ALABAMA INFANTRY, LAW'S BRIGADE

*Sturgis was part of a Confederate force—made up of Law's and Brigadier General Jerome Robertson's brigades—that was posted atop Smith's Hill, overlooking the Brown's Ferry road. From this point, the Rebels hoped to intercept and delay any reinforcements that Hooker might send to Wauhatchie from his main body bivouacked near the ferry. At 2:30 a.m., a Yankee force appeared, and soon a spirited melee was raging over the ridge's heavily wooded slopes.*

Law's and Robertson's brigades formed on the western slope of Lookout Mountain about nine o'clock at night. They threw up a protection of logs and such other things as could be picked up. We were not allowed to cut any timber, as that would have disclosed our position.

We had little time to work for soon we heard the battle raging on our left about a mile distant. Soon the Yankees came hurrying to reinforce their line. Our pickets fired into them and we could hear their orders: "Halt! Left face! Forward!" Then we had a regular "Kilkenny cat fight," a very bad one. We got mixed up sure enough. We were driven from our insecure breastworks, Robertson failing to connect with our lines. The loss on our part of the line was small, but we were greatly outnumbered. Twice we recovered our works and drove them down the hill.

I was cut off and found myself surrounded with men calling for a New York regiment. I quietly made my way around till I heard others calling for Law's Brigade. Our lieutenant colonel was twice stopped, and the cape of his overcoat torn off in an effort to stop him. Once when we recaptured our works a Federal and Confederate were seen with their left hands in each other's collar, grasping their guns with their right hands, neither being willing to surrender. A lieutenant, seeing the predicament, ordered the Yank to surrender, which he refused to do, when the deadlock was broken with a bullet.

I saw a man roll down the mountain side, started by a ball from my gun when only a few feet distant from its muzzle. He had the first shot at me, his ball passing through my hat.

*In this Travis depiction of the Battle of Wauhatchie, Knap's battery, posted on the hill to the right, scores a telling hit on the advancing Southern line at left, scattering in agony several ghostly Rebels. Though heavily outnumbered, the Yankees held out through numerous Confederate charges like the one illustrated here.*

## COLONEL ADIN B. UNDERWOOD

### 33D MASSACHUSETTS INFANTRY, O. SMITH'S BRIGADE

*Spearheading the Federal assault up Smith's Hill were the 33d Massachusetts, the 73d Ohio, and the 136th New York of the XI Corps. Underwood, who refers to himself in the third person here, was wounded by a bullet that shattered his upper leg and lodged in his penis. A surgeon removed the bullet, and Underwood gained a promotion to brigadier general for his bravery. He left the army in August 1865.*

That is business for Smith's brigade, leading the column. "Charge the devils, double-quick" is the message from Hooker. Double-quick it is, and the hill is reached. An order comes from Col. Orland Smith, "The Thirty-Third Massachusetts will form in line to the left of the Seventy-Third Ohio, in echelon with it, at thirty paces, advance up with it and take that hill." "We will try, sir." The Seventy-Third under Maj. Hurst forms in line, its right to follow the road. The Thirty-Third forms line to its left. "Forward, steadily now, Thirty-Third." Up the slippery slope. What a hill! almost perpendicular. Riders dismount, for no horse can get a foot hold. A sorry place, too, for men with knapsacks on their backs. (Why will they load down men with so much baggage for a fight?) Seize the tangled underbrush, anything, and pull and push on. Shots fall around. The Thirty-Third speedily strikes the enemy. The colonel on the right strains his eyes to keep sight of the Seventy-Third, but it is impossible in the forest, the darkness, and with the rough ground. An indistinct line is seen ahead, just made out in the glimmering moonlight. Then the old rebel trick, "Don't fire on us." Adjutant Mudge, just like him, risks himself to save any fatal mistake, and steps before the line. "Who is it?" he asks. "Who are you?" comes down from the crest. "The Thirty-Third Massachusetts" replies the adjutant. "Take that,"

757
HARPER'S WEEKLY.
NOVEMBER 28, 1863.]
THE ARMY OF THE CUMBERLAND—CAPTURE OF REBEL RIFLE-PITS IN LOOKOUT VALLEY BY THE THIRTY-THIRD MASSACHUSETTS AND SEVENTY-THIRD OHIO VOLUNTEERS, ON OCT. 28, 1863.—SKETCHED BY MR. R. DAVIS.—[SEE PAGE 764.]

*Although only a colonel, Orland Smith (above) led the brigade that attacked Smith's Hill. The Harper's Weekly engraving at left shows the soldiers of the 33d Massachusetts and the 73d Ohio—their battle lines disrupted by their rush over the rough, broken terrain in the dark—straining to reach the smoke-shrouded Rebel works on the hill's summit.*

# "The old flag of the regiment, and the white color, float in victory over those ugly rifle pits! Hurrah, boys! and thank God!"

replies the crest with a rebel yell, as the shower of lead falls. No Seventy-Third Ohio there. Up and forward, Thirty-Third, into the fearful storm, quick and steady. The encircling crest ablaze now, and the trees rattling with the hail. Gallantly on against great odds; men fall like leaves in the brave ranks. Now to meet them with cold steel. "Remember Massachusetts, fix ——!" the colonel commands. A bullet cuts short the order. He is one of the casualties, and the command devolves on the lieutenant-colonel. The adjutant is instantly at his side, and tenderly asks, "Good God, colonel, are you wounded?" But time is too precious for such courtesies. "Lead on the men," is the colonel's answer. Yet it is too hopeless for a minute; that fire was too deadly; too many gaps; the line must recoil a little, close up compactly again and take breath. A few words from Col. Smith. Now ready; another start. Men grasp the bayonet, set their teeth, and move steadily up again, maddened and determined; again into the tempest of fire and lead, almost too much for mortal men. Gallantly and generously, but too fearlessly, the adjutant springs before the line. "Forward, men, let us avenge our colonel," is his impulsive battle cry. Instantly he is a mark for rebel bullets, and the pride and the idol of the regiment lies dead in the beauty of his young manhood. Up, men of Massachusetts, avenge the dead now, these scores of young lives! Push on the stainless white color of your state, and the flag of your country, against these traitors who would trample them under their feet. Steady a moment, under that scorching fire; see Lieut. Shephard there, dashingly waves on his men, and Sergeant Williams, his captain being wounded, and lieutenant dead, calls, "forward, boys." A dash now; leap over into the rifle pits; follow the color, though the brave color-bearer drops; grapple with those villains who dare hold out, collar them, bayonet, club them with your muskets till they cry quarter. Look! They surrender at last and the rest—they run like sheep down the slope, and the hill is ours! The old flag of the regiment, and the white color, float in victory over those ugly rifle pits! Hurrah, boys! and thank God!

## PRIVATE GEORGE P. METCALF

136th New York Infantry, O. Smith's Brigade

*The left-most regiment in the Union assault, the 136th struggled up the slope to confront the 4th Texas of Robertson's brigade. The New Yorkers' determined charge set their foe to fleeing with, in the flowery words of one Texan, "a celerity and unanimity . . . , plung[ing] recklessly into the umbrageous and shadowy depths behind them, . . . followed by the loud huzzaing of the triumphant Yankees."*

We ran a few hundred rods and stopped in line of battle. The firing ceased, and we were soon ordered to move again and came to a halt at the foot of one of these ranges of foot-hills I have described. We were in a wagon-road. Our line was composed of our brigade, being the 55th Ohio, 73rd Ohio, 33rd Mass. and 136th N.Y. Maj. Gen. Steinwehr, a German, had charge of us. He came to our front and in broken English said, "What regiment is dat?" He was told. "That is a good line," he said. "We want you to take that hill. The rebels are on top of it. You go up. Don't you fire a gun. If you do, that will give them the range to shoot you. Don't say one word until you get right onto them, and then holler like the tuyfel. They will think the whole corps is behind you."

At the command, the whole line started up the steep hillside. The way was covered with thick woods, brush and fallen trees. It was stony and so steep in places that we had to cling to bushes to pull our way up. We kept steadily on; occasionally a flash and a report told us that the top was covered with rebels. At our right were the 73rd Ohio and 33rd Mass. They soon began to fire. This did the mischief for them. The enemy ahead of us and those ahead of them, seeing them coming by the flash of their guns, turned down upon them a deadly fire. The woods were filled with the cracking of rifles and the shouting of men. But still they pressed on and kept loading and firing and in line with us.

Nearer and nearer we came. It is impossible to tell in pitch-darkness how far away a flash of powder is. We could tell by the sound that we were getting near them, but our regiment, faithful to orders, fired no shot as yet. I heard the bullets occasionally fly over our heads.

It was slow work, and yet we were in no hurry to get to the top. All at once, we found ourselves within a rod of the rebel-line, as we came out of a thick growth of low bushes. I smelt the burnt powder. We gave a most unearthly yell. It was a yell of fright, of terror. We were face to face with death. We fired our guns and yelled, and roared and screamed. If the rebels were not frightened, I was. We ran toward them with our bayonets. They never stopped to ask who we were, or how we got there, or how long we had come to stay, or how many there were of us, or to bid us good-by. They just ran. They left their guns, their axes, and shovels, and breastworks that they were building.

We only fired a few shots apiece, for we only caught a glimpse of the rebels as they darted away in the darkness. Of course, we did not know where they went to. We knew nothing of the lay of the land on beyond us. But we were glad they had left.

## ANONYMOUS

4th Texas Infantry, Robertson's Brigade

*Although the author of this postwar account was able to look back with humor upon the flight of one of his bulkier comrades off of Smith's Hill, the retreat was in reality a terrified rush for safety by a seasoned regiment that had never before fled a battlefield. Another member of the 4th, Miles Smith, stated that the term "speedy" did not do justice to the velocity of the Texans' pell-mell plunge down the slope "densely covered with large and small timber."*

He was a litter-bearer, his name was Dennis, and he was six long feet in height, and Falstaffian in abdominal development. His position in the rear gave him the start in the stampede, and his avoirdupois enabled him to brush aside, or bear down, every obstacle encountered in his downward plunge. But his judgment was disastrously at fault. Forgetting the ditch-like drain that marked the line where descent of one hill ended and the ascent of the other began, he tumbled, broadcast, into it. The fall knocked all the breath out of him, and he could only wriggle over on his broad back, and make a pillow for his head of one bank of the drain, and a resting-place for his number twelve feet, of the other. Lying there, his big body looked, in the moon-light, like a rather short butt cut off of the trunk of a large tree.

The litter-bearer had barely got himself in the comfortable position described, when Bill Calhoun came plunging down the hill with a velocity that left a good-sized vacuum in his wake. Observant by nature, and made the more so by the fear that if he came to grief in his passage of the drain, the Yankees would capture him, Bill no sooner saw Dennis' recumbent body than, taking it for the log it appeared to be, and sure that it spanned the drain, he made a tremendous leap, and landed his foremost and heaviest foot right in the middle of Dennis' expansive corporosity, and on that particular part of it for which the owner had the most tender regard. The sudden compression produced by Bill's suddenly imposed weight, produced as sudden artificial respiration, and giving vent to a howl of agony, Dennis cried, "For the Lord Almighty's sake, man, don't make a bridge of me!" Bill was startled, but did not lose his presence of mind, and shouting back, "Lie still old fellow—lie still! The whole regiment has to cross yet, and you'll never have another such chance to serve your beloved country," continued his flight at a speed but little abated by the rising ground before him.

## LIEUTENANT COLONEL WILLIAM G. LEDUC

Chief Quartermaster, XI Corps

*Anticipating the success of the Brown's Ferry operation and Hooker's overland movement, LeDuc built several supply vessels at the Union's Bridgeport base, using scavenged materials and green lumber. On October 29 he set out on his first ration run to Chattanooga, thus opening the Cracker Line.*

I took charge of the boat myself, with a steersman named Williams who had run on a ferryboat from Cincinnati to Covington. A man by the name of Davis who had served as mate on a lake boat I put at the bow to watch for any drift. The engineer was familiar with the engines and we started up the river under a full head of steam. The carpenters were yet keeping on with their work, trying to finish up the boat.

After about five or six miles had been successfully accomplished, a hog chain broke and we floated down the current while we mended it with a rope. The vibration of the steamboat hull was so great that I feared she would break the rope in two. We had spliced it as well as we were able, and I had ordered the engineer to use only steam enough to keep in slow motion up the river. Thus we merely crawled along.

The rain commenced falling and continued to increase with the darkness of the night. Finally it became so thick we could hardly see two boat lengths ahead, and Davis came back from his watch at the bow and said that if we didn't land somewhere we would be sunk. But we kept a sharp lookout for drift and forged ahead. We crawled up the rapid river, keeping as near mid-channel as possible. About 1 o'clock a campfire was seen on the north bank, and as we approached a sentry was visible against the firelight. We didn't know whether they were our men or rebs; if rebs, we were in a tight place for the river was not musket-shot across.

When within hailing distance I called to the sentry: "What troops are those? Who's your Colonel?"

"Fifth Tennessee Cavalry," came the reply. "Billy Stokes is our Colonel, and he's a good one, you bet."

"Col. Stokes is on our side," I shouted to my crew, and we brought her over toward the fire.

I asked the Tennessee boys how far it was to Kelley's Ferry from there, and they pointed to a campfire about a mile farther and said that was the Ferry. "They have been waiting for you all night," they added.

We pulled out again and the boat was soon made fast at Kelley's Ferry, where the barges with the precious rations were unloaded. I went ashore and into the arms of my excellent Assistant Quartermaster, Joe Shoeninger, who helped me up the slippery bank. A messenger was sent off at once to notify Gen. Hooker of our arrival. Then I took a pull at his canteen and lay down by the fire to dry myself. I was soaked through and tired to death. I slept until the sun came looking over the crest of Raccoon Mountain; then before noon I mounted and rode to Gen. Hooker's camp to report.

The orderly that carried news of my arrival with the *Chattanooga* to Gen. Hooker notified the different camps as he passed, and the soldiers cheered him and shouted, "Cracker line's opened, boys; full bellies again!" They made as great a hurrah as if we had won a great victory.

*One of LeDuc's steamers, the Chattanooga, is shown above navigating the Tennessee River and, at left, piled high with supplies while docked at Kelley's Ferry. From Kelley's, supplies were hauled on a short overland trip to Brown's Ferry and thence into Chattanooga. When the Union troops saw the Chattanooga for the first time, they cried, "Hurrah for the bully little steamboat! Rations once more—hurrah!"*

# Bloody Sideshow at Knoxville

The Federal victory at Brown's Ferry and the botched Confederate counterattack at Wauhatchie worsened the already poisonous relationship between Bragg and Longstreet. Throughout that cold, wet, miserable October, President Jefferson Davis and Bragg's own restive generals had plied the commander of the Army of Tennessee with proposals for rooting the Federals out of Chattanooga, but Bragg had rejected them all.

On the other hand, a suggestion from Davis arrived on October 29 that Bragg endorsed wholeheartedly. "It has occurred to me," Davis wrote, "that you might advantageously assign General Longstreet with his two divisions to the task of expelling Burnside from Knoxville."

Bragg wasted no time in implementing the president's suggestion. Here at last was a way to rid himself of the most formidable of the critics around him. Sending Longstreet to east Tennessee, he confided frankly to Davis, "will be a great relief to me."

Longstreet was appalled. Attacking Knoxville now made no military sense to him. His force numbered 10,000 infantry—the divisions of Major General Lafayette McLaws and Brigadier General Micah Jenkins—along with Major General Joseph Wheeler's 5,000 cavalry. Without more men he would be at a disadvantage against Burnside's superior forces: 12,000 infantry and 8,500 cavalry.

More important, his departure would leave the Army of Tennessee with only about 40,000 men to confront an enemy growing in numbers and confidence. With the arrival of Sherman, Grant's army at Chattanooga would total about 60,000. By separating the Confederate forces, Longstreet argued unavailingly to Bragg, "We thus expose both to failure, and really take no chance to ourselves of great results."

As his troops packed to move north on November 5, Longstreet gloomily wrote to General Simon Buckner that "it was to be the fate of our army to wait until all good opportunities had passed, and then, in desperation, seize upon the least favorable movement."

The events of the next few days only deepened his pessimism. The East Tennessee &

*A Federal sentry stands atop the northwest wall of Fort Sanders in Knoxville. The main Confederate attack on the fort came from the right, over the flats, through telegraph wire entanglements, and into the ditch ringing the bastion.*

Georgia Railroad was so decrepit it took eight days to haul all of his regiments 60 miles to Sweetwater—about halfway to Knoxville. And contrary to promises Bragg had made, no surplus food or warm clothing awaited him there. "We found ourselves in a strange country," Longstreet later recalled, "not as much as a day's rations on hand, with hardly enough land transportation for ordinary camp equipage, the enemy in front to be captured, and our friends in rear putting in their paper bullets." It was beginning to look, he noted bitterly, "more like a campaign against Longstreet than against Burnside."

Longstreet's adversary, Major General Ambrose E. Burnside, had failed conspicuously fighting against him at Fredericksburg 11 months earlier. But Burnside had not ducked the well-deserved blame for that bloody disaster and had soldiered on, doing good service by leading the Army of the Ohio on a flawless advance from Cincinnati to Knoxville in mid-August. He had flanked the Rebels out of their position at Cumberland Gap and raced for Knoxville, covering as many as 30 miles a day.

East Tennessee was pro-Union country. Residents of the area had voted 2 to 1 to reject secession in 1861, and in the two years since, these staunch Unionist Southerners had suffered grievously at the hands of secessionists. Thus, when Burnside's Federals entered the town on September 2, most of its citizens gave them a joyous welcome.

Now, however, Longstreet's advance on Knoxville frightened the authorities in Washington, who began pressuring Grant to do something to help. But Burnside himself had no such fears. Announcing that his men were "ready to meet any force the enemy might send against us," he proposed engaging the Confederates south of Knoxville, then giving ground slowly to protract the affair, thereby keeping Longstreet's forces out of the forthcoming battle at Chattanooga. Grant gave his blessing to the plan, and Burnside set out with about 5,000 men, leaving the rest behind to complete Knoxville's defenses.

Burnside's troops met the Confederates on November 15 on the heights south of town. His cavalry force under Brigadier General William P. Sanders, although outnumbered, compelled three brigades of Confederate horsemen to pull back. Over the next few days, Longstreet tried his best to outflank the Federals and trap them outside Knoxville. But each time, first at Lenoir's Station, and then at Campbell's Station, the Yankees escaped. By November 17 they were safely back within the now well-fortified town.

But food and forage were scarce, and as the days passed both armies suffered. The Rebels, poorly supplied to begin with, far from their nearest base, and among hostile people, were, if anything, worse off than the Yankees.

After a week's deliberation, Longstreet decided to focus his attack on the redoubt at the northwest corner of town. The Federals had named it Fort Sanders in honor of Burnside's gallant cavalry chief, who had been mortally wounded in a skirmish on November 18. The fort had earthen walls eight feet high and was fronted by a 12-foot-wide ditch that was also—unknown to Longstreet—quite deep. Cannon projecting from the corners of the fort enfiladed the ditch, making it a deadly trap. But because the fort was situated only 120 yards from a creek bed where a large body of troops could assemble under cover, Longstreet chose it as the target of his attack.

All was ready by November 24. But when Longstreet learned that reinforcements were on the way from Bragg, he decided to wait for them. Then bad weather and further debate about where to focus the attack caused more delays. Finally, on November 28, upon hearing rumors of a Confederate disaster at Chattanooga, Longstreet decided he must attack that night. "There is neither safety nor honor in any other course," he declared.

Rebel skirmishers seized outlying Federal rifle pits sometime after midnight, November 29. A few hours later, McLaws' three brigades launched a bayonet charge. The morning air was wet and raw, the ground frozen. As the Confederates ran forward yelling, the defenders opened fire at point-blank range. The 79th New York Highlanders, a regiment of mostly Scottish-born immigrants, bore the brunt of the attack.

Suddenly the charging men began falling to the ground, entangled in a web of telegraph wire strung among the stumps left when the approaches to the fort were cleared. Once the wires were cleared away, the attackers leaped into the ditch, only to find themselves trapped by an ice-covered wall rising 16 feet before them. A murderous fire poured down on them. It was a massacre.

"The earth," wrote a Northern correspondent, "was sated in blood—men waded in blood, and struggled up the scarp, and slipping in blood fell back to join their mangled predecessors in the gory mud below. The shouts of the foiled and infuriate Rebels, the groans of the dying and shrieks of the wounded arose above the din of the cannon."

After about 20 minutes, Longstreet called a halt to the slaughter. By the time the firing died down, his men had suffered 813 casualties and done almost no damage to the enemy. It was, one Federal officer observed, "Fredericksburg reversed."

Shortly after this terrible repulse, a courier handed Longstreet a message from President Davis. Momentous events had occurred at Chattanooga that would alter the course of the war.

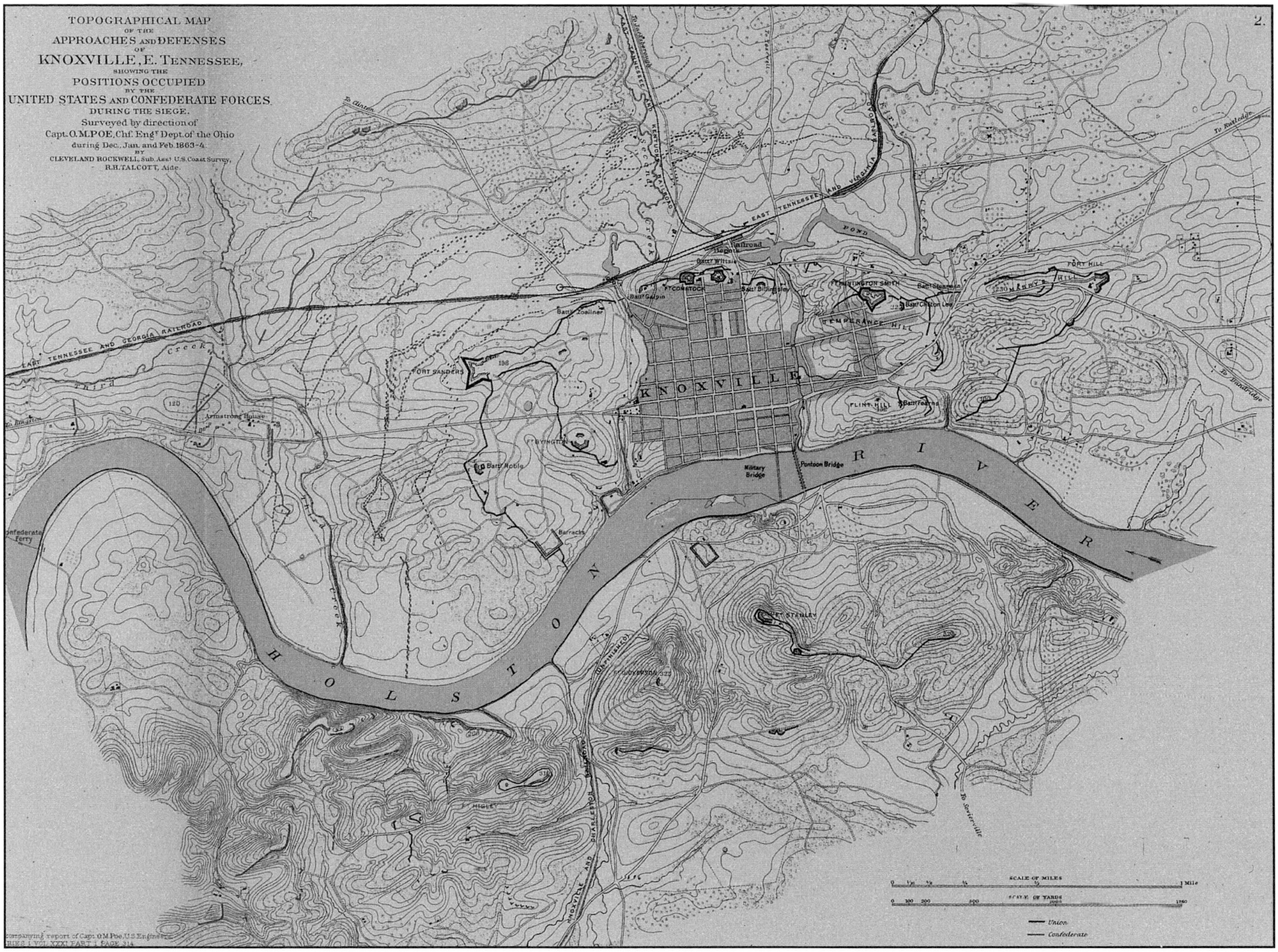


*In early September Burnside's Federals, after flanking the Rebels out of the Cumberland Gap to the north, entered Knoxville, a stronghold of Union sympathy in Confederate Tennessee. Informed in early November that Bragg was sending Longstreet to attack him, Burnside sallied forth to confront the Rebel force and fight a series of delaying actions, giving the rest of his army time to fortify the town. By November 18 Burnside had returned safely and Longstreet was encircling Knoxville, now ringed with the earthwork fortifications and rifle pits shown in this map prepared to accompany the Official Records of the War of the Rebellion. After about 10 days of skirmishes and probes, Longstreet launched a direct assault on Fort Sanders on the northwest corner of the Union defenses.*

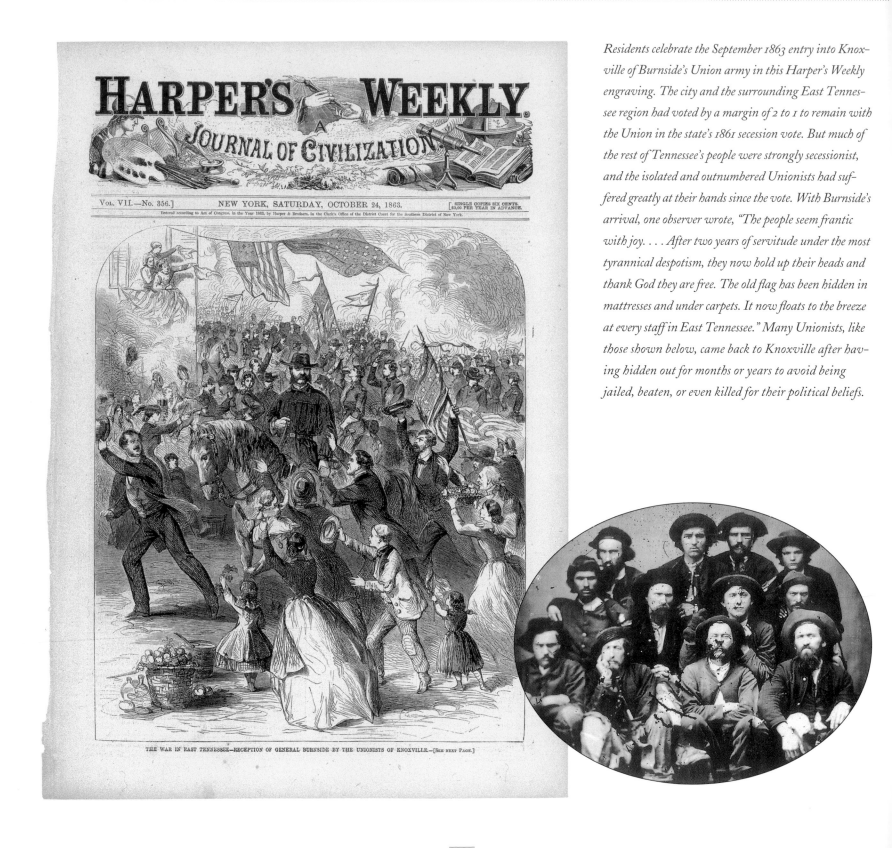

HARPER'S WEEKLY
A JOURNAL OF CIVILIZATION.

Vol. VII.—No. 356.] NEW YORK, SATURDAY, OCTOBER 24, 1863. [SINGLE COPIES SIX CENTS. $3,00 PER YEAR IN ADVANCE.

Entered according to Act of Congress, in the Year 1863, by Harper & Brothers, in the Clerk's Office of the District Court for the Southern District of New York.

THE WAR IN EAST TENNESSEE—RECEPTION OF GENERAL BURNSIDE BY THE UNIONISTS OF KNOXVILLE.—[See next Page.]

*Residents celebrate the September 1863 entry into Knoxville of Burnside's Union army in this Harper's Weekly engraving. The city and the surrounding East Tennessee region had voted by a margin of 2 to 1 to remain with the Union in the state's 1861 secession vote. But much of the rest of Tennessee's people were strongly secessionist, and the isolated and outnumbered Unionists had suffered greatly at their hands since the vote. With Burnside's arrival, one observer wrote, "The people seem frantic with joy. . . . After two years of servitude under the most tyrannical despotism, they now hold up their heads and thank God they are free. The old flag has been hidden in mattresses and under carpets. It now floats to the breeze at every staff in East Tennessee." Many Unionists, like those shown below, came back to Knoxville after having hidden out for months or years to avoid being jailed, beaten, or even killed for their political beliefs.*

## ELLEN RENSHAW HOUSE

Resident of Knoxville

*A staunch secessionist, House was appalled when the Yankees rode into Knoxville. Her devoted attention to the relief of Confederate prisoners and her open scorn for what she considered to be enemy invaders led the Federals, who suspected her of spying, to order her out of Knoxville in April 1864. She kept up her diary as she traveled about the South.*

Sept. 1 Tuesday. I think it is outrageous the Yankees are here. Just think. Here Here in Knoxville. Walked in without the least resistance on our part. Buckner evacuated it last week, took everything. There is one consolation we lost nothing in the way of eating, clothing, ordinance stores &c. But to let them have the place. I never never could have believed it. Only one regiment of the cavalry has come in yet. A Col Foster, I think, in command. He has taken up his quarters in Sneeds house and the good for nothing things have such comfortable quarters. How I hate them. Four came here and we had to give them something to eat. That was too much. . . .

Sept. 2 Wednesday. After dreaming of our boys, to wake and fine the Yankees here. Too bad—too bad. More came in today. I don't know how many there are or care. To know they are here is quite enough and more than enough. . . . This morning sister was sitting at her front window reading. Two men rode by with a flag. She turned her head. One of them said, "Did you see that girl. She would not look at our flag." And they both laughed.

Sept. 3 Thursday. They have been coming in today. They all ride two abrest. I suppose that is to string them out as much as possible. Our friend across the way come home today. Every union man in town, I believe, has been to see him. All looking perfectly delighted. They think they have everything their own way now, and I suppose they will for a time. A man came today to buy some bacon. Mother told him she had none to sell and very little. She could give them a piece. He was very polite. I don't suppose they will molest us if we keep quite. I certainly shall not let them think I am a Loncolnite but will behave as a lady. General Burnsides came in this afternoon and has taken up his quarters at Col Crozier house.

## LIEUTENANT COLONEL G. MOXLEY SORREL

Staff, Lieutenant General James Longstreet

*Sorrel, shown here as a brigadier general, a rank he received in October 1864, had served Longstreet since the Battle of First Manassas. After Knoxville he successfully led troops at the Wilderness and had his own brigade at Petersburg. Wounded severely in February 1865, he survived to become a businessman after the war.*

About November 3, Longstreet received his instructions. . . . . . . The troops of the expedition were to be the two divisions brought from Virginia and Alexander's fine battalion of artillery, six batteries; also Leyden's artillery, and Wheeler's powerful body of cavalry and horse artillery. We were also to take up all the loose bodies of troops to be found in the wide district to be covered. A force of about 3,000 men was promised from southwest Virginia.

It was an ill-disciplined body, not well organized, but accomplished wonders under Wheeler as a screen to the army, and an unceasing menace to the enemy's communications. . . .

. . . The expedition, glad to be on the move, set out smartly for Tyner's Station, where it was to be entrained for Sweetwater, but things went decidedly wrong. We had brought no transportation from Virginia and General Bragg's officers supplied us with wagons and teams, but

"The troops moved with the greatest coolness, deliberation and precision under a heavy and continuous fire, and resembled a drill rather than an actual battle."

held themselves under Bragg's order. A most inconvenient disposition then, and until we parted company with that commander for good.

With these and other difficulties it was November 12th before the last of our brigades came to Sweetwater. Here there were more disappointments as to rations, supplies, and transportation. We were dependent on Bragg's provisions, which cruelly failed us. Not to dwell too long on these mishaps, I need only add that they beset the entire campaign.

The cars and railway by which we helped the transportation were almost comical in their inefficiency. The railroad was of heavy grades and the engines light-powered. When a hill was reached the long train would be instantly emptied—platforms, roofs, doors, and windows—of our fellows, like ants out of a hill, who would ease things by trudging up the dirt road and catching on again at the top; and so it went on as far as the railroad would serve us.

A bridge train had been prepared by the engineers, and it had been our intention to use it across the Little Tennessee, or Halston, above its confluence and through Marysville. But here again was disappointment; there were pontoons but no train for hauling.

We were thus forced to throw our bridge across at Loudon, where, fortunately, the boats could be floated direct from cars without need of wagons, and there that curious bridge was laid by our worthy engineers. It was a sight to remember. The current was strong, the anchorage insufficient, the boats and indeed entire outfit quite primitive, and when lashed finally to both banks it might be imagined a bridge; but a huge letter "S" in effect it was with its graceful reverse curves. But no man should abuse the bridge by which he safely crosses, and this one took us over, using care and caution. I shall always love the looks of that queer bridge.

## MAJOR WILLIAM J. BOLTON

51ST PENNSYLVANIA INFANTRY, SCHALL'S BRIGADE

*Promoted to major the day he was wounded at Antietam in September 1862, Bolton eventually returned to service and went with Burnside to Knoxville. For his service there and in the Wilderness campaign, Bolton, shown here in a postwar dress uniform, was promoted to colonel and given command of the 51st.*

Nov 15 Regiment were aroused from their slumber at 2 A.M., formed on the color line, and in the mud and rain marched in direction of Loudon, reaching there about daylight. . . . The 1st Brigade of the 2d Division sent forward and deployed as skirmishers our brigade the 2d following in support. Our army gradually falling back on Lenoir, the scene very exciting and we are keeping the rebel advance in check. We reached Lenoir at 5 P.M., a running fight the whole distance some six miles, still have the enemy in check. Drew five days rations here, but did not have the time to cook them. . . .

After destroying the pontoon bridge, saw-mills, factories, one hundred wagons which had been corralled there loaded with provisions, a division of the 23d A.C. cut the spokes of the wheels, burnt the harness, tents and officers baggage. Barrels of bacon, coffee, and sugar were broken open and distributed to the men, and what could not be used was destroyed. The mules were needed for our artillery. The distruction of all this property was a military necessity, as it would certainly have fallen into the hands of the enemy.

Our brigade left here about dusk, taking the road leading to Knoxville, following Benjamin's battery of six 20 pounders. We marched all night through the rain and mud, and it was a severe and a laborious one. Men and horses were completely fagged out. The enemy were on our flank, and there was more or less musketry firing through the entire night. In fact it was a race with the contending forces for Knoxville, and Campbell Station was the key to the situation. The horses and mules gave out, and the men were compelled to drag the artillery over the deep gullies and steep hills, or abandon them, but with it all some of the ammunition had to be thrown away to lighten up the caissons. When daylight appeared, we found after our hard march that we had only made three miles in twelve hours from Lenoir. . . .

Nov 16 After partaking of something to eat, we moved off again about daylight, and we were more able to pick our road. We arrived at Campbell station . . . about 9 A.M. and not a moment too soon, as their advance skirmishers were on our heels, and fired into our rear. Hartranft had scarcely made his dispositions when McLaws appeared and at once attacked, but we steadfastly held our ground until the remainder of our troops and all our trains had safely passed. . . .

About noon, Longstreet unsuccessfully attacked our right, and afterwards our left centre. A white horse battery made its appearance on the outskirts of the woods in full view of us. Our artillery turned upon it at once and the very hills trembled under the reverberation. Almost immediately an attempt was made to turn our left, the enemy coming up evidently to strike Hartranft's left and rear. Again our artillery opened, and the enemy's broken ranks sought shelter in the woods. Burnside determined to retire to a new position about two-thirds of a mile to his rear. The difficult and hazardous undertaking was successfully accomplished in the face of the enemy. It was a grand sight. The troops moved with the greatest coolness, deliberation and precision under a heavy and continuous fire, and resembled a drill rather than an actual battle.

McLaws' Division promptly advanced to attack the new position whilst Jenkins continued his turning movement, but the difficulties of the ground delayed him until nightfall stopped his further progress. McLaws failed in his attack, and at the close of the action Burnside remained in possession of his own ground. Burnside's object was to fight long enough to give his trains time to reach Knoxville, and to gain cover of night under which to complete his withdrawal to that place, and therefore can fairly claim a victory. . . .

Under the cover of night the troops began falling back. 17 long muddy miles lay between us and Knoxville. Seventeen of the longest, weariest miles that it has ever been our misfortune to travel.

741
HARPER'S WEEKLY.
November 21, 1863.]
THE WAR IN EAST TENNESSEE—DRAWING ARTILLERY THROUGH THE MOUNTAINS.—[See Page 742.]


*The Harper's Weekly illustration at left depicts the difficulty of the march described by Bolton. One correspondent recounted that "a heavy rain commenced at daylight, and fell in unceasing torrents until late at night. The roads, so difficult of passage before, became now almost impassable. Wagons sank to their boxes in the liquid mud, mules fell exhausted in the traces and gave up the ghost; while drivers, teamsters, and artillerists became so covered with the spattering mud that it was difficult to distinguish them from the surrounding soil."*

## LIEUTENANT ROBERT T. COLES

4th Alabama Infantry, Law's Brigade

*Coles was an 18-year-old student at the LaGrange Military Academy when he enlisted in April 1861. Probably due to his education, he was named sergeant major when the regiment was mustered into service the following month. Wounded at Gaines' Mill, Coles surrendered at Appomattox and farmed in Alabama until his death in 1925.*

Brigadier-General Jenkins, commanding the division, had thrown out a strong line of skirmishers in his front from Bratton's brigade. All that was required of the 4th Alabama was to follow in the rear until we reached Lenoir's Station, where the enemy was found in force. Up to this time there had been constant skirmishing by our vanguard from the time we crossed the river at Loudon. It was now the 15th of November, and it was cold and raining. On very short rations, the regiment remained in line of battle all night.

On the next morning we discovered that our guide had placed us on the wrong road and the enemy had escaped during the night leaving a large number of cut down wagons loaded with commissary, ordnance and sutlers' stores. It was a race from here to Knoxville in our efforts to intercept and bring the enemy to bay. General McLaws' division was sent on one road and ours on another, both converging at Campbell's Station about twelve miles from Lenoir's. From some alleged mismanagement, which General Longstreet attributed to General McLaws' misconduct, we failed to accomplish anything after passing Campbell's Station. The enemy again escaped and continued on to his entrenchments at Knoxville.

Late that evening the regiment made a rapid march on the flank of the enemy, over stony ridges, through thick undergrowth of briars and scrub oak, without time to secure rations, with the hope of cutting off the rear of Burnside's army in its rapid retreat to Knoxville. We were sorely disappointed when finally, almost exhausted and ravenously hungry, we looked over the ridge down into the road to see the extreme rear guard of the enemy hastily disappearing. The men did their work cheerfully and zealously, but it appeared that our General Officers were at cross purposes, which, of course, caused all of our toils and hardships to result in failing to accomplish our object.

Before going into bivouac another effort was made to intercept and cut off a portion of the enemy's rear, but darkness coming on, we abandoned the movement and went into bivouac. . . .

Our march was so hurried we had no time to secure rations, except a few Irish potatoes, and it fell to my lot to divide them out equally to the officers and men. After a careful count, with the assistance of Lieutenant William Turner of D Company, it was found that each one was entitled to two potatoes. Lieutenant Turner suggested that he and I draw straws for who should have the four. It nearly broke my heart when Turner proved to be the winner, but, fortunately, one of the men, who had obtained from a citizen a small piece of fat bacon, generously gave me a slice. In some way Major Robbins had secured about a handful of peas. We boiled his peas and my meat in an oyster can, and these,

with the Major's two potatoes, which he kindly divided with me, was the menu of the Field and Staff of the 4th Alabama that night.

Early the next morning we followed on, driving the enemy towards Knoxville, arriving in front of that place on the 17th of November, 1863. For the first and only time during the war, we were issued two days back rations, which consisted of flour, bacon, mutton, sugar and coffee. We captured a large lot of sugar and coffee. The men were so hungry they ate too much and nearly all were made sick. Our surgeons attributed our illness to what they termed "sick flour."

*This two-image panorama, photographed during the siege, looks east from East Tennessee University toward downtown Knoxville. A Federal encampment appears to the left of the Second Presbyterian Church in the background at left center. Union earthworks line the hills in the distance and across the Holston River at right, and Union cannon can be seen in the right foreground. The Confederate attack came from the northwest, to the left rear of where the photographer was standing.*

## PRIVATE JOHN H. MANSUR

U.S. Army Signal Corps

*Mansur helped build the works at Fort Sanders, the strongest point in the defenses of Knoxville. Mansur joined the 75th Pennsylvania in August 1861 and transferred to the Signal Corps about six months later. He served in Knoxville for 11 months after the siege, then mustered out at the end of his three-year enlistment. A "Complete right hernia and disease of urinary organs" gained him a $12-a-month pension.*

The movements that resulted in our being cooped up in Knoxville extended over a couple of months. We had been chasing up the rebs and they chasing us alternately day about, in the neighborhood of Loudon, about 30 miles below Knoxville, since the middle of October. We had numerous skirmishes with them, notably at Lenoir's Station and Campbell's Station, on the East Tennessee & Virginia Railroad, and while we invariably beat them in the fighting, yet we just as invariably fell back during the night toward Knoxville, so that we reached our last ditch in that direction about the 18th of No-

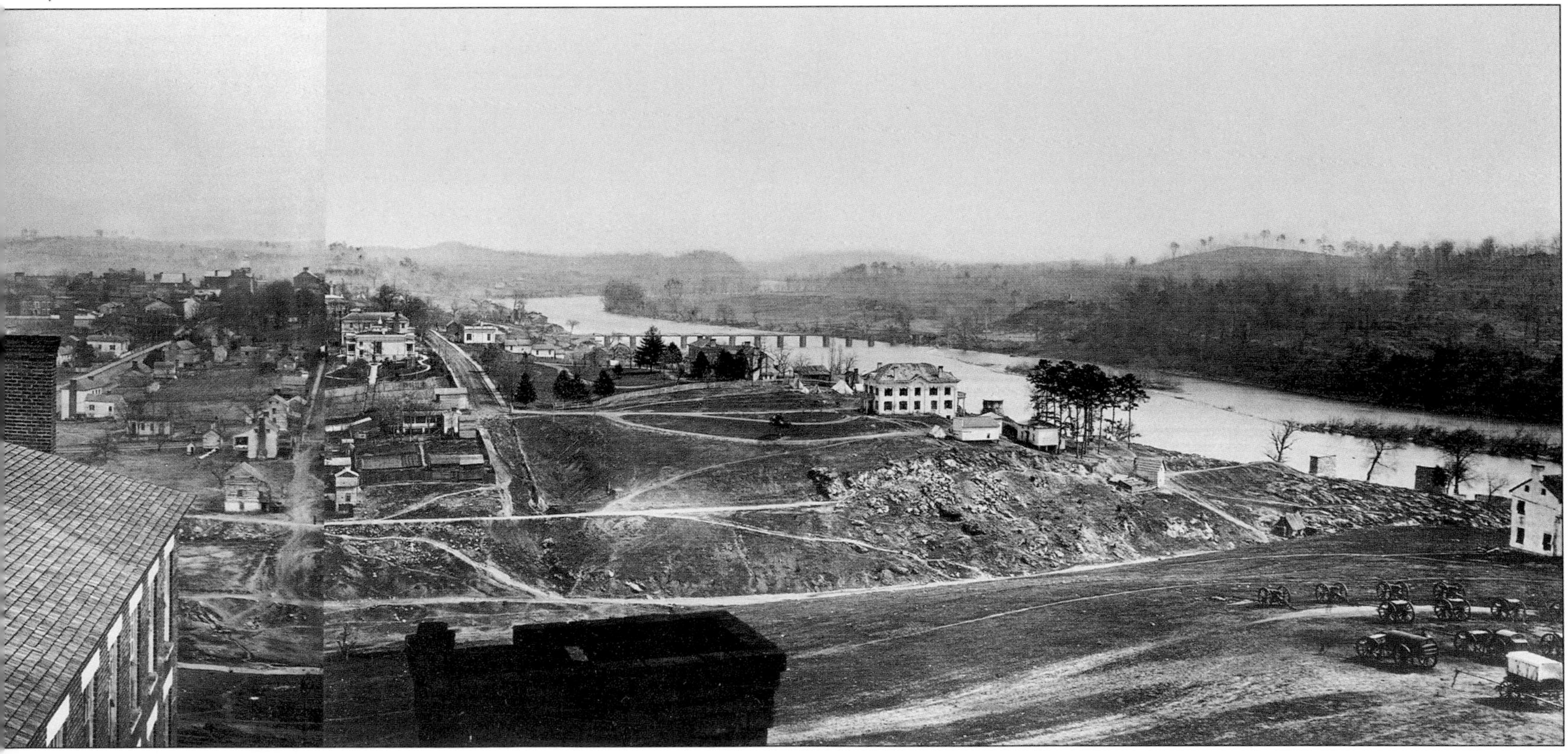

vember. It was during the last fight just outside of Knoxville that the gallant Gen. Sanders was killed. On the morning of the 18th, I was ordered to duty in a large fort on the right of the Kingston road, then without a name, but in a day or so afterward named Fort Sanders, after the brave soldier killed in front of it. . . . When we took possession of the fort it was only partially finished. The center of the inclosure was higher than the parapet, the bombproof was only about half done, and the side nearest the town was entirely open. We soon set to work to remedy this, and for several nights we had between 300 and 400 negroes digging and shoveling. It was hard work to keep them at it, for the rebs kept up a pretty lively shelling, and at the first alarm they would all lie down or run and hide. I recollect very clearly seeing one of them hiding behind an empty flour barrel, and I have been sorry a hundred times that I did not hit that barrel with a lump of dirt. While the inside of the fort was being strengthened we also were attending to the outside. We had with our detachment several miles of insulated telegraph wire, which was intended to be used in putting up a portable telegraph line, but had never yet been taken off the reel. This wire we wound around the stumps of the trees on the slope of the hill in front of us in two lines about 100 yards apart, forming a fence that was almost invisible, but, as it proved, a very serious obstacle to an advancing column. . . . We still kept on strengthening the fort where it was thought necessary, and the rebs, with the most commendable patience, waited till we had everything in the very best order, and then tried to do what they should have done at the start, before we had time to fortify—namely, carry the place by assault.

*Major William M. Gist of the 15th South Carolina Infantry (left) was slain instantly by a Yankee sharpshooter's bullet on November 19 as he prepared to lead his regiment in a charge against the Knoxville fortifications two days after Burnside's withdrawal back into the city. Gist was one of the first Confederate officers to die in the siege of Knoxville. His uniform hat displays the palmetto insignia of his native state.*

## SERGEANT WILLIAM TODD

### 79TH NEW YORK INFANTRY, MORRISON'S BRIGADE

*Todd's regiment, composed mostly of Scottish immigrants, was known as the Highlanders. Its first colonel, James Cameron, brother of Secretary of War Simon Cameron, was killed at First Manassas, where the regiment suffered 198 losses. Ravaged again at James Island, in 1862, the 79th lost 110. At Second Manassas and Chantilly, 105 more fell. The Highlanders were the primary defenders of Fort Sanders.*

Friday, 20th. Third day.—All quiet during the night. Morning cool and misty. Picket firing began as soon as the fog lifted. At nine o'clock the new picket were ordered out; their appearance caused the enemy to fire with renewed vigor, and there was considerable ducking and dodging before the relieved men were safe in the fort. Gangs of negroes are busily engaged in rolling bales of cotton on the parapets of the fort, for the better protection of the men. The interior crest being only about four feet above the banquette tread, the upper parts of our bodies were exposed to the enemy's fire. The cotton bales were covered with rawhides, to prevent their being ignited by our musket fire. It was announced that strict garrison rules had been adopted for the government of the fort, and that roll-call at five o'clock each morning must find every man at his post. The enemy must have advanced his picket line, for the bullets are now singing over the fort in very unpleasant frequency, which causes all hands, from General Ferrero down to drummer boy, to duck and dodge in a manner not at all creditable to old soldiers. Rain began to fall in the afternoon and continued all the evening, rendering our situation very disagreeable. It was impossible to move about without getting over ankles in mud, and our clothing and accoutrements were soon in a very disreputable condition. There was not room enough for all the men to pitch their shelter-tents, and many of us received a thorough drenching, which added greatly to our discomfort.

# "We were so near the town that we could hear the tunes played by the band at Fort Sanders. The favorite air then was: 'When this Cruel War is Over.' "

## LIEUTENANT FRANCIS W. DAWSON

STAFF, LIEUTENANT GENERAL JAMES LONGSTREET

*Born Austin J. Reeks in London, Dawson emigrated in 1861 expressly to fight for the Confederacy, changing his name to honor an army captain uncle killed in India. After a brief stint in the C.S. navy, he joined the artillery and by June 1862 was on Longstreet's staff as an ordnance officer.*

Burnside fell back to Knoxville, and we went into camp around the town. The principal defensive work was Fort Sanders, which had walls twenty feet high, with a ditch ten feet deep. Efforts were made to guard the river, both below and above Knoxville, so as to prevent Burnside from receiving supplies or reinforcements, and the works were occasionally shelled. There was a good deal of delay, for one reason and another, and we were so near the town that we could hear the tunes played by the band at Fort Sanders. The favorite air then was: "When this Cruel War is Over." Finally, an attack was ordered to be made on Fort Sanders, but, although our men fought with their usual gallantry, they were driven back. This was on the 29th of November. In front of the fort trees had been cut, so as to fall with their branches outward, and wires had been stretched from stump to stump to trip up any assailants.

## SERGEANT PHILIP G. WOODWARD

36TH MASSACHUSETTS INFANTRY, MORRISON'S BRIGADE

*As the defensive preparations described here ended, Woodward recorded that "November 26th was our National Thanksgiving, and General Burnside issued an order reminding us of the debt of gratitude which we owed to Him who had prospered our Arms and preserved our lives. We ate our corn bread, and thought of home and loved ones, who, uncertain of our fate, would find little cheer at the table and by the fireside." Wounded at Cold Harbor, Woodward returned home a captain at war's end.*

Meanwhile, our men were busy strengthening our works with chevaux-de-frise, the stakes being bound together by wires to prevent their being torn apart. They were about five feet in height. The north side chevaux-de-frise was made with two thousand pikes captured at Cumberland Gap a few weeks before. . . . Still further, were wire entanglements stretched a few inches above the ground and fastened to stakes and stumps. At other points, dams were constructed across the creek, throwing back the water. The whole being a line of defense which could not be passed except with fearful loss.

Fort Sanders was garrisoned by the 79th New York Highlanders. The 45th Pennsylvania had its left on the river, on its right was the 36th Massachusetts, then the 8th Michigan and the 100th Pennsylvania, Colonel Leasure's Roundheads, with its right on the Fort.

The siege had now continued several days, and we felt that the strength of our position would enable us to repel an assault from any quarter, but the question of supplies was a serious one. Bread made from wheat and corn mixed was issued to the men in only half and then quarter rations. No sugar nor coffee. A few times a very little piece of fresh pork was issued. Some days we had an ear of corn per day, which was parched and pounded, stirred up in water and baked. In some instances we saw men picking up kernels of corn under the feet of the mules and eating them.

The Fort had now been made as strong as the means at our disposal admitted. At distances of eighty and thirty yards in front, rifle pits were constructed, to be used in case our lines were driven in from the outer line. Sandbags were so arranged at the Fort, as to cover the embrasures. Traverses were built for passing from one position to another. In the Fort were four 20-pound Parrot guns, four light 12-pound guns, and two 3-inch steel rifle guns.

On the 28th there was little firing, but our pickets had been driven in in front of the Fort. It was evident that the enemy intended an attack. All through that long, cold night we were in the trenches, without overcoats, and suffered severely. Many had chills and fever. But the night finally wore away, and at about six o'clock on the morning of the 29th the enemy suddenly opened a furious cannonade against Fort Sanders.

## COLONEL E. PORTER ALEXANDER

CHIEF OF ARTILLERY, LONGSTREET'S CORPS

*Having taught at West Point before the war, Alexander joined the Confederate army as a captain of artillery. Considered to be a genius at the placement of cannon, he commanded the guns on Marye's Heights at Fredericksburg. Alexander was promoted to brigadier general three months after Knoxville.*

On the way back the party stopped opposite Fort Sanders, and while watching it with glasses, saw a man cross the ditch in front of the northwest salient, showing the depth of it at that point as less than five feet. This encouraged a hope that the ditch of the fort would not be found a formidable obstacle, and as there was now no alternative, and Leadbetter was urgent against further delay, the attack was ordered at noon on the 28th, this time being necessary to return Parker's battery to its enfilading position on the south side, whence Leadbetter had had it withdrawn the night before.

At noon the next day all was ready, but the day was rainy, and very unfavorable for artillery practice, so Longstreet again decided to postpone the attack until the next morning, the 29th. . . .

At the earliest sign of light in eastern sky, three successive guns fired from different batteries gave the signal to the sharpshooters to open fire and for the storming columns to advance. Their shells were visible like meteors in the air and they exploded high above the fort. For a few minutes about a dozen guns poured a hot fire on the fort and into the angle of the lines behind it. This was intended only to encourage the storming columns, and was discontinued in a few minutes. At once the sharpshooters opened their fire upon the parapet, and orders were given the storming columns to move. . . .

. . . As the two columns advanced on converging lines, they presently ran into an entanglement of telegraph wires stretched between stumps which threw down the leading files and caused a little delay. But these

*Captain Orlando M. Poe leans against one of the stumps that impeded the Confederate assault on Fort Sanders as he confers with Colonel Orville E. Babcock, Burnside's senior engineer. Both men, key participants in the development of the defenses of Washington, D.C., in 1861, were primarily responsible for devising and preparing the Knoxville fortifications. In the background a sentry stands on the fort's northwest bastion, which took the brunt of the Rebel attack on November 29.*

were soon torn away and with very little loss. . . . The two columns were soon found to have converged in the darkness too much, and being already deep columns, one of four lines and one of five, they simply coalesced in the darkness into a mass whose officers could no longer separate or distinguish their own men. To this mass was presently added Anderson's brigade, ordered to carry the breastworks east of the fort. Through some mistake, some minutes later, they came in from the left, in two lines, where already nine lines were crowding each other. The ditch was found to be from four to eight feet deep, and about twelve feet in width, without any berm at the top of the counterscarp, and with steep sides rendered slippery by freezing weather and the rain of the previous day. Yet many officers and men were able to cross the ditch and scale the parapet, but not in such numbers as to overcome the 150 infantry defending the fort with fine tenacity. A few shells were lighted . . . and thrown by hand into the ditch as hand grenades, and axes and billets of wood were thrown over the parapets. . . .

Meanwhile fully 20 minutes elapsed and daylight began to make things dimly visible. Nearly 200 men had gotten into the ditch and not finding it easy to advance, now preferred to surrender. The fire from the fort had ceased except an occasional musket fired over the parapet exposing only a hand of the man holding it. But at a point 500 yards to the south of the fort, an offset 200 yards long, running nearly west from the Federal breastworks, gave a fair enfilade fire upon the crowd of men along the counterscarp of the west front of the fort, and from this point the increasing daylight was bringing a fire which rapidly multiplied the casualties.

Longstreet, about this time, was advancing with the brigades of Johnson and Gracie, with those of Jenkins and Benning upon the left, when he received an exaggerated report of the wire entanglement which had been first encountered. Without a second thought Longstreet ordered the recall. Johnson begged to be allowed to go on, as also did Jenkins, but Longstreet, giving full faith to the report, forbade.

*In this engraving of the assault on Fort Sanders, attacking Confederate troops attempt to charge up a slope to the fort's northwestern rampart but find themselves entangled in a web of telegraph wire strung among fallen trees and tree stumps. In the background, Federal enfilading fire repulses other attackers as they try to climb out of the deep ditch in front of the fort and scale the ice-slicked earthen walls.*

## SERGEANT ANDREW A. WERTS

3D SOUTH CAROLINA INFANTRY, KERSHAW'S BRIGADE

*Kershaw's brigade was positioned as part of the reserve to the south of Fort Sanders. It was to rush to the support of Humphreys' and Wofford's brigades once the fort was overrun, but the assault failed, and Kershaw's men were not ordered into battle. While Werts had a good view of the action he describes, he is mistaken in thinking that the Federals had virtually abandoned their strong defensive positions.*

Early on the morning of the 29th Nov. the general attack was to be made on Ft. Sanders. The troops were in motion long before day, splashing through the water and mud their clothing wet and fingers were benumbed. Ft. Sanders as a large fort covering several acres, surrounded by a deep mote which measured from bottom to top some 18 to 20 feet. Wofford and Humphrey were to make the direct attack on the fort. Kershaw was placed to their right. Should the fort fall in the hands of the attacking party, Kershaw was to go forward, capture the breastworks in his front. The crash came with the signal guns from Alexander's battery, followed by 20 guns from our battery. Burnside returned the salute with 50 guns. The shells shrieking, bursting into the fort. After the artillery duel had been kept up some fifteen or twenty minutes, Wofford and Humphrey throwed forward their brigade through brush and treetops encountering a wire entanglement. This was soon overcome and the Confederates found themselves on the cress of the 12 foot abyss. Some jumped into the moat and began to climb the steep walls on the shoulders of others. Our sharpshooters stationed back of the line, all the time, picking off the cannoneers by shooting over the heads of our columns. The enemy throwing hand bombs over to explode in the moat. The enemy had nearly all left the fort. Just at that critical moment, Major Gogans, of Longstreet's staff, rode up and reported the fort impregnable without ladders and axes. We evacuated Knoxville at midnight on Dec. 4th.

*Longstreet chose the Mississippi brigade of Brigadier General Benjamin G. Humphreys (bottom left) and the Georgia brigade of Brigadier General William T. Wofford, who was absent due to illness at the time, to lead the main assault on Fort Sanders. It was to be a bayonet charge; none except sharpshooters were to fire during the advance. Thus, not one weapon was loaded in Wofford's and Humphreys' brigades, or in Kershaw's support brigade, when the charge began. As the troops ran forward screaming the Rebel yell, Yankee guns and muskets opened up a withering fire on them at point-blank range. While "stunned for a moment by the torrent of canister and lead," a Northern correspondent reported, the attackers kept coming.*

"I saw those brave men—for they were brave even if they were the enemy—marching up there as if nothing would stop them."

## SERGEANT JAMES B. KENNEDY

100TH PENNSYLVANIA INFANTRY, W. HUMPHREY'S BRIGADE

*Kennedy had enlisted in the 100th for three years at Washington, Pennsylvania, in August 1861. During his part in the fierce fighting to defend Fort Sanders, which he describes here, he was severely wounded. A Minié ball passed through his face and neck, destroying the left side of his jaw and leaving him permanently disfigured. He saw no more action and was mustered out at the end of his enlistment in October 1864 after nearly a year of convalescence.*

It was about 6:30 a.m. when the boys gave the alarm and shouted: "They are coming!" I sprang to the parapet. I had to get on top, for cotton bales had been placed on end on the outer edge of the parapet, so as to protect us as much as possible. There was a space in the extreme corner which did not have any cotton bales, but instead had branches of trees stuck in the outer edge for a screen, but they were no protection, as it was there that two of company A were killed—Aaron Templeton and Isaac R. W. Garrison. When I looked over the cotton bale I saw those brave men—for they were brave even if they were the enemy—marching up there as if nothing would stop them; but they made a mistake that time, for when they came to the wire entanglements the first line commenced falling, while we were giving them the best we had. That kind of demoralized them, but did not stop them, for they came on, filling the ditch in front of fort and climbing up on each other's shoulders. I saw there what I consider as daring an act as any performed during the war by two rebels, by which both lost their lives —one climbing to the top of the parapet and planting their colors there, and urging the "boys to come on, the fort is ours!" He was shot by members of company A. The other was that of a captain who attempted to come in at the embrasure, demanding of us to "surrender."

Just as he made this demand, and was partly through the embrasure, the cannon, double-shotted with grape and canister, was set off. That was the last I saw of him. I was then standing on the parapet, on the left of that gun, and one of the 79th New York boys, who was between me and the embrasure, was killed, and fell against me, and then down near or under the cannon. About that time my gun was so damaged by a shot which struck the barrel that I could not use it. I got down and got his gun; fired about five rounds from that, when I had to retire to hospital. . . .

. . . When the alarm was given, Lieutenant S. N. Benjamin made his appearance, as he always did when there was any fighting to be done, but as his guns could not be used at so short a range, he called to one of his sergeants—O'Keefe, I understood him to say—to "bring me some of those 20-pound shells." He cut the fuse short, and lit it with a brand taken from a fire we had been trying to keep warm at near the parapet. Some of the boys say he lit it with a cigar; he was smoking at the time. As he threw them over among the rebs, I heard him say, "Look out over there, or some of you will get hurt."

While the attack was raging, the cotton bales caught fire, and Captain Buckley got on top and put it out. I expected to see him killed, but he was not.

## CAPTAIN WILEY G. JOHNSON

18TH MISSISSIPPI INFANTRY, B. HUMPHREYS' BRIGADE

*Johnson's unit was to attack around midnight, clear the Federal pickets from in front of the fort, and dig in. Once that was completed, the 13th and 17th Mississippi were to charge past their fellows and overrun the fort. Humphreys had selected the two young colonels mentioned below to lead the assault, "that they might win new laurels." Johnson wrote later that the attack on Fort Sanders "was short, but one of the most desperate struggles of the war, and deserved better success."*

The hour of twelve came. We were at the appointed place, drawn up in skirmish line, so that as we neared the fort we would not crowd each other by concentration. The stars shone brightly and the ground was freezing rapidly. . . . I walked along the line and told the boys to meet me on the other side of those yankee picket lines under that fort, and it would be all right. . . .

At the command we moved forward through brush, briers, and thorns, in the face of the picket firing, capturing or driving all the pickets into the fort, and getting pretty close to the fort itself. Then came the fun, if there is any fun in such things. I called for my pick and spade man, and true to his trust here was my faithful Irishman, Pat Burns, with his arms full of the implements, in addition to his fighting accoutrements. The line was marked the full length of the regiment for our earth work. Then you ought to have seen the fire fly out of those rocks. The enemy in the fort, only a few rods off, tried to depress their guns so as to shell us, but every shell went over our heads, and served only to add increased zest to the work. We had to get into that ground before day, and we did.

We had accomplished our part of the contract, and were prepared to hold the position taken, and being so close to the fort, we could aid our assalting friends from the rear, till they passed over us, by picking off the gunners in the fort.

At the dawn of day up came the two gallant regiments, steady and determined. Fizer of the Seventeenth, with a hatchet buckled on to his sword belt, with which he had vowed beforehand to cut down the tall flag-staff on top of the fort, and McElroy of the Thirteenth, the very picture of chivalry, were at the head of their respective regiments. They moved quietly till they passed over us and our embankment, then with the rebel yell they rushed for the fort. It was as grand a charge as I ever saw, but success was impossible under the circumstances, and ought to have been foreseen before the attempt was made.

The assaulting force was composed of regiments from different brigades with no general officer in immediate command. These regiments, instead of moving on parallel lines till they enveloped the fort, began to converge from the start; so when they got to the deep ditch or moat at the base of the fort, they were in the condition of Napoleon's Old Guard at the battle of Waterloo, when they came to the sunken road of Ohain. They knew nothing of it till they came suddenly upon it; hence, they rushed headlong into it. There was no help for it. Companies and regiments were so mixed and jumbled it was utterly impossible for the officers to tell their men from others. It was in the midst of this confusion that Colonel McElroy got back out of the ditch and asked a Georgia colonel on his left to move his regiment further to the left, in order to make room for his Mississippi regiment. The Georgia colonel (I forget his name), a brave and good man, questioned the right of an officer of his own rank to command him. Neither knew which ranked the other. They were discussing the matter in pretty sharp terms, when they were both shot down in their tracks. . . .

In the meantime Colonel Fizer had had a little better success. True to his purpose, with hatchet in hand, he had climbed to the top of the parapet, and was making for the flag-staff, when a ball shattered his arm, and he rolled back into the ditch. Many more tried the same thing, and I think a few got over but never to return. A close inspection showed the face of the fort too steep to climb.

*This engraving depicts Rebel troops attempting to climb out of the ditch and scale the front wall of Fort Sanders. The ditch was, on average, eight feet deep; once in it the men were confronted by an almost vertical, slippery wall rising 16 feet. Some soldiers leaped onto the shoulders of others to try to reach the top of the wall. Those who made it were shot down. Men, one observer wrote, "struggled up the scarp, and slipping in blood fell back to join their mangled predecessors in the gory mud below."*

## SERGEANT WILLIAM TODD

79TH NEW YORK INFANTRY, MORRISON'S BRIGADE

*In the hand-to-hand defense of Fort Sanders described here by Todd, almost anything that could be used as a weapon was. Major William Bolton of the 51st Pennsylvania recalled seeing Private James Dunne, out of ammunition, thrust an artillerist's long-handled worm into a Confederate as the attacker tried to charge through an embrasure. The skewered Rebel was pulled inside the wall and captured.*

The attacking party had reached the ditch before we gained our positions, and a scene was being enacted difficult for pen to describe. The artillery, depressed to the lowest point, was hurling double and triple charges of canister into the masses of the enemy. Some of our men were firing over the cotton bales and others through the embrasures occupied by the artillery; still others were pouring a destructive flank fire from their rifles, and enfilading the ditch on both the north and west fronts. Both officers and men were shouting and encouraging each other. . . . The enemy, finding that the ditch barred their progress, seemed at fault. They crowded about the edge, and, hoping to escape the murderous fire of our artillery and rifles, many jumped into the ditch! Now was Benjamin's opportunity, and, assisted by Captain Baird, who held a burning stick, the twenty-pound shells were ignited and rolled down among the living mass below. As they burst, yells, shrieks and groans attested the bloody work! Now the enemy's fire slackens and we can see that many of them are hurrying to the rear. A cheer goes up from our throats, but is instantly answered by a chorus of yells from a fresh column of the enemy, who, nothing daunted by the repulse of their first line, now crowd up to the assault. The wires trip many and break their lines; many fall to rise no more, but the living press forward.

. . . the second assaulting party was now raining bullets through the embrasures, and along the edge of the cotton bales, and the fire from within was renewed. There was no need to take careful aim; the brave rebels crowded up to the ditch, as the first line had done, and almost every bullet fired by us found a death mark. Shells were bursting in the ditch, literally tearing the poor fellows limb from limb and scattering the fragments far and near. Many tried to scramble out by making a platform of the bodies of their dead comrades, but few came out alive, and those only to be a mark for our unerring rifles. To most of those who entered, it was indeed the "Last Ditch."

*The 79th New York Highlanders had marched to war in 1861 proudly wearing kilts or tartan pants called trews. By 1863 the battle-scarred veterans had given up their costumes for blue uniforms. As can be seen in this photograph of Highlander James Berry, only the soft caps called glengarries remained of their regalia.*

Our twelve-pound howitzer had ceased firing for some time, owing to a lack of ammunition, the last charge having been left in the gun for the greatest emergency; it came when half a dozen of the bravest of our foes, thinking the gun was silenced, had managed to scale the counterscarp and present themselves at the embrasure. The demand—"Surrender, you d——d Yankees!"—was all the gunner, who lay under the piece close to the parapet, was waiting for. "Yes! we'll surrender *this* to you!" was his reply. The lanyard was pulled, and when the smoke cleared away the bodies of the brave rebels had been scattered to the winds!

The gun was now run up into the embrasure and the gunners armed themselves with rifles. No second attempt was made at that point.

But a yell louder than usual causes us to glance in the direction of the sound. There, on the very angle of the bastion, we see a rebel flag rising above the exterior crest, and soon appears the head and shoulders of the bearer! Brave fellow! but your last moment is at hand! A dozen rifles are discharged, and with the flag-staff clutched in a death-grip, he rolls to the bottom of the ditch, riddled with Yankee bullets. Another tries to succeed him and shares the same fate. Still others crowd on. They have formed a temporary bridge over the ditch, and are making a desperate effort to scale the parapet! A curious incident now occurs, which, were it not for the terrible and deadly work now going on, would be laughable. Sergeant Dunn, of Company K, owing to the excitement, had forgotten to withdraw his ramrod when last he loaded his piece, and it was fired off with the charge. On attempting to reload he was unable to ram home the cartridge. Two of the enemy were making their appearance above the crest within a dozen feet of him. Clubbing his rifle he flung it at them, but failed to hit either. No other piece was within reach; his comrades were busy with their own work—the enemy were nearly upon him—time was precious. Looking hastily about he espied an axe; it was but the work of a moment to seize and swing it about his head and hurl it at the approaching foe; it hit and knocked one down, while the other fell at the same instant, pierced by a bullet!

## LIEUTENANT WILLIAM A. MCCLENDON

### 15TH ALABAMA INFANTRY, LAW'S BRIGADE

*During the siege of Knoxville, First Sergeant McClendon was elected second lieutenant to replace an officer who had been disabled. He later recalled, "So I turned in my rifle, and donned a sword, with one stripe on my collar. I entered immediately on my duties as lieutenant, but I never did feel right in battle with only a sword, and always provided something to shoot with." McClendon fought on through the duration of the war and surrendered with Lee at Appomattox in April 1865.*

As a last resort to caputure Knoxville Longstreet decided to storm Fort Sanders and we were hurried back across the river in supporting distance, and in sight of the devoted Georgians of Woffords and Bryans Brigades of McLaw's Division, who had been ordered to make the assault. It was a strong fort built upon a commanding position and the large and small timber had been felled with their tops outwardly, making the route to the fort almost impassible. The fort itself was well nigh impregnable, and could not be occupied from the front unless the assaulting column was well provided with ladders to scale the wall after the large ditch in front was occupied. We stood in position under arms, and watched the brave Georgians as they moved out to the assault. I knew from what I could see that it would be a desperate undertaking, and many a brave Georgian would bite the dust.

*This flag of the 16th Georgia was captured when, according to a soldier of the 17th Michigan, the Confederate officer carrying it stepped "in the embrazure in front of a cannon, laid his hand on the muzzle of the gun, and called out to the gunners to surrender; the gun was discharged, and the man was blown to atoms, his flag falling into the fort." The colors of the 13th and 17th Mississippi were taken at about the same time.*

The blood within me became chilled with fear of the result of that charge as I imagined the carnage to be in the ranks of them brave fellows, but I kept silent and made no comment. The Georgians moves on, until they come in range of the numerous cannons that could be brought to bear upon them when they began to send forth missles of destruction into their ranks. Without wavering they move on, until they become entangled in the brush, when they lost their organization, and each man picked his own way to advance, but they move on, shot, shell, grape and cannister dealing death at every step, but they move on, until they get near enough to receive the fire from the small arms in the fort, they gave the "Rebel Yell," and firing as they advanced they made a dash for the fort. They reached the ditch and could go no farther, and all the commanding officer could do was to order a retreat. There was no effort as I saw, made to reinforce them, and they were repulsed with heavy loss, but the charge upon "Fort Sanders" by them Georgians will ever live in the memory of the living, and will adorn a page in history testifying to the devotion of them Georgians to the "Lost Cause." There was no other effort made to capture Knoxville, and upon information that reinforcements were coming to Burnside, Longstreet raised the siege, and moved off up towards Bristol.

## LIEUTENANT CHARLES W. WALTON

51st New York Infantry, Fry's Brigade

*Within a few days of being wounded at Antietam, Walton was promoted from corporal directly to second lieutenant and six months later was named a first lieutenant. By April 1864 he was a captain. Here Walton describes the horrible slaughter visited on Longstreet's attackers in front of Fort Sanders. In an action that lasted barely a half hour, Confederate casualties were 813 to a Federal loss of only 13.*

Across the railroad, up the gentle slope, and through the stumps they came, while our guns were making havoc among their ranks. On they came, never faltering, with that well-known war yell; the stumps that the wires were attached to are reached, and down they fall amid charges of grape and canister, while the steady fire of the infantry from the adjoining rifle-pits, although destructive, did not deter them from rushing forward. They filled the ditch, and every foot of ground gave evidence of their great courage. Lighted shells with short fuses and hand grenades were thrown over in the ditch, and in another moment through the smoke we discovered another brigade closed en masse rushing on to meet the same fate, as our guns opened on them with renewed vigor. Yells mingled with groans as they fell and, unable to stand such a scorching fire, they broke and fled to the rear; the few who returned in safety were truly fortunate. One or two leaped the ditch, climbed the parapet, and planted the colors on the fort, but only for a moment, as they were instantly hauled in by our men. Such deeds of heroism are rarely recorded, and we could not help but admire their pluck as they were marched off as prisoners of war.

"I knew from what I could see that it would be a desperate undertaking, and many a brave Georgian would bite the dust."

Before the smell of powder and smoke had passed away, I, with a few others, passed out of the fort over the ditch on a plank and looked on that scene of slaughter. Such a spectacle I never again want to witness! Men literally torn to pieces lay all around—some in the last throes of death, others groaning and their faces distorted under the severe pains from their ghastly wounds. Arms and limbs, torn from their bodies, lay scattered around, while at every footstep we trod in pools of blood. The ground also was strewn with split guns, bayonets and equipments, not to speak of hats and boots. Over a hundred dead bodies were taken from the ditch alone while the vast number of the wounded were being carefully carried within the lines to receive the best care in our hospitals; as they passed by us on stretchers their moanings were pitiful to hear. Three hundred prisoners fell into our hands, representing eleven regiments, and it was evident to us that the enemy had met with a fearful loss, while ours was comparatively slight.

A flag of truce having been granted the enemy until 5 o'clock, burial parties were sent out, and for an hour or two they were busy burying their dead, who were laid in rows and covered over with the soil. At the appointed time the signal gun from the fort was fired, the truce was at an end, and Fort Sanders resumed its wonted aspect.

## LIEUTENANT FRANCIS W. DAWSON

STAFF, LIEUTENANT GENERAL JAMES LONGSTREET

*Dawson wrote candidly that Longstreet's "reputation . . . as a fighting man was unquestionably deserved, . . . there was no lack of energy or of quickness of perception, but he was somewhat sluggish by nature, and I saw nothing . . . to make me believe that his capacity went beyond the power to conduct a square hard fight. . . . whenever he had an independent command, he was unsuccessful."*

In one of the attacks we made, Captain Winthrop, of the 44th Foot, in the English army, who was on leave of absence, and had been with us for some time, behaved with the most brilliant gallantry. We were taking a hasty lunch in the breastworks under fire as the assault began, and Winthrop rode off to see what was going on. Finding that the troops were advancing, he rode out in front of the line and right up to the enemy's works, striking with his sword at the soldiers who held them. In less time than it takes to tell it he was lying on the ground with a big hole in his collar bone. It was a very painful wound, but he recovered.

The attack on Knoxville having failed utterly, and tidings having been received of the defeat of Bragg, at Missionary Ridge, Longstreet raised the siege, and retreated to Virginia.

## ASSISTANT SURGEON ROBERT P. MYERS

16TH GEORGIA INFANTRY, WOFFORD'S BRIGADE

*The wet, cold weather had taken a toll on the Rebel soldiers before the assault and, as Myers recounts, increased the suffering of the wounded, making the task of caring for them even more difficult. During the two-hour truce on November 29, Burnside graciously loaned ambulances to the enemy to transport their wounded and assigned Yankee soldiers to assist surgeons like Myers in their grim work.*

Before day light we were in line between the R.R. & fort Loudon the latter on outskirts of Knoxville—as soon as there was light enough our Artillery open'd—at 6 am our Infantry commenced fireing & charged the works with severe loss on our side—Col Ruff kill'd in first charge at the ditch which surrounded the fort. Col Thomas kill'd & fell in ditch his overcoat pierced with 19 holes Adjt Cumming taken prisoner in the fort which tis said he entered through port hole—Capt Nash Co A killed—our regt's loss in killed, wounded & prisoners 85 as far as known—Maj Hamilton Comdg Phillips Legion wounded in arm above elbow—Adjt Porter of Cobb Legion thigh—the fight was soon over—the weather was intensely cold & the wounded suffer'd much—I had large fires built on the field to keep them warm—my hands became so cold while dressing the wounded I had to heat water to warm them after the attack we fell back—Capt B. E. Stiles not in the battle, & I was the only medical officer of Wofford Brigd on the field.

30th. The Brigd was with-drawn at 12 M yesterday & we returned to Camp where all was quiet & sad—the feeling just after a battle is very depressing—the excitement intense at the time but after its all over you get into Camp and look around & miss so many familiar faces it makes the stoutest hearts quiver—After the attack the enemy suspended hostilities until 5 PM—so that we might bury the dead and get those most

*In this engraving based on a painting by famed cartoonist Thomas Nast, the attack on Fort Sanders is shown from the defenders' perspective. A wave of Rebels tries to scramble up the steep wall while Federal soldiers behind the parapet fire directly at them. One Yankee (center left) prepares to hurl a fused shot like a hand grenade into the mass of Confederates. A soldier in the fort noted that the attackers were so close and so packed together that "there was no need to take aim."*

*This rope-tension wood-shell drum was used by Confederates during the Knoxville campaign. The routines of camp life, from roll call to taps, were regulated on both sides by such drums. There were also drumrolls for tactical maneuvers during battle, although the roar of cannon and musket fire often drowned them out.*

severely wounded off their hands—I went with Lieut. Ed: Thomas while the flag of truce was up to get his fathers body which brought to us by four Yankees on a litter—we were not allow'd to go near the fort which they had surrounded by a strong line of pickets Lt Col G Moxley Sorrel of Savannah A.D.C. to Genl Longstreet was in chge flag of truce—the whole day was intensely cold—this morning as I would wash the water would freeze on my hair & beard before I could wipe it off altho I was before a large fire—reports are numerous some say Genl. Bragg whip'd Thomas others the reverse—its reported also that the enemy got into our rear and destroyed the E.T. & Ga RR between Charleston & Cleveland Tennessee every thing quiet on the lines—

December 1st 1863. This morning Ed Thomas caused his fathers remains to be disinterred from Field Infirmary & buried at the private graveyard of a Mrs Crawford about a mile from our Camp & 3 M fr: Knoxville. Col Ruff was buried alongside Col Thomas—I marked both of the graves with head boards & cut their names on them—The weather somewhat moderated tho the ground frozen hard.

## PRIVATE JOSEPH B. POLLEY

### 4th Texas Infantry, Robertson's Brigade

*Like many in Longstreet's corps, Polley was frustrated at having failed to vanquish the Yankees yet glad to be heading back to the eastern theater. In Virginia the corps would face some of the toughest fighting of the war in the upcoming Wilderness campaign and around Petersburg, where Polley would be wounded in the Darbytown road fight and lose his right foot to amputation.*

Half an hour after the fighting ceased, General Longstreet received positive information that the battle of Missionary Ridge had been fought and was won by the Federals, then under command of General Grant, and that Bragg's army was in retreat. With this information came an order directing him to rejoin Bragg. As a march to the south and to Bragg's army would not only be over a mountainous and extremely rugged country, but also expose him to pursuit by Burnside and a Federal force then approaching Knoxville from Cumberland Gap, he decided to move north, up the Holston River, into a field offering admirable opportunities for the maneuvering of a small army and soldierly enterprise; moreover, it would take him beyond the reach of Bragg's authority.

To mask the withdrawal of the Texas and Law's brigades from the east side of the Holston, they and the cavalry on their right, on the morning of December 3, made a vigorous demonstration against the Federals in their front. These stood their ground well until about noon; then they abandoned their first line of intrenchments, and took cover in another nearer the river. Night coming on, the two brigades quietly marched to the ferry over the Holston, crossed the river, and, moving around the city, went northward toward Strawberry Plains, as the advance guard of their little army. Silence prevailed and the utmost caution was observed among the Texans and Arkansans until they were well beyond sight and hearing of the Union soldiers they had so long helped to hold in practical captivity. Then, giving expression to their feelings, they made the woods ring and resound with loud and unchecked rejoicings that they were on their way to rejoin "Marse Robert's" army. Some enthusiastic broke into song, and as the opening words of the old melody, "Carry me back to ole Virginny," floated in musical cadence from his lips, a shout went up that made the welkin ring, and there was not a man "with music in his soul" but joined hopefully in the chorus.

# The Battles for Chattanooga

Ulysses S. Grant was an offensive-minded soldier, and he found it intolerable to remain cooped up in Chattanooga, surrounded by towering hills infested with the enemy. Shortly after opening up the Cracker Line, he advised General in Chief Henry W. Halleck: "If the rebels give me one week more time, all danger of losing territory now held by us will have passed and preparations may commence for offensive operations."

All that was needed was the arrival of General William Tecumseh Sherman's Army of the Tennessee. Sherman's march from Memphis had been slowed to a snail's pace by Halleck's order to repair the Memphis & Charleston Railroad line along the way. On November 2 Grant countermanded the order, directing Sherman to turn over the task to Brigadier General Grenville M. Dodge, an experienced railroad builder, and "hurry eastward with all possible dispatch toward Bridgeport."

*Federal troops of General Philip H. Sheridan's division sweep up Missionary Ridge in this photograph of part of a lost cyclorama. A lone Rebel defender fires off a round as others surrender and an entire unit withdraws eastward over the crest.*

To defeat the Confederates, Grant would have to attack an enemy entrenched on high ground, and he planned his offensive carefully. Upon Sherman's arrival, Grant would have three forces at his disposal; he would give the pivotal role in the assault to the army led by his old friend. There were few men in the world Grant trusted as he did Sherman—and he had great faith in the Army of the Tennessee, for it was his own former command.

Grant viewed his other two forces with skepticism. He suspected that Hooker's XI and XII Corps had been sent to him as castoffs from the Army of the Potomac, and the Army of the Cumberland had just suffered a defeat. According to Sherman, Grant thought that the latter force "had been so demoralized by the battle of Chickamauga that he feared they could not be got out of their trenches to assume the offensive."

Sherman's target would be Bragg's strategic flank, his right—at the junction of the Confederate supply line from the south and line of communication with Longstreet in the north. Sherman would march from Bridgeport to Brown's Ferry, cross to the north side of the Tennessee River, and move into the hills north of Chattanooga.

This movement could not be concealed from Confederate observers on Lookout Mountain, but Grant hoped to confuse them about where the Federals were going. Once out of sight, Sherman would make camp. Then, in a rapid nighttime move, he would bridge the river—General William Smith was already building the necessary pontoons—whisk his men across, and before Bragg knew what was happening, roll up the Confederate right along Missionary Ridge. Bragg would thus be cut off from his supply base at Chickamauga Station and driven away, if not destroyed.

Grant gave Hooker and Thomas supporting roles. He ordered Hooker's XII Corps to move around Lookout Mountain and threaten the Confederate left at Rossville Gap while the XI Corps, under Howard, remained in reserve on the north side of the river, opposite Chattanooga. Thomas was to give artillery support to Sherman and later to assault the Confederate center.

On November 15 Sherman, traveling well in advance of his army, finally reached Chattanooga. The next day Grant took him to study the terrain at the north end of Missionary Ridge—the objective Grant had chosen for him. Sherman stared through a telescope for a few moments, then closed up the glass with a snap and pronounced: "I can do it!" Soon he was on the move again, retracing his route to Bridgeport to marshal his forces.

The attack was scheduled for dawn on November 21. On November 19 the Army of the Tennessee set out from Bridgeport for the 35-to-40-mile march to its jumping-off point. But the weather did not cooperate. A heavy rain turned the roads to mud, and the march slowed to a crawl. It was November 20 before Sherman's vanguard reached Brown's Ferry, and the rest of the army was strung out all the way back to Bridgeport. Grant decided to postpone the attack.

A fresh downpour began on November 20 and continued through the following day. The river began to rise, threatening the pontoon bridge at Brown's Ferry. When all of Sherman's divisions but one were across, the bridge gave way—stranding the remaining men, commanded by Brigadier General Peter J. Osterhaus. Grant ordered Osterhaus to join Hooker in Lookout Valley. Meanwhile, Sherman's other divisions disappeared into the hills above Chattanooga, and Howard's XI Corps crossed the bridge at Chattanooga and moved in behind Thomas' defenses.

Grant hoped that the Confederates, having first seen Sherman's troops crossing at Brown's Ferry and then, a short time later, Howard's troops moving across the river into Chattanooga, would conclude that they were the same force. To make up for the loss of Osterhaus, Grant assigned Sherman one of Thomas' divisions, commanded by Brigadier General Jefferson C. Davis, and rescheduled the attack for November 24.

As Grant had hoped, the Confederates were thoroughly confused. Bragg, watching all those enemy troops moving around, fretted about Sherman's location and intentions. He finally concluded that Sherman was marching on Knoxville, and, on November 22, ordered Buckner's and Major General Patrick R. Cleburne's divisions to entrain north to reinforce Longstreet. Buckner left immediately. Cleburne marched his troops to Chickamauga Station to await the return of the train carrying Buckner.

Bragg then tried a ruse of his own. Under a flag of truce, he sent Grant a letter. "As there may still be some noncombatants in Chattanooga," Bragg wrote, "I deem it proper to notify you that prudence would dictate their early withdrawal." Grant puzzled over the message. For some reason Bragg wanted him to think he was planning an attack. The mystery deepened when a Confederate deserter falsely reported that Bragg was pulling back from Missionary Ridge. The deserter's report galvanized Grant. He urgently needed to know if the Confederates were actually withdrawing. If so, this would be an ideal time to strike. Someone had to test the Rebel reflexes. Sherman was not yet ready, but Thomas was.

Early on the morning of November 23, Grant gave Thomas his instructions. In Chattanooga Valley, the plain lying between the city and Missionary Ridge, rose a wooded mound about 100 feet high called Orchard Knob. For weeks Bragg's men had held the valley, including the hill. Now Grant wanted Thomas to conduct a reconnaissance in force to see if the Rebels were still there.

The Chattanooga Valley and its surrounding hills formed a magnificent natural amphitheater. Grant wrote later that it was "the first battle field I have ever seen where a plan could be followed, and from one place the whole field be within one view."

Onto this stage at noon on November 23 marched the division of Thomas J. Wood. On Wood's right was Major General Philip H. Sheridan's division. Still smarting over their rout at Chickamauga, the men were determined to prove their mettle.

As Wood's and Sheridan's men marched onto the plain, soldiers on both sides stopped to watch. On the hills looming over the plain, clusters of Confederates could be seen gazing at the display. Like many of the Federals, they believed for a moment that Thomas was holding a grand review. At about 2:00 p.m., a signal cannon boomed, and the blue-clad lines surged forward. Suddenly the Confederate pickets realized they were under attack by a force many times their number. In just a few hours it was all over. Thomas' men had seized Orchard Knob and driven a mile-deep salient into the center of Bragg's line. Thomas moved swiftly to strengthen the position. The

Rebel earthworks on the hill were reversed to face the Confederates and a six-gun battery brought up.

Orchard Knob had been a minor but instructive action. It showed Grant that Bragg had not withdrawn, and Bragg now knew that Grant was intent on attack. Hastily, Bragg recalled Cleburne's division from Chickamauga Station and pulled Brigadier General William H. T. Walker's division off Lookout Mountain and placed it about a mile from the north end of Missionary Ridge.

By now Sherman's men were safely hidden in the woods eight miles northwest of Chattanooga, ready for a nighttime river crossing and a morning attack. Late that night Grant told Hooker that instead of simply making a demonstration against Lookout Mountain, he should now attempt to capture it. In the game of cat and mouse that Grant and Bragg were playing, Grant had seized an advantage, and he intended to keep it.

*During November, Bragg maintained his stranglehold on the Federals in Chattanooga. But his army was in disarray because of disaffection among his commanders, and he had weakened it further by sending Longstreet's corps north to attack Burnside at Knoxville. Meanwhile, Grant was gaining strength. The Brown's Ferry and Wauhatchie operations had opened his supply lines, and Sherman had arrived with reinforcements about November 20. On November 23 Thomas' men stormed and captured Orchard Knob, east of town. By midnight Sherman's forces were positioned to the north for a night attack across the Tennessee River against Missionary Ridge, and Hooker's troops were preparing to strike Lookout Mountain to the south. The Yankees were set to try to root the Rebels out of their positions around Chattanooga.*

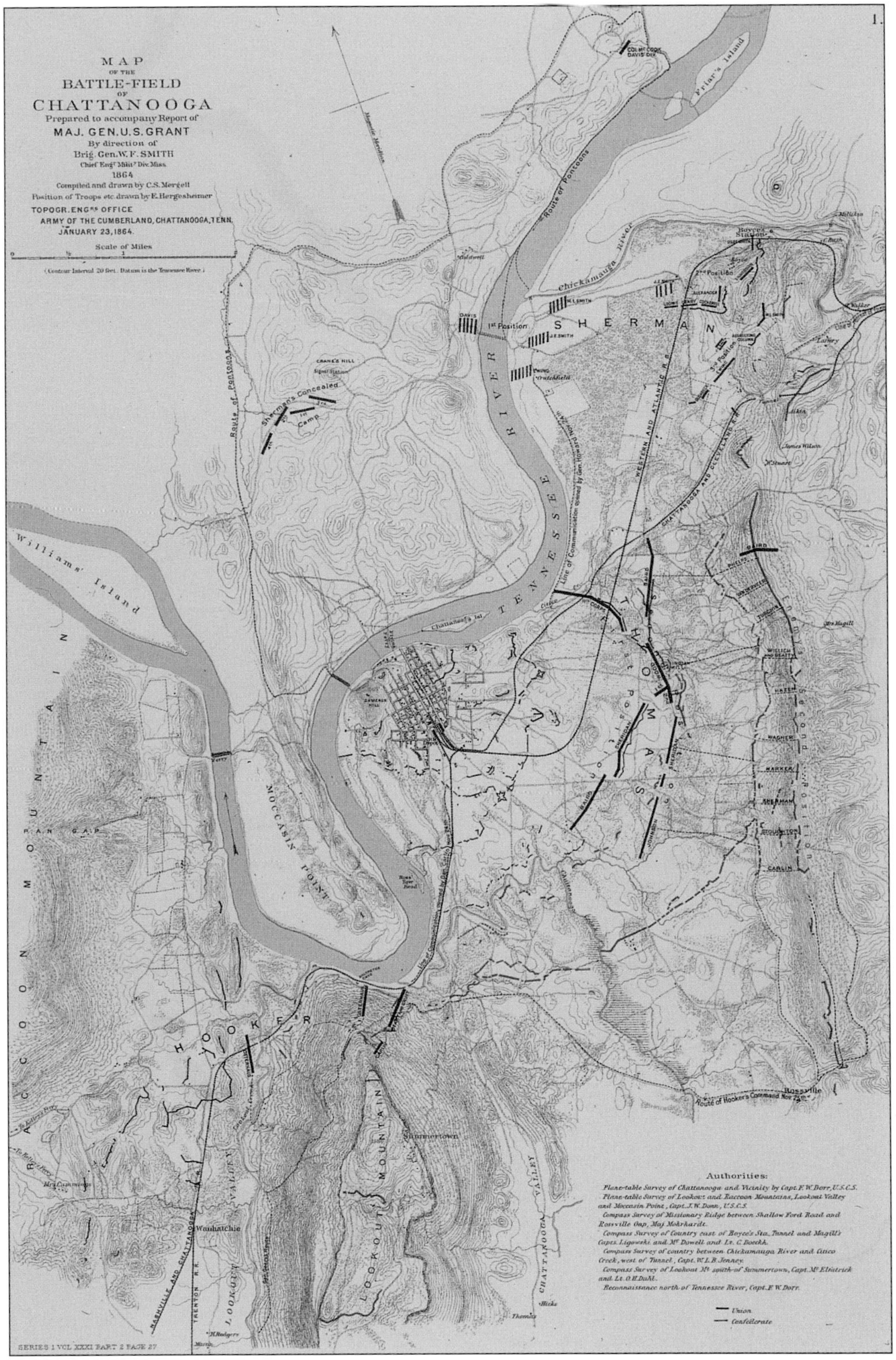

## PRIVATE ROBERT A. JARMAN

27TH MISSISSIPPI INFANTRY, WALTHALL'S BRIGADE

*After Grant opened the Cracker Line, the once starving Yankees began again to enjoy full bellies while, as Jarman describes, the men of Bragg's army felt the increasingly tight crimp of low rations. In the meantime, thousands of Union reinforcements were steadily advancing toward Chattanooga.*

We continued to do guard duty for the month of October, or at least the greater part, when our command was moved back a short distance and the men fixed up more comfortable for a few days, when it was said we would go into winter quarters. While here I received my overcoat and some other things from home, and some money, by the courtesy of a Mr. Drake, who had to refugee from Tennessee and had gone to the army to visit his sons in the Tennessee regiment.

We did not, however, remain in this position very long, but our brigade was sent to the front on Lookout Mountain to relieve part of Longstreet's corps that was ordered to Knoxville; and here it was on Lookout Mountain that rations became very scarce during our ten days stay there in Nov. One day our issue of rations consisted of three crackers and about two tablespoons of sugar, but thanks to Rafe, who was with the wagon train, we, that is my mess, kept a full supply of bacon on hand for each day. While here on Lookout Mountain, we did picket duty at the foot of the mountain, on a creek, we called Lookout Creek, and near the railroad. While here the two picket lines at many places were not more than forty yards apart. We could see and hear them relieving their pickets, and they could see us. Each party kept fire at the vidette post day and night. We even met half way in the creek, where it was shallow and shoally; to swap newspapers, canteens, and tobacco for coffee. And I have seen some swap hats and shoes, and talk for half an hour at a time, but this was only when no officer was present on either side.

## CAPTAIN WILLIAM L. JENNEY

STAFF, MAJOR GENERAL WILLIAM T. SHERMAN

*Jenney's mysterious cake became part of the spoils of war when, on October 11, a division of Nathan Bedford Forrest's Rebel cavalry under General James R. Chalmers attacked the transport train hastening William T. Sherman from Memphis to confer with Grant at Chattanooga. The Union troops held onto their train after a spirited fight, but not before the daring horse soldiers took more than 100 Union prisoners and captured or burned most of the Federal supplies on the freight cars.*

General Grant ordered General Sherman to report with his army with the greatest possible haste at Chattanooga. Sherman embarked on boats and landed at Memphis, where the march began. As the railroads were fully occupied in carrying supplies, the troops were forced to go on foot.

Sherman had a special train to take himself, staff and escort to Corinth. Just as we were leaving Memphis a German, with a large cheese box in his hands, appeared at the train, inquiring for Captain Jenney. I announced myself and asked him what he wished. "Oh, Captain, I told my wife what you had done for me, and she sent you this cake. Take it."

"What did I do for you?" I asked. "I don't remember anything."

"Yes, you did, here is the cake."

Just at this moment the train started. About noon we made preparations for lunch and opened the box which contained a large, handsomely frosted cake. Just as we were about to cut it the train stopped and someone ran in and called to us: "Get out of here as quickly as you can. The road is cut ahead of us and we are stopped by Chalmers' cavalry."

We got out of the cars as quickly as we could. Directly above us on the bank was the redoubt of Collierville, of which we took possession. Sherman immediately stepped into the telegraph office and telegraphed to Corse, who was some dozen miles away, stating the situation and ordering him to come to our relief double quick. Corse happened to be within easy reach and replied at once, "I am coming," so that we felt sure of relief ere long.

The enemy immediately commenced an attack on the redoubt and bombarded us with eight pieces of artillery for four hours. They had about 8,000 men and eight guns. We had some 600 men and no guns. Twice they got possession of our train when an assault from the ditch cleaned them out. On top of the cars we had brought a battalion of the

"They had about 8,000 men and eight guns. We had some 600 men and no guns."

Thirteenth United States Infantry. Numerous assaults were made by the enemy, which were always repulsed.

Two or three times one of the men would scream out: "There is a rebel who is trying to steal our knapsacks!" which were left on the top of the car, and would fire at him. "No," said the officer, "that is our man, Tom Smith, who is dead drunk and did not get off with us." As soon as the firing was over, some of his comrades climbed onto the car to see how many times Tom, who had been under the cross fire from both sides, had been shot. To their astonishment he was found to be entirely uninjured and woke up quite sober.

Our horses had not escaped so well. My own was wounded in the car and the train was generally riddled with bullets, broken glass, etc., and there was a cannon shot through the engine so that we were obliged to wait all night till a train could be sent for us from Corinth. I went down to our car which I found had been pretty well cleaned out by the enemy. Everything of any value had been taken—among other things, my cake. As I stood on the platform a soldier passed along with a large piece of cake in his hand. He called out, "Who had the cake?" I replied that I did, but it was all gone, and asked him where he had got that piece. "Took it out of the hand of a dead rebel—there under the fence. It is real good. He had his mouth full but I let him keep that."

I never was able to learn who presented me with that cake, nor could I recall the German nor anything that I had ever done for him.

## LIEUTENANT JAMES DINKINS

STAFF, BRIGADIER GENERAL JAMES R. CHALMERS

*As Dinkins sorted his plunder, he discovered that he had captured the sword of Lieutenant Colonel Charles Ewing, Sherman's foster brother and his assistant inspector general. During the battle, Sherman had taken cover in the railroad station. Had the Confederates been aware of this, claimed James Young of the 7th Tennessee Cavalry, they could have used their artillery to blow the building to bits.*

A long train of freight cars rolled into the station from Memphis, from which the Thirteenth Regulars disembarked and ran into the fort. We knew, of course, that Major Cousins had failed to cut the road on the west as ordered, otherwise the train could not have passed him. General Chalmers knew that any further delay would be ruinous and, therefore, gave the order to charge. Our men moved forward in fine style, but were met by a hot fire. They charged within about sixty yards of the fort. We could see nothing of the enemy except the tops of their heads. General Chalmers saw it would be a great sacrifice to storm the fort and, therefore, withdrew under cover of the woods.

General Chalmers' plans were well laid, and had McGuirk charged the fort before the arrival of the Thirteenth Regulars, instead of halting in the cavalry camp, the garrison would, unquestionably, have been captured. Or had Major Cousins cut the road, as ordered, the Thirteenth Regulars could not have reinforced the garrison, and in that event we would have captured it.

After the line had fallen back and was resting in the woods, I was sent to find Lieutenant Banks and Major McGuirk. Arriving at the point where the rear of the train rested, I noticed a number of our men in the cars throwing out saddles, bridles, blankets and bundles. I dismounted, hitched my horse to a telegraph pole and boarded the coach at the end of the train. I wanted some of the plunder. The coach was empty, but on the seat was a handsome sword which I picked up. I ran out to where the men were busy getting saddles. In one of the cars were several horses. It had not occurred to the men that the horses could be gotten out. I said, "Make them jump out," and with that I pulled myself into the car, untied a fine horse and led him to the door. After much urging the horse jumped out. It did not require much time for the boys to get the others out. With their plunder, they all galloped off to catch the command which had retired about a mile back, where the general waited in vain for the Federals to follow.

Through the baggage taken from the cars, we discovered that General Sherman and staff were passengers on the train. We captured all their personal baggage. The sword which I found had the name of "Lieut.-Col. Ewing, Gen. Sherman's Staff" on the cover. It was a very handsome one. The horse which I captured was also a fine animal, and most likely was the one ridden by General Sherman. I was very proud of this horse, but my pride of ownership was short lived, for the general ordered the quartermaster to take charge of him, as well as the others captured.

As soon as we ascertained that General Sherman was in the fort, the failure was doubly regretted. Burton, one of my negroes, named the captured horse "Sherman," and often said his "marster captured Old Sherman."

*Brigadier General James R. Chalmers (left) had led infantry brigades at the Battles of Shiloh, Perryville, and Murfreesboro before transferring to Forrest's cavalry early in 1863. At Collierville Chalmers was struck and dazed by a spent ball. He later expressed disappointment at the performance of his men during this engagement, claiming that their eagerness to get at the train's rich booty had produced a delay that cost them a chance to capture the town.*

## CORPORAL RICE C. BULL

123D NEW YORK INFANTRY, KNIPE'S BRIGADE

*As former soldiers of the Army of the Potomac, Bull and his comrades, now on guard duty at Bridgeport, Alabama, were used to maintaining a spit-and-polish appearance for the benefit of Washington officials. They gazed in amazement as the Army of the Tennessee's crusty and disheveled veterans of Vicksburg sauntered past on their way to the relief of Chattanooga.*

On November 20th the Army of General Sherman known as the Army of the Tennessee, consisting of the 15th and 17th Corps, passed our camp. It was on its way to reinforce General Grant, who had been placed in supreme command and was then with General Thomas. This Army looked quite unlike our own that had originally been a part of the Army of the Potomac. They all wore large hats instead of caps; were carelessly dressed, both officers and men; and marched in a very irregular way, seemingly not caring to keep well closed up and in regular order. These were faults in marching which we had been taught to avoid. They could be excused for their loose marching, however, as they had just made a three hundred mile movement on the way to join Grant. We found their boast was that they "put on no style." They were a large fine type of men, all westerners; it was easy to see that at any serious time they would close up and be there. As they passed by we viewed their line and a good deal of friendly chaffing was done. They expressed their opinion that we were tin soldiers. "Oh look at their little caps. Where are your paper collars? Oh how clean you look, do you have soap?" and so on. We took it good-naturedly. They came to know and respect us later on, after the first battle, where we stood in line together. As the war went on we had no better friends than the men in those two Corps that were with Sherman's Army in the Atlanta Campaign, the March to the Sea and on until we finally parted after the Grand Review of that Army in Washington.

## BRIGADIER GENERAL ARTHUR M. MANIGAULT

### Brigade Commander, Army of Tennessee

*Throughout November, Manigault and Bragg's other commanders watched with mounting concern from their perches overlooking Chattanooga as the Union army below, once again well fed and resupplied with ordnance, commenced a regular shelling of the Rebel lines. The reawakening of the blue-clad war machine produced an upswing in Federal morale; one Yankee, Captain Rodney Bowen of the 100th Illinois, boasted that the Union now had the "inside track on Mr. Bragg."*

From about the 10th of November, it began to appear that the enemy was receiving supplies. He began now to open with his artillery whenever a favorable opportunity offered, and it became unsafe to expose a regiment or company of dress parade or inspection, as we had formerly done. His batteries at Moccasin Point kept up a constant fire on the troops and working parties on Lookout Mountain and in that vicinity. . . . Many of their guns were mounted on platforms, and threw their shells from the point below across the river, and to [the] tableland on the summit or over the mountain. They were so well protected that our batteries could make no impression on them, although having the advantage of a plunging fire. At this portion of the line, the skirmishing was at times very sharp, also on our extreme right, when the line was lengthened to the river by a body of cavalry, there not being a sufficient number of infantry for the purpose; but all along the centre, there was no infantry firing. Although they frequently cannonaded us, our guns seldom replied. They did us very little harm. Such prisoners as we from time to time captured, gave a much worse account of matters for us than was agreeable to hear. They represented their supplies as ample, and the quality of their subsistance good, acknowledging at the same time that their sufferings, occasioned by a deficiency of food, during the earlier part of the investment had been very great; and they also gave the much more alarming intelligence that reinforcements were daily arriving. This was evident to all, for new encampments were almost daily visible, even without a glass, not only on our side, but also across the river. Their works had long since been completed, and were of a most formidable character. From the crest of the Missionary Ridge, the eye commanded a full view of Chattanooga and of the country surrounding it. The enemy's works, lines, and the troops defending them, were plainly visible, and the sight of their army became as familiar to us as that of our own, but two miles off.

Most of the timber on the ridge had been, by this time, cut away, used for fuel, building purposes, and breastworks at the foot of the hill. Such trees as were left standing had completely lost their leaves, and in the valley or level land below, the same conditions of things existed, so that our view was uninterrupted, and at one glance you could take in the position of both armies, numbering perhaps from 120,000 to 130,000 men.

At night just after dark, when all the camp fires were lighted, the effect was very grand and imposing, and such a one as had seldom, I take it, been witnessed. Over and over again I have spent an hour or more in the quiet of the evening on a large, prominent rock that jutted out from the face of the ridge, and one of its highest points (the place is as familiar to me now as though it were but yesterday) admiring this grand illumination, thinking of home, family, and friends, or speculating as to the future.

## MAJOR GENERAL WILLIAM T. SHERMAN

### Commander, Army of the Tennessee

*Sherman, grieving over the death of his son, Willy, from typhoid fever in late September, arrived in Chattanooga on November 15. After learning he was to assault the northern end of Missionary Ridge, Sherman reconnoitered the ground of the proposed attack and returned to his army confident of success.*

In company with Generals Thomas, W. F. Smith, Brannan, and others, we crossed by the flying-bridge, rode back of the hills some four miles, left our horses, and got on a hill overlooking the whole ground about the mouth of the Chickamauga River, and across to the Missionary Hills near the tunnel. Smith and I crept down behind a fringe of trees that lined the river-bank, to the very point selected for the new bridge, where we sat for some time, seeing the rebel pickets on the opposite bank, and almost hearing their words.

Having seen enough, we returned to Chattanooga; and in order to hurry up my command, on which so much depended, I started back to Kelly's in hopes to catch the steamboat that same evening; but on my arrival the boat had gone. I applied to the commanding officer, got a rough boat manned by four soldiers, and started down the river by night. I occasionally took a turn at the oars to relieve some tired man, and about midnight we reached Shell Mound, where General Whittaker, of Kentucky, furnished us a new and good crew, with which we reached Bridgeport by daylight. I started Ewing's division in advance, with orders to turn aside toward Trenton, to make the enemy believe we were going to turn Bragg's left by pretty much the same road Rosecrans had followed; but with the other three divisions I followed the main road, *via* the Big Trestle at Whitesides, and reached General Hooker's headquarters, just above Wauhatchee, on the 20th; my troops strung all the way back to Bridgeport. It was on this occasion that the Fifteenth Corps gained its peculiar badge: as the men were trudging along the deeply-cut, muddy road, of a cold, drizzly day, one of our Western soldiers left his ranks and joined a party of the Twelfth Corps at their camp-fire. They got into conversation, the Twelfth Corps men asking what troops we were, etc., etc. In turn, our fellow (who had never seen a corps-badge, and noticed that every thing was marked with a star) asked if they were all brigadier-generals. Of course they were not, but the star was their corps-badge, and every wagon, tent, hat, etc., had its star. Then the Twelfth Corps men inquired what corps he belonged to, and he answered, "The Fifteenth Corps." "What is your badge?" "Why," said he (and he was an Irishman), suiting the action to the word, "forty rounds in the cartridge-box, and twenty in the pocket!" At that time Blair commanded the corps; but Logan succeeded soon after, and, hearing the story, adopted the cartridge-box and forty rounds as the corps-badge.

*The town of Bridgeport, Alabama, lines the far bank of the Tennessee River in this photograph taken across the Nashville & Chattanooga Railroad bridge. The original railway bridge had been burned by the Confederates before the Battle of Chickamauga, and the Yankees had quickly constructed a pontoon bridge at the same location. The sturdy bridge pictured here was built after the siege had been lifted, when supplies could travel safely again by rail from Bridgeport to Chattanooga.*

*Although corps badges like the XII Corps's star insignia (near left) had been part of the Army of the Potomac's trappings since early 1863, Thomas' and Sherman's troops saw them for the first time at Chattanooga. This XII Corps pin belonged to Frederick Davis of the 28th Pennsylvania Infantry, who had battle honors inscribed upon it later. The westerners at first poked fun at the emblems but soon recognized the pride such items could instill and later adopted their own. The XV Corps based its "forty rounds" badge (far left) on the story related in Sherman's account (opposite).*

## MAJOR HENRY S. DEAN

22D MICHIGAN INFANTRY, ENGINEERS BRIGADE

*The plan for Sherman's assault on Missionary Ridge's northern tip called for his army to leave its hidden camp north of Chattanooga, move eastward, and cross the Tennessee on a pontoon bridge. The responsibility for building this bridge fell to Dean, who wisely relied on the advice of a junior officer to help him get the pontoon train close to the river without revealing its presence.*

At nine o'clock p.m., November 20th, Capt. Fox sent the pontoon train from under cover of Cameron Hill to the north side of the river, where it was delivered to me. At that time I did not know as much about pontoon trains as I did at the close of the war. That the train was to be taken to its destination without permitting the enemy to get sight of it we all understood, but of how it was to be arranged after it got there I was as ignorant as a child, so I asked Capt. Fox how he wanted it parked. He hesitated, and I repeated the question. Finally he said: "It is a delicate matter for an officer of inferior rank to give orders to a superior who is in command."

I looked squarely into that honest face of his and said: "I am the smallest major in the army. If you know how this train ought to be parked, tell me."

He said: "Place the balk here, the chess plank there, the spring lines so and so, the head line in such a place and the anchors. . . . "

"Hold on," I said, "I know what an anchor is, but don't know anything about your balk, chess plank and spring lines. Show me what they are."

He did, and we started out with the train. It was raining and the night very dark. In many places the wagon would go down in the mud to the axletree. The poor, weak mules would get stalled in the mud and men would have to pull them out. Wagon wheels would give out, and the men supplied their places with wheels taken from General Palmer's ammunition train, which was parked on the north side of the river opposite Chattanooga. Wagons would upset and men, by means of ropes, would right them.

As the first grey of morning appeared in the east the wagons were quickly concealed in ravines and behind hills, or if they could not be gotten out of sight in that way, they were concealed by piling brush over them. The men and animals were moved behind the hills and not permitted to show themselves during the day. At 2 o'clock a.m., November 22d, we had the train parked in the ravine leading down to the river where the crossing was to be made, a thick growth of underbrush concealing it from the enemy's pickets on the other side of the river. On November 23d, concealed from the view of the enemy, the men rested behind the hills. The strict guard established to prevent any of them from showing themselves was hardly necessary; they were completely worn out by three nights of labor, such as I have never seen performed by men before or since.

# "Not one straggler lagged behind to sully the magnificence and perfectness of the grand battle array."

## BRIGADIER GENERAL THOMAS J. WOOD

DIVISION COMMANDER,
ARMY OF THE CUMBERLAND

*A fiery commander who was often in the thick of combat, Wood was twice wounded in the left foot—at Murfreesboro and near Atlanta in 1864. In both cases Wood, although bleeding and in pain, refused to leave the field until the fighting ended. At Chattanooga, Grant selected Wood's division to lead a reconnaissance in force on November 23 that captured the prominence known as Orchard Knob.*

Troops in line and column checkered the broad plain of Chattanooga. In front, plainly to be seen, was the enemy, who was soon to be encountered in deadly conflict. My division seemed to drink in the inspiration of the scene, and, when the advance was sounded, moved forward in the perfect order of a holiday parade. . . . I should do injustice to the brave men who thus moved forward to the conflict in such perfect order, were I to omit to say that not one straggler lagged behind to sully the magnificence and perfectness of the grand battle array.

From Fort Wood to the railroad the country is open. South of the railroad the country passed over is partly open and partly wooded. Hazen's brigade had to pass over the open field, several hundred yards in breadth, and Willich's through the woods. On the southern side of the field the enemy's front line of pickets was posted. Orchard Knob, given in the order directing the reconnoissance as the guiding point, is a steep, craggy knoll, rising some hundred feet above the general level of the valley of Chattanooga. It is twenty-one hundred yards from Fort Wood, and had been held by the rebels as an outpost since the investment was first established. The position being naturally so strong, they had done but little to strengthen it by intrenchments on its summit. To the right of Orchard Knob, looking toward the South, a rocky, abrupt, wooded ridge extends several hundred yards toward the southwest, but is not so elevated as the knob. The enemy had formed rude but strong barricades on the northern slope, just beyond the crest of the ridge. To the left of the knob, still looking toward the south, a long line of rifle-pits extended away off to the north-east, and, trending round, reached almost to Citico Creek. Orchard Knob was the citadel of this line of intrenchments.

General Willich was ordered to direct his brigade on the knob, and General Hazen his brigade on the intrenchments on the right of it. As soon as the skirmishers moved forward, the enemy opened fire. Across the open field, and through the woods, the skirmishers kept up a sharp, rattling fire, steadily and rapidly driving in the enemy. As the knob and intrenchments were neared, the fire became hotter, and the resistance of the rebels more determined, but the majestic advance of our lines was not for a moment stayed. Finally, Willich's brigade, which had met with less opposition than Hazen's, having arrived quite near the knob, "by a bold brush" ascended its steep acclivity, crowned its summit, and it was ours. In the meantime, Hazen's brigade was encountering a determined resistance from the enemy, sheltered by his breastworks, on the rocky ridge to the right. For a few moments the fire was sharp and destructive. More than a hundred casualties in the leading regiments attest the severity of the fire. But nothing could restrain the impetuosity of the troops, and in a few moments after Willich's brigade had carried Orchard Knob, Hazen's skirmishers poured over the enemy's barricades.

*Yankee skirmishers in the foreground of this Harper's Weekly engraving engage Rebel pickets of the 24th Alabama—whose positions are indicated by the puffs of smoke issuing from their weapons—atop Orchard Knob. The rounded hillock and the small but rugged ridge that ran southward from it, also visible in this illustration, were terrain anomalies in the otherwise flat plain that stretched between Chattanooga and Missionary Ridge. By capturing this high ground the afternoon of November 23, the Union gained a launching point for their attacks on Missionary Ridge.*

THE CAPTURE OF ORCHARD KNOB, CHATTANOOGA, BY HAZEN'S AND WILLICH'S BRIGADES, DEPLOYED AS SKIRMISHERS, NOVEMBER 23, 1863.
SKETCHED BY MR. THEODORE R. DAVIS.—[SEE PAGE 813.]

"I thought from the pain which I experienced that the bullet had passed through my body, and was rather disgusted when an examination revealed the fact that I was knocked out without a scar to show for it."

## CAPTAIN JOSEPH T. PATTON

93D OHIO INFANTRY, HAZEN'S BRIGADE

*While Willich's brigade charged directly at Orchard Knob, Hazen's men—fresh from victory at Brown's Ferry—attacked the ridge on the right, defended by the 28th Alabama. Although the 93d eventually helped overrun the position, Patton and 56 other members of the regiment fell before the vicious fusillades of musketry delivered by the Alabamians.*

On Nov. 23d we issued sixty rounds of ammunition to the men and turned out as if for drill. The rebels from their position in our front were enabled to watch our every move; and supposing that we were turning out for a grand review, took no measure to meet the advance which soon followed.

The 93d was a part of the front line, and when the word "forward" was given, advanced in battle line without skirmishers. The rebel pickets fired and fled at our approach. When within charging distance of their line of breastworks, "Fix bayonets! Forward, double quick!" were the orders which followed in quick succession. The enemy were now fully alive as to the purpose of our movements, and opened fire from sixty pieces of artillery from Missionary Ridge; the infantry from behind their breastworks also opened a most destructive musketry fire, but the gallant boys pressed forward through this terrible storm of iron and lead which was rained upon them, without a halt or waver.

The rebel works were reached and over them the boys went, capturing many prisoners. Our Lieutenant Colonel, Bowman, was on the right of the regiment; as he passed around the end of the works he encountered a rebel with his gun aimed at him. With drawn sword the Colonel rushed at the fellow with the exclamation, "Damn you, you shoot me and I'll cut your head off." The force of the Colonel's remark had the desired effect as the reb dropped his gun and surrendered.

Orchard Knob and the first line of works were ours, but not without heavy loss, as more than one-third of our regiment were killed or wounded in the charge. Three color-bearers fell, the fourth planting *Old Glory* on the enemy's works.

As we started on the charge, I was turning toward the left of my company when a bullet struck a diary which was in the right breast pocket of my blouse, glanced downward and struck my sword belt-plate, which was bent until it was of no further use. Fortunately for my present usefulness, I had buckled my belt under my blouse before starting, which saved my life, as the diary stopped the bullet from passing through my right breast, and the belt-plate prevented it passing through my bowels.

The blow sent me to grass and left me insensible. When the stretcher bearers discovered me, they decided that I was dead and that they would first care for the wounded. (My name appeared in the newspapers as among the killed). How long I remained there I have no means of knowing, but was finally removed to camp where I had comfortable quarters and my colored boy to care for me. The blow had broken my ribs and injured my spine. I thought from the pain which I experienced that the bullet had passed through my body, and was rather disgusted when an examination revealed the fact that I was knocked out without a scar to show for it.

## CAPTAIN GEORGE W. LEWIS

124TH OHIO INFANTRY, HAZEN'S BRIGADE

*As the Union troops came out of their earthworks and deployed for the attack on Orchard Knob, they presented a breathtaking spectacle that most of Bragg's men mistook for a dress parade. Lewis, a teacher from Spencer, Ohio, survived the fighting at Chattanooga without incident but was severely wounded in the left elbow at the Battle of Nashville on December 16, 1864. The joint was damaged beyond repair, and surgeons had to amputate Lewis' mangled arm.*

The twenty-third day of November, 1863, the Army of the Cumberland moved out late in the afternoon, none of us knowing the purpose. We formed in continuous line of battle with a heavy skirmish line well in the front. At the word of command we all moved in the direction of the ridge.

Before the rebels seemed to be aware of what was intended we had come up to our picket line, and that also advanced with our skirmishers, when the rebel outposts in most places gave way without showing much resistance. But where the rebel line crossed Orchard Knob they had quite respectable rifle pits which they defended with some spirit, causing the 41st O.V.I. some trouble in dislodging them, and thereby we had some few men wounded in our brigade. This line, formerly occupied by the rebel outposts, we at once commenced fortifying by throwing up strong rifle pits of earth and stone. We then advanced our skirmish line well out toward the base of the ridge. One of the prisoners that we captured said: "Weuns thought youns was coming out for a review, we didn't think youns was coming out to fight weuns." We informed the Johnny that General Grant was commanding us, and he was not a review general.

## BRIGADIER GENERAL ARTHUR M. MANIGAULT

BRIGADE COMMANDER, ARMY OF TENNESSEE

*Although proud of the way his outnumbered troops had defended Orchard Knob, which he refers to here as Cedar Hill, Manigault was disappointed by the lack of support given to his regiments. Even worse, later that day he was ordered to retake the knob with the remainder of his brigade. Just as they were about to undertake this hopeless task, the attack was canceled, causing his soldiers, said Manigault, to issue "a general sigh of relief" and heartfelt exclamations of "Thank God!"*

At that time my picket line occupied a front of about 800 yards, and a high and commanding eminence known as "The Cedar Hill" was a part of the ground held. It was the most prominent point between the Ridge and Chattanooga, and one of much importance. The 24th and 28th Alabama regiments were on duty that day, and held the picket line. They numbered together about 600 men on duty, both of them being small regiments. The picket line was entrenched with a shallow ditch and low earthwork, with rifle pits a little in advance.

About 4:30 o'clock the enemy formed two lines of battle with a skirmish line in front, and began to move forward. About five o'clock, their skirmishers came within range of ours, and the fight commenced. Our advanced troops were soon driven in by their line of battle, who moved steadily to the attack. Their first line was checked by our fire, but the second line coming to their assistance, together they moved forward in spite of our fire, which was not heavy enough to deter them, and came in contact with the reserve line of skirmishers. Both regiments behaved well, particularly the 28th, which resisted obstinately, and with great gallantry, many of them fighting hand to hand; but the odds against them were irresistible, and Lieut. Col. Butler, 28th Ala., Commanding, in order to save his Regiment, was forced to give the order to retire. The other regiment, 24th Alabama, had already given way. Had they contended much longer, they would have been killed or captured to a man, as the lines to their right and left had broken, and the enemy were getting to their rear. The 28th lost a good many, the 24th fewer—in all about 175 men.

Having obtained possession of our picket line and the hill mentioned, the enemy seemed satisfied, and pushed forward no further. Our skirmishers retired about 350 or 400 yards and halted. Whilst the enemy advanced large numbers immediately in front of the hill to protect and

*This photograph, taken from Missionary Ridge, shows Orchard Knob in the middle distance, one of an 1864 series of pictures by Northern photographer George N. Barnard depicting the crucial features of the Chattanooga campaign. Framed by the trees in the foreground, the hill, because of the steep angle of the photographer's viewpoint, appears "flatter" than it actually is. Bragg and his staff had a similar view on November 23, as they gazed upon the assembling Union troops and tried to guess their intentions.*

hold it, he set large parties to work upon it, building breastworks and batteries for their artillery. In rear also was a large reserve force, and for the security of this point to which they seemed to attach much importance, they must have held in front at least 6,000 men, exclusive of the two lines in front.

Whilst this combat was going on, all remained silent spectators. No effort to reinforce our advance posts was made, and as our lines were very weak and we had not men enough to man them, and not knowing what was the ulterior intention of the enemy, I do not know that it would have been wise to risk more men to the front. Our skirmish line was lost and to recover it a general engagement would have to be fought.

## LIEUTENANT ALBION W. TOURGEE

105TH OHIO INFANTRY, VAN DERVEER'S BRIGADE

*As Tourgée does here, many Union soldiers wrote admiringly of the spectacle of Union military might at Orchard Knob. According to Lieutenant Colonel Joseph S. Fullerton of the IV Corps, for example, "Flags were flying; the quick earnest step of thousands beat equal time. . . . the bright sun lighting up ten thousand polished bayonets till they glistened and flashed like a shower of electrical sparks—all looked like preparations for a peaceful pageant, rather than for the bloody work of death."*

The enemy fired on us with some heavy guns on the Ridge, but their shots fell short. We saw them standing on their works and watching our maneuvers. It must have been an imposing sight to them. There were mustered on the plain that day, in full view of the enemy, nigh fifty thousand men, with more than one hundred guns, including the heavy guns in the forts along our line. The movements of these forces must have greatly magnified their apparent numbers.

We waited and speculated—Colonel Tolles standing beside his black horse, impatient for the fray to begin. Now and then a shot from the crest of Lookout was answered by our guns on Moccasin Point. Neither did any harm, but the echoes, rolling back and forth, added to the romantic character of the battle-scene. About noon the fire grew hotter on our left. Half an hour later Wood's Division moved to the assault of Orchard Knob. We followed, supporting their right. It was nigh half a mile away; but when we reached the hills and looked back, the whole world seemed alive. Waves of blue were swelling over hillock and plain; the great guns of the forts were belching harmless shots over our heads. The enemy were fleeing to their next line of works, a mile away, at the foot of the Ridge. We had captured four hundred men, and had left one hundred dead and wounded on the way.

From end to end of our line; from those who remained in the works; from the Army of the Cumberland and the Army of the Potomac; from all who saw and all who heard, rose clamorous cheers over this first success in a movement which was to be so full of wonderful spectacles. The enemy looked down upon us from the crest of the Ridge and yelled back defiance. We thought there was a note of doubt in the yell, as, no doubt, there was.

*This Union forage cap, bedecked with a company letter and a regimental numeral, was worn by one of Albion Tourgée's compatriots in the 105th Ohio.*

## PRIVATE GEORGE P. METCALF

### 136th New York Infantry, O. Smith's Brigade

*At Orchard Knob, Grant ordered two divisions of the XI Corps to move forward on the left of the Union line and support the assault by Wood's division. Although Metcalf, whose regiment was part of this movement, does not openly admit it in this account, the XI Corps troops performed poorly, advancing only a short distance before diving for cover. One regiment, the 33d New Jersey, cowered behind a barn during the attack, refusing the entreaties of its officers to move forward.*

In the afternoon the long column began to move toward Mission Ridge. Our regiment's position was almost opposite Fort Wood, and between that and the ridge shells could be sent from this fort onto the top of both Mission Ridge and Lookout Mountain. We soon reached the picket-line of the enemy, and they fled hastily to the top of Mission Ridge.

The long line kept steadily moving forward, and soon the bullets came flying over our heads from the skirmish-line of the rebels. As we steadily took our column toward the base of the hill, I could see long lines of soldiers keeping our brigade company. To the left and right, as far as the lay of the country would permit, men were seen marching forward. The bullets came now with more telling effect. Men were wounded here and there. . . .

We hurried along, occasionally being frightened by a shell sent tearing through the air over our heads, either from our own force in the rear or the enemy on the ridge. We crossed a railroad-track and drove the skirmish-line before us back up the slope. Here we halted in an old corn-field from which the corn had been cut off the stalks. We were not told to lie down, but we knew enough to do that without orders. We did not get down any too quick either, as a shower of bullets went over our heads, quickly followed by another and another. We tried to see how close it was possible for one to lie on the ground. I tried making myself as thin as possible. But, do all I could, it seemed to me that every part of my body stuck up in plain view and would surely get hit by some of the many bullets that were flying over us. We soon found, however, that we were lying in a little depression, or sag, in the field, and if we only lay down flat no bullet could hit us. But a foot above our heads we could see the standing stubs of corn-stalks cut off by flying bullets.

We lay here over an hour. During all the time the bullets kept zipping over our heads, close to me lay a member of my company with his nose flattened on the ground. Out of sport I got hold of a dry stalk of a weed and hit him on his ear. He jumped as if shot and put his hand up to feel the blood that wasn't there. Others began to toss little stones, without exposing themselves to danger, onto the heads of their comrades that dared not look up and did not understand that we were safe if we only kept down below the range of the rebel rifles. I saw one of our officers lying with one foot purposely stuck up in the air, as I believe, hoping to be shot in this non-vital spot and so have an excuse not to go into the main fight.

Night soon came on, and we fell back a few rods and built a strong line of breastworks. I worked nearly all night carrying rails and logs and shoveling dirt. When morning came, we had a line of earthworks three feet thick and six feet high.

# "Now, boys, lie low, you know, and let 'em come up close, you know, and then rise up and give 'em hell, you know."

## LIEUTENANT JOHN K. SHELLENBERGER

64TH OHIO INFANTRY, HARKER'S BRIGADE

*As Shellenberger's account shows, the capture of Orchard Knob picked up the spirits of the Army of the Cumberland and erased some of the sting of Chickamauga. A large task still remained before the Federals, however, for Lookout Mountain and Missionary Ridge were still firmly in Confederate hands.*

On this 23d day of November, our pickets, who were to act as our skirmish line, had been carefully instructed, and when the bugles suddenly sounded the charge, they sprang forward with such a dash that they actually ran over some of the Confederate pickets before the latter had recovered from their astonishment. Their intrenched picket line was carried with a surprisingly small amount of resistance and with a correspondingly small loss to our side.

A little later, after the Confederates had recovered their self-possession, and the two skirmish lines were spitefully pecking away at each other, one of the Confederates called over:

"Hello, Yanks, what's got the matter with you all over there?"

One of our men called back: "We're out of wood." This was literally true; for not only all the timber inside our picket line had been cut off, but the stumps and the roots of the trees had been dug out of the ground in the growing scarcity of fuel. The Confederate called back:

"If you wanted wood why didn't you say so? We have more than we need out here, and if you had only asked us you might have sent out your teams and got all the wood you wanted without kicking up such a hell of a fuss about it."

Our battle line followed up the advance of our picket line until it reached the foot of the hill, where a halt was called. At this time heavy firing had broken out along the skirmish line, and the inference was that the main body of the Confederates had swarmed out of their camps and were advancing to drive us back. The position of the Sixty-fourth Ohio, where the line had halted, was a most unsatisfactory one. The ground ascended in our front for a couple of hundred yards, and this slope was nearly bare, while at the top of the rise the timber was heavy enough to afford good shelter. If the enemy should drive back our skirmish line and occupy this timber, they would have us at a great disadvantage.

The men were growling discontentedly and asking why we were not advanced to the top of the slope, when General Sheridan appeared upon the scene. He came dashing along from the left and immediately in front of our line, which was lying down, riding the same black horse which, with his rider, achieved such deathless fame nearly a year later at Cedar Creek. When he reached the front of the colors he pulled up so abruptly as to almost seat the horse on his haunches. His eyes were beaming as if he could scarcely refrain from bursting out laughing at some idea that was amusing him, and he leaned over toward us and began speaking in a suppressed sort of way, as if he was about to communicate in strict confidence something that we would find intensely funny.

He said: "Now, boys, lie low, you know, and let 'em come up close, you know, and then rise up and give 'em hell, you know."

It was probably the contemplation of the surprise of the enemy when we should unexpectedly "rise up and give 'em hell, you know," that was tickling him, and it certainly did seem an easy thing to do, the way he had of putting it. He paused an instant to flash his eyes along our line, the eyes of the men catching fire from his as they met, and then as if satisfied with his scrutiny, he nodded and smiled in a way that plainly said, "I know that I can rely upon you to do it," and dashed on to the next regiment.

It was a false alarm, for no enemy came, but if they had come . . . the Sixty-fourth would have obeyed the general's instructions to the letter. . . . We afterward took up a position that evening . . . which was fortified by throwing up a light line of earthworks. We remained quietly behind these works until the afternoon of the 25th.

# Lookout Mountain

Shortly after midnight on November 24, the Federal offensive began. A pontoon boat filled with 30 men pushed off from the mouth of North Chickamauga Creek into the swift current of the Tennessee River and drifted downstream. Near the mouth of South Chickamauga Creek, the oarsmen rowed to the Confederate side of the river. The small force scrambled ashore and easily overcame the handful of Rebel pickets.

Within 15 minutes 1,000 men were floating toward landing sites. A steamer from Chattanooga helped ferry more troops across. As each pontoon boat unloaded, it was attached to the preceding one, and by noon a bridge 1,350 feet long was in place, allowing the rest of Sherman's three divisions to cross.

About 1:00 p.m., Sherman deployed his troops in three columns and sent them up the hill just east of the river. Astonishingly, there was virtually no opposition. It was not until the attackers had reached the summit that enemy batteries fired on them. The Federals dragged their own artillery up to the top and returned fire. Peering about in the rain and mist, Sherman checked his bearings. He received a ghastly shock—he was on the wrong hill!

Sherman's objective had been the northernmost part of Missionary Ridge, known locally as Tunnel Hill because of the railroad tunnel that passed through its base. His maps showed Missionary Ridge as a continuous range, and the visual observation he had made a few days before had seemed to confirm this. In fact, the stunned general could now see that there was a break in the ridge, and the hill closest to the river—the one on which he was standing—was a separate peak. A deep valley about a mile wide separated him from Tunnel Hill.

Thus, despite the perfect river crossing, Sherman's men remained as far from their objective as ever—and all chance of surprise was now lost. Not knowing the extent of the forces opposing him, and with daylight fast fading, Sherman ordered his men to dig in for the night.

As it happened, his three divisions were opposed only by a single brigade of Texans from Cleburne's division who had rushed to the area that afternoon after Bragg got word that Sherman had crossed the Tennessee. Just a day earlier, Cleburne and his men had been at Chickamauga Station waiting to entrain for Knoxville to help Longstreet when Bragg recalled them. Bragg ordered Cleburne to take the high ground near the mouth of the South Chickamauaga and hold it "at all hazards."

Cleburne galloped to the Tunnel Hill area and hastily made what he called "a moonlight survey of the ground." He had heard word of a Confederate "disaster" at Lookout Mountain earlier that day, which convinced him that he would see fierce fighting in the morning.

That disaster—a Union victory at Lookout Mountain—had come as a surprise to everyone. While Sherman was launching what was to have been the main attack that morning, Hooker advanced across Lookout Creek and around Lookout Mountain through a narrow gap between its lower slopes and the Tennessee River. Grant had told Hooker that if he saw an opportunity, he could seize the mountain, but his primary mission was to push beyond it and clear the Rebels from Chattanooga Valley, which lay in between Lookout Mountain and Missionary Ridge. Hooker was then to take Rossville Gap and be in position to threaten Bragg's left and rear.

Hooker had 10,000 men in three divisions, one from each of the Federal armies at Chattanooga: Geary's from the Army of the Potomac, Brigadier General Charles Cruft's from the Army of the Cumberland, and Osterhaus' from the Army of the Tennessee.

Hooker began the movement across Lookout Creek about 8:00 a.m. He divided his forces, sending Geary's division and one of Cruft's two brigades, commanded by Brigadier General Walter C. Whitaker, south to Wauhatchie, where the creek was fordable. There the Federals waded across, capturing some 40 Rebel pickets and driving off the rest.

Feeling their way through the dense fog, Geary's troops tramped halfway up the western slope. Then they worked their way northward, along the base of an almost vertical cliff, toward a rendezvous with the rest of Hooker's force at the gap between the mountain and the river. Resistance was light, but the march was "laborious and extremely toilsome," Whitaker reported later, "over the steep, rocky, ravine-seamed, torrent-torn sides of the mountain."

Meanwhile, Osterhaus' division and Cruft's other brigade crossed a bridge a mile and a half north of the ford that Geary had used.

Bragg's forces on Lookout Mountain numbered about 7,000, but they were widely scattered, and only a fraction were in position to defend the plateau at the northern end of the pinnacle. Earlier, Bragg had moved most of Hardee's corps to Missionary Ridge to deal with Sherman's threat. To compensate, Breckinridge had extended the left of his corps under Major General Carter L. Stevenson to cover Lookout. But Stevenson did not arrive until a few hours before Hooker's attack began, and he was unfamiliar with the terrain.

About 10:00 a.m. Geary's troops rounded the shoulder of the mountain at the Cravens farm and encountered a Confederate force led by Brigadier General Edward C. Walthall. As sharp fighting erupted, Geary anchored his right on the base of some nearby cliffs and wheeled his line forward until his left joined with the right of Osterhaus' oncoming division. Now the Federal line extended about a half-mile from the Cravens farm down the slope to the Chattanooga road at the foot of the mountain.

To resist the advance of this 10,000-man juggernaut, Walthall had only 1,489 men. And the Confederate batteries on the summit could not depress their guns enough to help. Federal artillery, meanwhile, had found the range and began pounding the enemy. By 1:00 p.m., after three hours of fighting, the Rebels had pulled back into a second line of entrenchments 400 yards east of the Cravens house. Shortly afterward, they received reinforcements, and as darkness fell the battered defenders still held their ground.

Despite their doughty stand, however, Bragg feared they might soon be overwhelmed, and in the night he withdrew them. Next morning a small detail of Yankees from a Kentucky regiment climbed up and unfurled the Stars and Stripes high on a cliff top, evoking round after round of cheers from the thousands of men on the spreading plains below. Whatever frustrations Sherman was experiencing at Missionary Ridge, Lookout Mountain was now in Federal hands.

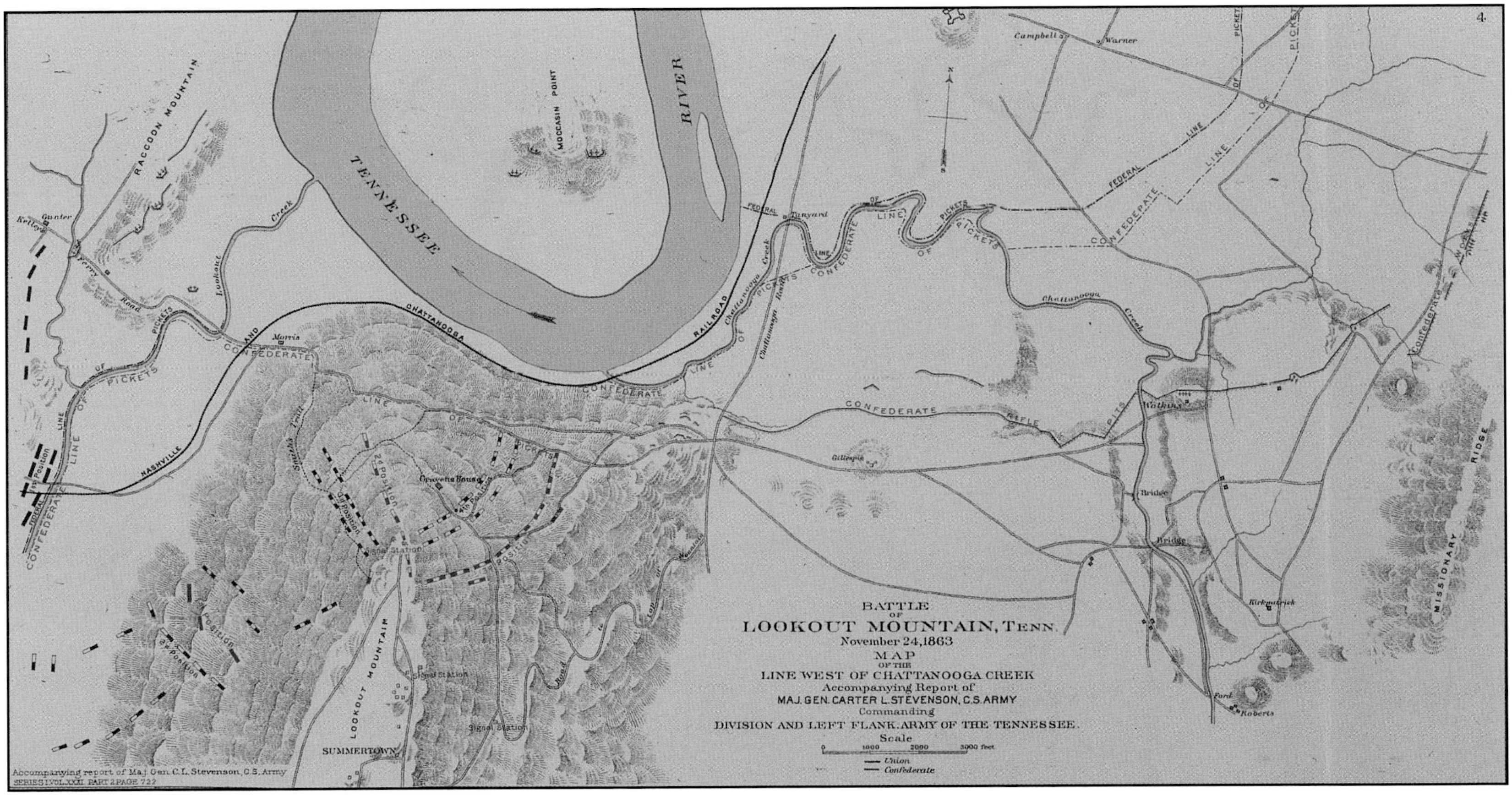


*After midnight on November 24 Sherman's army floated down the Tennessee, landed and took Billy Goat Hill, and dug in. To the south, Hooker's men crossed Lookout Creek and moved north along the western face of Lookout Mountain, driving Bragg's force, composed of Walthall's, Brigadier General John C. Moore's, and Brigadier General Edmund W. Pettus' brigades, before them. During the day fog on Lookout Mountain hid the fighting from those below, giving rise to the name Battle above the Clouds. The clash continued through the night, as small Rebel contingents held Hooker's army at bay while the main Confederate force on Lookout withdrew to reinforce Missionary Ridge in preparation for the next day.*

# "General Sherman, who was on horseback surrounded by his staff, was so pleased that he took off his hat and cheered."

## DRUMMER JOHN S. KOUNTZ

37TH OHIO INFANTRY, LIGHTBURN'S BRIGADE

*Kountz describes Sherman's operation to attack Missionary Ridge in the early hours of November 24. A small flotilla of troop-filled pontoon boats bobbed out of North Chickamauga Creek, crossed the Tennessee, and landed near the mouth of South Chickamauga Creek. After these men overwhelmed the Rebel pickets, the empty pontoons were used to bring across Lightburn's brigade, and the Federals soon had an entrenched bridgehead on the east bank of the river.*

The night was dark with a drizzling rain. About midnight all was ready and the signal given to cross, Major Hipp's boat leading the fleet, John Hess and others of Company E, 37th, being his companions. The Major pushed well into the river, and, after awhile, headed straight for the south shore, and on nearing the point where it was proposed to land, a picket fire was discovered and our troops headed directly for it. The men hurried out of the boats and up the bank, surprising and capturing all of the Confederate pickets but one. The surprise was so complete that the "Johnnies" scarcely realized the situation. At this time a Confederate vidette came up at full speed, shouting "The Yanks are coming!" He was promptly dismounted and compelled to join his comrades just captured.

Major Hipp recrossed the river followed by the flat boats. On getting back the darkness made it difficult for him to find our troops and he shouted for the second division of the Fifteenth Corps, when he was immediately answered in suppressed voices to keep quiet or he would be arrested. Having no time for explanation and becoming impatient, the Major cried out, "Where is General Sherman?" The answer came promptly through the darkness from the General himself, who was not more than 50 feet away, "What do you want?" The Major answered, "I want a brigade, the boats are in waiting." The General at once asked, "Did you make a landing?" Major Hipp answered, "Yes, and captured the pickets." General Sherman, who was on horseback surrounded by his staff, was so pleased that he took off his hat and cheered.

At this time we embarked and after a short, though seemingly long ride, landed on the south bank of the river. Our Major continued the work of crossing and recrossing with fresh troops until morning, when two full divisions were on the east bank of the Tennessee. Meantime, our men put in splendid work digging entrenchments. General Sherman, who had crossed in one of the flat boats, personally superintended the work, and I well remember the General's remark, "Pitch in, boys; this is the last ditch," as he walked up and down the line. At the dawn of day a pontoon bridge was built over the Tennessee River and another over Chickamauga Creek near its mouth. That night's undertaking had been grandly accomplished and General Sherman was one of the happiest men in Grant's army.

At daybreak we were on the south side of the Tennessee River, strongly entrenched, prepared to meet any force General Bragg might pit against us. It must have been both a surprise and a mortification to the Confederate commander when he saw Sherman's army on the morning of the 24th securely fortified on the south bank of the Tennessee.

On the 24th we moved forward, with skirmishers in advance, over an open field to the hill near the railroad tunnel, where we fortified for the night. From our position we could see Hooker's men "above the clouds" on Lookout Mountain and also had a good view of the Army of the Cumberland on our right.

## CHAPLAIN WILLIAM G. KEPHART

10th Iowa Infantry, Matthies' Brigade

*Kephart told the story of the crossing to his local newspaper, the Burlington (Iowa) Hawkeye. As his account indicates, this riverine expedition was similar to the successful Brown's Ferry mission. Both were conducted under the cover of darkness and further assisted by a dense fog that blanketed the river valley—and both were perilous. Each soldier at the oars, recalled one of Sherman's men, "rowed as though his own life and that of his country was at stake."*

At 12 o'clock on Monday night Sherman's corps was put in motion. We were encamped in a small valley, surrounded by high hills, about two and a half miles from the contemplated crossing of the Tennessee River. There had been concealed in Chickamauga creek about 120 pontoon boats to transport us to the opposite side. Gen. Morgan L. Smith's Division (2d) was first crossed over, with instructions to capture, if possible, the rebel pickets. This was done with complete success. The 8th Missouri was assigned this duty. Guided by a citizen, they came upon the pickets so unexpectedly that the Colonel of the 8th walked up to the officer of the guard and challenged him, supposing it to be their own officer, he was about to order out the guard to give him the salute, when the Colonel informed him that he had not the password, but would nevertheless *relieve him.* For the first time he discovered his mistake, but too late. One of the pickets only made his escape on horse back, but was taken before he reached the camp. They said they never dreamed of our crossing at that point. Some of them were evidently dreaming *of something* when taken, perhaps of feasting upon broiled Yankees. It is said that the Lieutenant in command was taken in amorous dalliance with one of the *virtuous* daughters of chivalry.

Before it was fairly light our Division (3d, John E. Smith's) and Ewing's Division had crossed over. It was a novel and *romantic* sight to see that fleet of boats blackening the waters of the Tennessee.—No time could have been more favorable.—It was misting, foggy and cloudy. The moon just gave us light enough to see plainly how to make our crossing. We landed just below the mouth of Chickamauga, at a large open plantation, surrounded by dense woods on every side.—The men went to work as those who felt that their scalps depended upon their industry, and it seemed to me that in less than an hour a breast-work and rifle-pit was made about a mile in length, extending clear across the open space.

*Tunnel Hill, on the north end of Missionary Ridge, rises in the left middle distance of this photograph taken from Billy Goat Hill. Sherman's men had swarmed up the latter peak on the morning of November 24, believing they were assaulting Missionary Ridge, only to find to their dismay that a broad and rugged valley still separated them from their objective. Sherman was justifiably vexed when he realized his mistake; despite bloody fighting, his troops would prove unable to dislodge the Rebels from Tunnel Hill.*

## PRIVATE JENKIN L. JONES

6TH WISCONSIN BATTERY, J. E. SMITH'S DIVISION

*Born in Wales in 1843, Jones came to the United States with his parents as an infant. Unlike many soldiers his age, Jones did not "pant for the fray." Deeply religious, he claimed that he had only entered the "dreaded" service because his conscience, which he referred to as the "daughter of the voice of God," impelled him to do so.*

Nov. 24. 6 A.M. Two divisions were safely across and a more beautiful scene I never witnessed. Through the gray dawn a long line of infantry could be seen drawn up on the opposite bank a mile long, while the waters were covered with boats busily going and coming, loaded with men, the regimental colors standing in the center of the boat. The bridge was now covered, boats brought up, anchored in line, and the floor laid without any delay, the 4th Division marching in the boats and the artillery covering the field. Fires were allowed to be built now and we soon had coffee. It commenced raining, as cold and disagreeable as the day could be. A steamboat was due at 4 a.m. to take us across, but did not come till 6:30 a.m. Taylor's Battery crossed the river first, and as we were not pressed we waited for the bridge to be built. It was very disagreeable, and I felt almost sick; late hours and irregular meals having brought on diarrhea, etc. A large constellation of stars were gathered on the bank, watching the progress of the bridge, among which were Sherman, Blair, W. F. Smith, etc. The line on the other side in one hour had a line of breastworks up and advanced out of sight to form another.

12 M. The bridge completed and we crossed it, being the second battery to do so. The dread of crossing had passed. Halted at a corn crib and the cannoneers got as much corn as they could, but the infantry was formed and advanced in column of division at secure arms, it raining very heavy. This savage-looking column moved forward with caution, crossed a forty-acre lot and halted. The skirmishers went out but

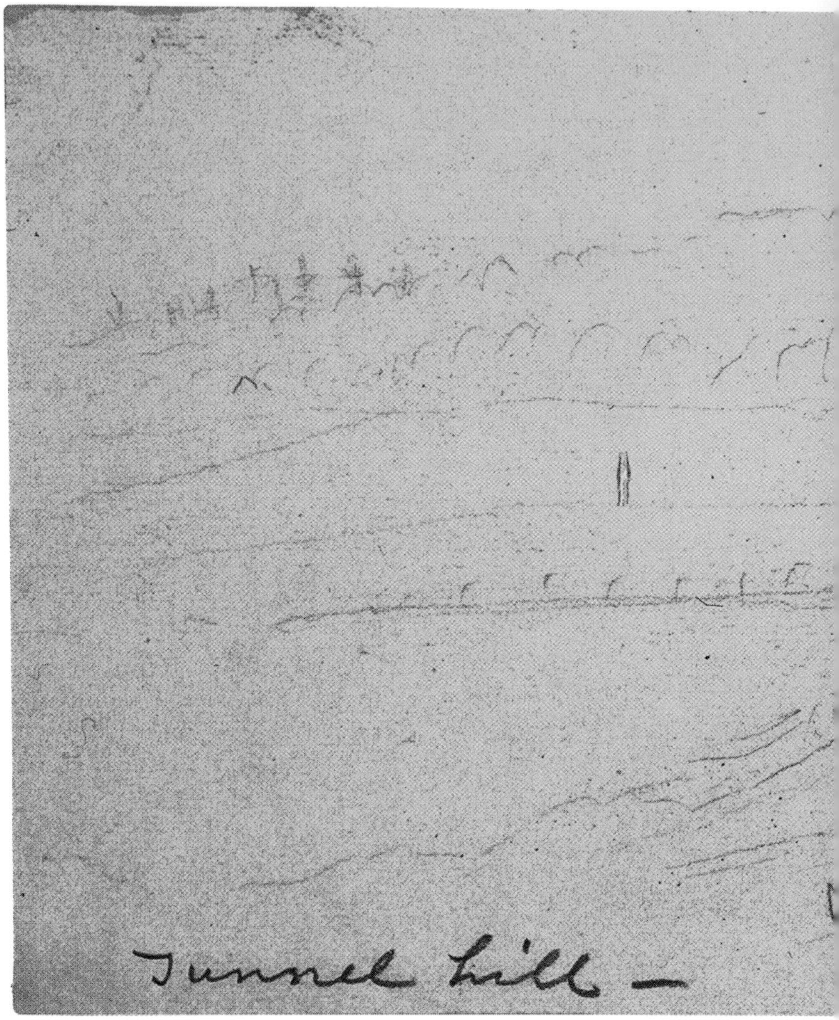


not a gun was fired. Advanced again. . . . An occasional gun shot, but we advanced until we were directly under Mission Ridge. Not a reb seen. . . . Our battery started for the left . . . we had four teams on a carriage, but the hill was too steep for us and two more teams were put on the pieces, and caissons left behind.

A detail of two hundred men was sent to our aid with axes, the enemy sending shells over us quite thick. 1st piece failed to advance with the horses. Ropes brought forward and it was hauled up by hand, we following with all haste. By this time a very brisk skirmishing was going on right to our left and rear quite close, and General Matthies came down at the head of his brigade at double quick, the old general on foot, making fine time. Captain Dillon ordered the howitzer section

and Cogswell's Battery to the rear in all haste. The extra teams were unhitched and the pieces unlimbered, and with great difficulty we made a left about, the hill being so steep that it shoved our horses down amongst the infantry that were pouring down. But the cannoneers fastened a rope to the axle-tree, and down we went in good earnest. Halted at the R.R. crossing in a complete jam of infantry, artillery and ambulances near General Smith's headquarters, who knew nothing of our movements and demanded by whose orders we came down.

We stood there in the cold damp evening for half an hour, got a feed of shelled corn from an out-house close by, when we moved back into the first field above General Matthies, and came into camp alongside of Cogswell's Battery and the 2nd and 3rd brigades of our Division.

*Tunnel Hill, at the northern end of Missionary Ridge, was so named for the Chattanooga & Cleveland Railroad tunnel cut through it. This view, sketched by Alfred R. Waud, clearly shows the rail line and the tunnel's entrance in the hill's western face. The soldiers of Major General Patrick R. Cleburne's division—some of the Army of Tennessee's best fighters—fought Sherman to a standstill here.*

Unhitched but did not unharness. Our rations were entirely out with the exception of coffee and some cornmeal picked up, so we ate hastily of unsifted mush and coffee.

. . . Returned to camp by 9 p.m. I was nearly exhausted from cold and lack of sleep, having been up since 1 a.m. Lay down in cold and wet blankets.

## LIEUTENANT ROBERT M. COLLINS

15TH TEXAS CAVALRY (DISMOUNTED), J. A. SMITH'S BRIGADE

*Surprised by the Federal thrust at his right flank, Bragg reacted in time to halt the movement of Smith's brigade and other units of Cleburne's division to Knoxville, redirecting them toward Tunnel Hill. Collins, who had been captured and exchanged earlier in 1863, was later wounded during the Atlanta campaign. His regiment was one of several at Chattanooga that, lacking mounts, fought as infantry.*

On the evening of November 23d, our division was put in motion moving in the direction of Cleveland. We marched about eight miles, went into camp and it is said were waiting for transportation by railroad to Knoxville. At this time Gen. Grant was in command of the Federal army, and as soon as Bragg moved out our division he commenced at once to press our line. . . . All night of the 23d Gen. Bragg had details of men to keep up fires on that part of the line we had left, beating drums as if he had a big force on that part of the line; but Gen. Grant was too old a bird to be caught with that kind of chaff, and just kept on pressing. While it was yet dark, on the morning of the 24th, our division was moved back and took position just in rear of our old line, and east of the ridge. The writer with permission went to the top of the ridge, and from where we were, we could see over the whole valley, and it was alive and working with long lines of blue infantry, bristling with bayonets; it was a fine view of the pomp and splendor of glorious war, and we felt it in our very bones, that the ground was going to be torn up and lots of people hurt in the neighborhood before many days. All at once, about 4:30 in the afternoon, we were put in line and started off at a double quick, to the right. We knew from the way couriers were dashing around, the serious expression on the face of those in high place, the haste with which we were being moved, and the old decks of playing cards the boys ahead of us were throwing away, that somebody was getting hurt, or we were on a race with the Federals for some important point. Referring to the playing cards, it is strange that men will carry something in their pockets they are ashamed to be found dead with. We had seen this throwing of cards away before . . . we crossed the mountain right over the Chattanooga and Cleveland Railroad tunnel, and formed in line in a valley between the mountain proper and a high point of mountain that seemed to jut down between Missionary Ridge and the river. We moved forward up the mountain, but the Federals were already there; they had beaten us to the position. We fell back and took position on the main range, and formed a line with the left of our brigade resting over the tunnel already referred to, and extending along the mountain to the right. . . .

It was now dark, the night is cold and crisp, and being so close to the enemy, we could have no fires and we had to just grin and bear it.

## LIEUTENANT COLONEL EUGENE POWELL

66TH OHIO INFANTRY, CANDY'S BRIGADE

*As Sherman moved against Missionary Ridge, a force under Major General Joseph Hooker prepared to assail the Rebel left on Lookout Mountain. To reach the enemy the Yankees had to cross Lookout Creek, a narrow but deep and steep-banked stream that wound along the mountain's western base.*

It struck me, as I stepped into Geary's tent, that I had seldom looked upon a more silent, solemn party, but Geary broke the silence by saying, "Colonel, I have sent for you. I have orders to make a demonstration upon Lookout Mountain. I wish to know where and how I can cross that creek with my command." . . .

Gen. Geary's inquiry of me as to where he could cross Lookout creek caused the situation at the dam to flash across my mind, and I described it to him and stated that I thought I could lash rails, boards, etc., to those knees and make a good foot bridge. Geary accepted the proposition at once, told me to return to my picket line, take the reserve pickets and build the bridge, and by that time he would be at the little mill just back of that point with his division, and would cross over upon Lookout Mountain.

I withdrew at once, mounted my horse and was soon moving with my pickets to carry out the orders. When I reached the open space at

*This sketch shows Federal troops of the XII Corps rushing through thickets in the early morning hours of November 24, carrying rails to help bridge Lookout Creek. As Colonel Powell recounts, the men lashed such planks to the foundation of an unfinished mill dam, quietly completing the task without the use of a single nail to avoid making noises that could have alerted Rebel pickets.*

the dam, the moon was shining, making it quite light, but soon thereafter clouds of mist settled down upon the mountain side and it grew quite dark. I halted the pickets at the site of the proposed bridge and told the men what the orders were. I said that it was probable that as soon as we began building the bridge the Confederates would begin firing upon us, as we then could hear the enemy moving in the underbrush beyond. I said that I wanted half of my force to cross the creek by climbing from knee to knee, and when over to form a half circle for the protection of the bridge builders who necessarily would be unarmed and defenceless, and that the men who should go over must draw the fire of the enemy upon themselves and return such fire as effectually as possible and thus protect the men at work.

I called for volunteers to cross the creek; there was complete silence for a time, when a soldier stated he would go, then another, and it was evident that the whole command would go, so I divided my command as nearly equal as to numbers as I could and directed the right to sling their guns across their shoulders and climb across the knees. This was done, and soon a part of my force was on the enemy's side of the stream, being the first Union soldiers to reach there.

Then I placed a soldier on each knee and directed the others on our side of the stream to get rails, boards, etc., and pieces of rope from the mill. These were handed out to the soldiers on the knees and there tied securely, and soon we had a good solid foot bridge made, upon which men in single rank could move safely and rapidly across. This bridge was made without hammer, nails or saw, simply by lashing timbers to the knees, and as the boards had been torn off of the dam the water passed under the foot bridge without any resistance from it. During this time, much to our surprise, not a shot had been fired by the enemy. . . .

Then another foot bridge was easily made by our pontooneers further down the stream, upon which Osterhaus' division and other troops crossed and joined Geary, thus making his force on the battlefield near the point of the mountain much stronger than that of the enemy.

## PRIVATE DAVID MONAT

### 29th Pennsylvania Infantry, Cobham's Brigade

*After Geary's men crossed Lookout Creek, they toiled up steep, narrow trails toward Lookout Mountain's fog-shrouded summit. Upon reaching the sheer limestone cliffs known as the palisades, Monat and the other troops faced to the left and began moving laterally across the mountain's ravine-scarred slope toward a confrontation with Brigadier General Edward C. Walthall's unwitting Rebel infantry.*

The 109th [Pennsylvania] Regt. of our Brigade were left in the works. Col. Cobham of the 111th Penna. commanding our Brigade rode past and said, "Boys, how would you like to have a fight this morning?" I said "It would be damn rough without any chance for breakfast." He replied "That's so, but I guess we'll get one." We then heard that one Regt. from each Brigade of our Division was to be left in the works we had vacated and that we were to assault Lookout Mountain.

It was a cold chilly day and a misty rain falling and we could not see very far up the mountain. Neither could the Rebs see us. After crossing the rail road and moving some distance down along Lookout Creek at the foot of the mountain we came to a halt near a mill. Genl Hooker & Geary with their staffs passed by in our rear. Shortly orders came for all the officers of our Regiment to report at the mill. They soon came back, our Captain looking very serious, and told us we were ordered to take the mountain and that our Regiment was to be the first to cross the creek. Our Chaplain came along and "God blessed us" and said "If any of you have any messages or valuables to send to your friends I will take them and see they are safely delivered." I said to Jack MacLauchlan, "Jack, I've got about 3 or 4 dollars. If I go, look out for them and if you get a chance take a drink and say 'here's to a good fellow.' "

The pioneers were then ordered forward to lay boards & planks across the mill dam and we started across the creek with orders to keep straight up the mountain till we reached the Palisades at the top, which looked like a wall on top of the mountain. The Rebs were up on the slope of the mountain towards Chattanooga where they had a line of breastworks around their camp.

When we reached the Palisades we halted and came to a front and passed the word down the line. Orders came to throw out Companies C & E as skirmishers and to move forward. It was hard travelling over the rocks & fallen trees & up & down gullies. We soon reached the Reb pickets when the firing commenced and the skirmishers halted. Capt. Woeltge of the 111th on Cobham's staff shouted to Capt. Millison of Co. C in charge of the skirmish line to forward the skirmishers. Millison replied "The Rebs are in force in our front." Woeltge shouted "Damn it, dats what we want. Forward!" Millison gave the order to move forward and we had not gone far when he was shot in 2 places.

By this time we were all up with the skirmish line and kept on driving the Johnnies back and soon reached a position where we could look down the mountain at the Rebs in their works and they soon started to leave. The left of our line had some heavier fighting than us as that was where the main body of Johnnies laid. It appears they were so busy watching some of our troops who were making a show of crossing [at the foot of the mountain] that they had no idea we had gone down the creek and crossed there, and when we showed up above them they got demoralized and skedaddled. . . .

We kept on and drove the Rebs around to the face of the mountain overlooking Chattanooga. Just then the sun broke out and the mist lifted and our fellows over in the valley in front of Chattanooga saw us and gave such a shout and cheers as I never heard before. As Col. Rickards, Capt. Woeltge and several others joined us we took a drink from my canteen.

*This photograph, reportedly taken on November 24 during the Battle of Lookout Mountain, shows General Hooker (standing, third from right) with his staff at the base of the mountain. After leading the Army of the Potomac to defeat at Chancellorsville, Hooker had languished without a command until given the XI and XII Corps in September 1863. Despite Hooker's success on Lookout Mountain, Sherman passed him over for promotion, and in 1864 he was relieved from field service at his own request.*

## LIEUTENANT JOHN R. BOYLE

111TH PENNSYLVANIA INFANTRY, COBHAM'S BRIGADE

*Boyle's regiment and the 29th Pennsylvania were on the extreme right of the Union advance, some men literally scraping against the palisades as they moved forward. Their brigade commander, Colonel George A. Cobham, wrote proudly that although the "fighting was desperate," his men drove the Rebels from their fortifications.*

"In five minutes a wall of flaming steel surrounded the besieged line, and within fifteen minutes the enemy threw down his arms."

The early morning was damp and raw, and clouds and mist enveloped the mountain side. The men had one day's rations. The creek was too deep to be forded, but in a few minutes it was bridged, and a picket post of forty-two men was captured by Cobham's brigade, which was in the advance. A section of Knap's battery was posted and left at a point to command the creek. The troops were scaling the steep and rugged mountain side by the right flank at eight-thirty o'clock, until the base of the crest was reached . . . the line stretched perpendicularly down the hill from the palisades to the creek. . . . The mountain sloped downward at an angle of nearly forty-five degrees, and was covered with underbrush and heavy bowlders, and broken by yawning ravines from fifty to one hundred feet deep.

At nine o'clock a charge began that continued for three miles in the fog and over these formidable natural obstacles. Some distance above the mouth of the creek the left captured a line of rifle pits, and drove the enemy into and then out of a second line, thus uncovering the fords where Cruft and Osterhaus were waiting to join Geary. . . . Owing to the nature of the ground the right advanced more rapidly than the left, and Candy half-wheeled to the right and obliquely upward. The line was a concave dragnet scooping in everything that was on the mountain side. When the right and center had advanced somewhat more than a mile pickets were found in strong natural defenses, and were driven in on a line of battle that stretched across the plateau and was sheltered in intrenchments of rocks and earth breastworks, protected by tangled slashings. It was Walthall's Mississippi brigade. With magnificent enthusiasm the One Hundred and Eleventh Pennsylvania and Ireland's brigade charged these works on double-quick and with the bayonet, while the Twenty-ninth Pennsylvania swept gallantly around on their flank. In five minutes a wall of flaming steel surrounded the besieged line, and within fifteen minutes the enemy threw down his arms. A few tried to escape, but Reynolds's battery beyond the creek rendered the way out so dangerous that they also preferred to surrender. Four stands of colors were taken, and the prisoners were sent back to Whittaker, whose men were near enough to see and cheer the clever victory.

Over these captured intrenchments the line dashed, unmindful of fatigue, and rounding the point of the mountain came in sight of the Craven farm. In its dooryard were two pieces of artillery, and protecting it from the front was Maney's Confederate brigade within another mass of strong defenses. As the right swerved a little from the palisades to flank these works a regiment struck it from above, but the Twenty-ninth Pennsylvania about-faced and gave it such a volley at short range that it surrendered before a second round could be served. A squad of a dozen or more rose up from the rocks in front of the One Hundred and Eleventh Regiment and threw up their hands. . . . The regiment and Ireland's brigade charged Maney's works as they had charged Walthall's, on front and flank, while Candy came upon them from below. Three guns from the top of the palisades endeavored in vain to reach the Union line, but shells and hand grenades were hurled down by hand upon our men. In a few minutes the Craven house, its intrenchments and cannon were in our hands.

## COLONEL WILLIAM F. DOWD

24TH MISSISSIPPI INFANTRY, WALTHALL'S BRIGADE

*As Federals bore down upon them, the brigade's five Mississippi regiments, on orders from Dowd, crouched behind logs and boulders to weather the fire. Wrote Henry Woodson of the 34th Mississippi, the "face of the mountain was lurid with bursting shells and seemed to belch smoke from every crevice, while the mountain itself seemed to howl and shriek as if a million demons had been aroused in its caverns."*

General Walthall appreciated to the fullest extent the situation, feeling that if his brigade gave way, the Federal forces could push round past the Cravens House and cut the large body of Confederates from the rest of the army on Missionary Ridge. I felt and knew that, if necessary, the brigade must be sacrificed to save the army. I knew, too, that it would take many hours to bring the Confederate forces from the top of Lookout Mountain to our support.

While General Walthall and I (as senior colonel of the brigade) were yet conversing, and as he was about to leave, our videttes were driven in and the fire became hot. General Walthall left the brigade in my command, and left to hurry the troops down from the mountain. I realized that everything depended upon the holding of this position until the descending troops could reach and support us.

I ordered my men behind rocks, trees and every cover that nature afforded, and instructed them not to fire until the enemy moved out in the open space in my immediate front. In the meantime the Federal troops advanced cautiously and carefully, yet following our videttes and pickets so closely, and driving them in so rapidly, that I was obliged to give the order to fire, thereby killing, I have no doubt, some of my own men. As soon as the enemy reached the open space a deadly and destructive fire was opened upon him, which soon drove him back under shelter of the rocks and trees.

The battle continued without a moment's intermission, at close quarters, until between 12 and 1 o'clock. Failing in his repeated attacks in front, the enemy moved a considerable force under cover of the rocks and trees close along the base of the rock, and before I discovered this movement, opened fire on my flank and rear, which killed and wounded several men. A powerful battery . . . and several others on the north side of the creek were pouring shot and shell into our right flank and rear. The slaughter was terrible on both sides. I saw our color-bearer shot down within a few feet of me, but the colors were immediately taken up and held by one of the color-guard. The battle-flag, rent and torn, was carried to Missionary Ridge the next day.

General Walthall had ordered me early in the morning "to hold my post till hell froze over," and thinking at this juncture that the ice was about five feet over it, I went up the line and ordered my regiment to retire slowly in a skirmish line, taking every advantage of the rocks, trees and other shelter, and to re-form in the rear of the Cravens House at the point where the roads from the house and mountain top intersected.

In the meantime, other brigades were formed in line of battle south of the Cravens House, extending from the base of the high rock to the foot of the mountain. Our brigade was formed behind this line as a reserve. The enemy advanced with inconceivable slowness and caution, but in the afternoon he began a severe attack on our line at very short range. Both lines were sheltered by the overhanging rocks. The battle raged without intermission until a late hour in the night, probably about 2 o'clock a.m.

## BRIGADIER GENERAL JOHN C. MOORE

BRIGADE COMMANDER, ARMY OF TENNESSEE

*Moore's acting divisional commander, Brigadier General John Jackson—derisively nicknamed Mudwall—remained far from the fighting at Lookout Mountain, leaving Moore and Walthall to fend for themselves. Here, Moore criticizes Jackson and describes how he moved his three Alabama regiments into position near the Cravens house.*

Our division commander, Gen. Cheatham, was absent on leave the day of the assault, and Gen. John K. Jackson, as ranking brigadier, was in command. I had not seen the division commander but once from the day we arrived until late on the night I was ordered to evacuate our position and after the movement had been accomplished. Up to the hour of assault I had never received a word of

*This photograph shows a portion of the "bench road," mentioned by General Moore, over which his men rushed to join the battle. The narrow road began at the mountain's northeastern end and wound its way up to a natural shelf, or bench, below the summit. From this point, the road snaked around the northern face of Lookout Mountain, continuing southward along the western slope. This view looks nearly due north; the Tennessee River flows by in the distant lowlands and Chattanooga lies in the right rear, obscured by haze.*

instruction as to the disposition of my command or the proposed line of defense, if any had even been determined, in case of attack.

. . . November 24, was very cloudy, partially obscuring the sunlight, but clear enough in the lower atmosphere to observe with field glass the conditions of the enemy. I saw that their pontoon bridges had disappeared, which was evidence that the long-continued monotony of inaction would be speedily ended. As there was no evidence at Chattanooga of an intended attack on our Missionary Ridge lines, I hastened around to the northern slope of the mountain and found that the Federals were massing their forces in Lookout Valley, a half mile away. Hastening back to headquarters, I dispatched a staff officer to the division commander, asking for orders.

In the meantime I formed my brigade in line ready to move. My messenger soon returned and reported that he could find no one at division headquarters, only four or five hundred yards distant. By this time firing had commenced on the picket lines and I sent him again, with the same result. The firing soon became very heavy. Gen. Walthall and I had consulted, as neither had instructions as to disposition of forces in case of attack. It was agreed that my left should rest at the Craven house and my line extend to the mouth of Chattanooga Creek, unless otherwise instructed by the division commander when ordered into line, and Gen. Walthall's brigade would have charge of the line to the left and beyond the Craven house. Gen. Walthall remarked that he would hold his advanced position on the north slope of the mountain till forced back, and would still contest every inch of ground, and would then make connection with my left. This resolution was worthy of that daring and gallant officer, but, knowing his greatly exposed position and the narrow passage open for the withdrawal of his men, I greatly feared the daring effort might have a disastrous ending.

The firing had become very severe, both by small arms and the Federal battery on Moccasin Point and the ridge north of Lookout Creek. At this time a division staff officer dashed up, giving orders to place my men immediately in the so-called rifle pits. My brigade moved by flank at a double-quick, under heavy fire from the Moccasin Point battery. Soon after the assault began a dense fog gathered about the mountain and continued much of the day. The Federal gunners did some

> "Under cover of the fog a few of our sharpshooters, concealed behind trees and large stones, soon picked off every Johnny that dared show his head on the top of the cliff."

remarkably good guessing, however, as to about "where we were at." Just as our rear files turned out of the bench road near the Craven house we met the remnant of Walthall's brigade rushing to the rear in inextricable disorder. The officers seemed to be using every effort to arrest their flight, but the men rushed past them in spite of threats and even blows. Where or when they stopped I never learned.

## PRIVATE ELISHA C. LUCAS

8TH KENTUCKY (U.S.) INFANTRY, WHITAKER'S BRIGADE

*During the battle near the Cravens house, Lucas and his comrades crouched in the damp shrubbery, forming a reserve for the Federal regiments hammering at Walthall's Confederates. The Kentuckians, lying exposed and vulnerable at the base of the palisades, had to endure the deadly fire of enemy sharpshooters and dodge unnerving rockslides started by Rebels on the heights above. Lucas, a native of Louisville, joined the 8th in March 1862 and served until the end of the war.*

Early on the morning of the 24th of November, our brigade moved up Lookout Valley into a dense forest where the enemy lost sight of us for a few hours. In the forest we piled our knapsacks, blankets and part of our rations, and left them under guard. We filed off to the left, crossed Lookout Creek on an old mill-dam, and commenced the difficult task of ascending the mountain through a thicket of cedars. Up, still up, meeting with no opposition except inanimate nature, pulling up by shrubs and projecting rocks. At last we reached the inaccessible walls of limestone, a perfect palisade several hundred feet high. This movement was still unobserved by the enemy, who were expecting us to attack them in front.

We faced north, the 8th Kentucky forming the extreme right wing of the line. A heavy skirmish line was put forward. We moved forward, keeping well up with our skirmishers. Thus we swept along the steep, rugged mountain side over huge rocks, fallen trees and deep ravines, regardless of the scattering shot sent at us from the mountain top.

A heavy fog that hovered over the mountain enabled us to attack the enemy by surprise in the flank and rear of their works. Their evident confusion was so great that they made but a feeble, unorganized resistance—their defense being principally Indian fighting from behind trees and large rocks. We gleaned a large harvest of prisoners. Those of the enemy that were not captured fled around the nose of the mountain and took a strong position on the southeastern slope, just under a towering cliff. About this time two of our heavy guns on Moccasin Point opened fire, and were replied to by those of the enemy on the point of Lookout, almost immediately over our heads.

By this time, 3 p.m., a dense cloud enveloped the mountain. The enemy made a determined stand, as they were strongly reinforced in their fortified position. A good many of the 8th having been sent back to Lookout Valley, in charge of prisoners, we were left in reserve at the nose of the mountain. Being near the wall or palisade, the enemy not only shot at us whenever the cloud would lift, so as to enable them to see, but resorted to an awful mode of warfare—rolling down loose stones at us. Under cover of the fog a few of our sharpshooters, concealed behind trees and large stones, soon picked off every Johnny that dared show his head on the top of the cliff. Though their ordnance made a terrific noise, their heavy missiles passed harmlessly over our heads as their pieces could not be depressed to a sufficient angle to reach us.

B. F. Wood, an excellent shot, succeeded in silencing a particularly annoying sharpshooter who had secreted himself in a niche of the irregular crown of the precipice. The rapidity of his shots were only accounted for by his comrades behind loading for him. Ben maneuvered until he obtained a view of the annoying rebel's head. As the fog lifted from the mountain Ben's unerring rifle cracked. The rebel sharpshooter sprang forward and fell on the edge of a rock 20 feet below. His hat, with a bullet hole in it, came to the base of the cliff. Ben laid there a long while, but no other daring rebel showed his head at that point.

820
HARPER'S WEEKLY.
[December 26, 1863.
THE ARMY OF THE CUMBERLAND—CAPTURE OF REBEL WORKS AT THE WHITE HOUSE, ON LOOKOUT MOUNTAIN, NOVEMBER 24, 1863.—[See Page 828.]

*Riflemen of Geary's division, sheltering behind the wall in the foreground, fire toward the Confederate line by the Cravens house. Additional Union troops—probably from New York regiments—charge down the wooded slope to the right, flanking the Rebels and forcing them to retreat. The house's yard is littered with Confederate dead and wounded, as is the adjacent Bench road.*

## CAPTAIN MAX VAN DEN CORPUT

Cherokee (Georgia) Battery, Stevenson's Division

*Posted on the top of Lookout Mountain, Corput had two guns rolled to the western edge of the summit. To bombard the enemy, the Rebel gunners had to raise the trails of these pieces to fully depress their barrels. Despite Corput's claims, however, the great elevation of his position and the heavy fog that obscured the Federals prevented him from greatly hampering the Union assault.*

About 10 a.m. the fog on the side of Lookout Creek had disappeared enough to show us the Federals moving in three different bodies from the foot of Raccoon Mountain toward Lookout Creek. The pickets had been firing from about sunrise toward the creek. We could hear very distinctly cutting of timber in the valley, but presuming that the pickets would give notice of any work going on on the side of the Federals, I took no notice of it.

The longest fuse that I had with my guns was 7, which time would carry my shells only 1 mile. The position of the Federals being far over that distance, I did not open fire on them then. After their first charge on our infantry—who instantly gave way, the enemy pursuing them—

I opened fire on the Federals, having brought my section in position on the left of the mountain. I fired 33 shells, doing in many instances good execution. The Federals were, however, soon under cover of the rocks, [and I was] unable to depress my guns enough. The fog during all that time was very dense on the right and in front of the point. When the enemy made their charge I discovered two places over the creek where they had made bridges by cutting timber, which answered for the cutting that I heard in the morning.

At about 2 p.m. General Brown gave me orders to fire toward the Craven house if I could ascertain the direction, the enemy being reported in force in that direction. I obtained from the signal corps the position of the house, and fired about thirty times at intervals in that direction and toward the right. In the opinion of General Brown, then present, and according to my own judgment, I believe I did some good firing.

*In this photograph taken after the Battle of Lookout Mountain, Union soldiers amble among the large boulders on the grounds of the Cravens house looking for souvenirs. These stone outcroppings provided natural breastworks for the Confederates defending the area. The home itself stands to the right, destroyed by the ravages of Union artillery firing from Moccasin Point and Yankees scavenging for firewood. The sheer cliffs in the background are a portion of the famous palisades.*

## LIEUTENANT CHESLEY A. MOSMAN

59TH ILLINOIS INFANTRY, GROSE'S BRIGADE

*Mosman's regiment and the rest of the brigade were on the extreme left of the Federal line as it converged on the Cravens house. Mosman, who enlisted as a private, was hit in the right forearm and hip at Pea Ridge in 1862 and suffered another wound when he fought in the Battle of Nashville in 1864.*

We had driven the Rebels around to the east so that our line lay nearly due north and south from the palisades to the river. . . . Just as we got within 50 yards of the line the men, by a common impulse, ran forward to a depression seemingly formed by the water running down the mountain. It was about five feet deep, a natural protection, and the men had hardly gotten into it when a perfect storm of balls flew over our heads. The slope of the mountain is very irregular with great detached, irregular shaped rocks lying on it, sometimes ten to twenty feet high and big as a house. Some of them we have to round and the Rebels get behind them to fire at us. We have to shoot at the flash of their guns, the mist or cloud is so heavy. The fog and smoke were so thick we could not see a man two paces from us, but the Rebel bullets flew over us in showers and it was necessary for us to keep firing to keep them from advancing. Some men fired from 50 to 80 rounds each. A big cur dog followed the Regiment in and stood with his head sticking over a log some fifteen inches in diameter that protected his body very well, and when the Rebels gave us the volley he could not understand what it was all about. The balls would hit the log and he would look to see what it was. The bullets hitting the rocks were flattened into all sorts of shapes and they would whistle all sorts of tunes or shrieks, and the dog just kept looking everywhere, in every direction to see what was making the noise. It was comical to see him.

## LIEUTENANT ALBERT R. GREENE

78TH NEW YORK INFANTRY, GREENE'S BRIGADE

*As Greene and his fellow Yankees swarmed around the haze-shrouded Cravens house, the Rebels fled in panic. Private Robert A. Jarman of the 27th Mississippi remembered that he "skedaddled" before the onrushing bluecoats, running past the house and avoiding capture by jumping down "over two cliffs nearly twenty feet high." After the battle the despondent Jarman claimed that his decimated brigade had been "simply crushed by numbers" and now resembled a "small regiment."*

A little before the fog bank reached us the color-bearers, as by a common impulse, rushed ahead, and with a great shout the whole line broke cover and followed them. On they went in the face of a nasty rain of bullets. The rebels broke and ran and we ran after them, heedless of the bullets from the summit. Into holes, over rocks and stumps and logs, over a slight line of earthworks, past a ravine in which were huddled our foes to the number of two hundred or three hundred, who were speedily made prisoners and put under guard,—through a camp of huts and shelter-tents, and over fires where rebel breakfasts were cooking, on, capturing squads of the fleeing enemy, till the dense fog shut in again over and around us, and we must stop and feel our way. The battery did not change front as fast as we advanced, and it exploded one shell in the line of the One Hundred and Forty-ninth, doing some harm, and others too close in front of us, and for a while threw them to our rear. . . .

It grew lighter again and the bullets again began to sing amongst us. The fog seemed to break where we were; we could not see the valley, but it got clear on our level and above us. An earthwork was sighted ahead. Behind the last knoll the line was steadied and well closed up. As we showed over this knoll we were greeted with a sharp fusilade, which developed into a steady fire. Our line stopped and commenced firing. This was not what was wanted, but the resistance was heavy for our light line. Cobham again helped us by his crossfire. Barnum of the One Hundred and Forty-ninth, shouting to his men to follow him, rushed up the knoll, waving his sword above his head. A bullet struck his sword arm and it fell by his side, but the line had caught his spirit, and it went on now across good ground and with a regular front. The little white house on the point came in sight; we could see Chattanooga, and the watchers there could see us. All energies were bent to reach the house. Again the rebel line broke and ran. . . .

*The Battle of Lookout Mountain, fought in a misty drizzle that thickened as the day wore on, was romanticized by Northern artists and newspapermen as the Battle above the Clouds. The lithograph below fancifully conveys the essence of that idea, depicting Union troops crossing a fictionalized terrain toward an enemy position. In the inset tableau, General Hooker is portrayed coolly observing the progress of his troops as members of his staff seek shelter from Rebel fire behind trees. In actuality, Hooker had remained safely to the rear during the engagement, as was expected of the commander of a large force.*

# "The two vast armies of Grant and Bragg, in breathless suspense, awaited the outcome of the contest which both realized was no 'feint,' but a fight to the death."

In the yard at this farm-house were two Napoleon guns, and their caissons hard by were well supplied with ammunition. Our line here wheeled sharp to the right, following the enemy in plain view, and entered some woods. The fog closed in on us again. The whole of this charge could be plainly seen with glasses from Chattanooga, for while the fog was thick below, shutting in the sides of the mountain, our elevation was in plain sight. It is said that as we rounded the point in this last rush, the watchers in Chattanooga and on Orchard Knob, anxiously awaiting our appearance, were almost beside themselves with exultation, and that even Thomas so far forgot his gravity as to throw his hat into the air with a great shout.

## LIEUTENANT ALBION W. TOURGEE

105TH OHIO INFANTRY, VAN DERVEER'S BRIGADE

*Tourgée and the soldiers of the Army of the Cumberland had an unparalleled view of the fighting taking place on Lookout Mountain, hundreds of feet above their position on the plain east of Chattanooga. But when the fog closed over the action, the anxious Yankees below cocked their ears, straining to hear the faint sounds of combat. In this account, Tourgée mistakenly claims that he saw Hooker in the fight; it was most likely a regimental or brigade commander whom he saw riding by.*

After a little it became apparent that the fire was coming nearer. A white mist, the remnant of the night's storm, still hung about the nose of Lookout. Now and then, the wind swept it aside, till we could see the crest; sometimes the palisades below. Anon, the white veil would settle over it all and only the rattle of musketry would come out of the sunlit cloud. All at once it flashed upon us that this demonstration against the Ridge in our front was a feint and that Hooker was trying to take the Lookout—was taking it as we were soon assured. After a while faint cheers could be heard. How intently we listened. "That's no corn bread yell" went along the line, as every eye and every field-glass was turned toward the cloud-veiled Mountain. The artillery ceased firing and the two vast armies of Grant and Bragg, in breathless suspense, awaited the outcome of the contest which both realized was no "feint," but a fight to the death. Again and again, the "mudsill" cheer rang, out, each time nearer the palisaded crest. Soon a faint grey line appeared in the open field on the slope of Lookout. Even with the naked eye, it was apparent that it was disorganized and falling back. Through the smoke and mist, the colors sometimes flashed. The gray masses fell slowly back, and a line of blue appeared. As the crimson of the old flag was recognized, Grant's army broke out into cheer after cheer, which must have been inspiring to Hooker's men, and appalling to the enemy. With scarcely a halt to reform, the line of blue moved forward, General Hooker riding his white horse, following close upon the charging column. The Confederates, fell slowly back, rallying and breaking again, until with a sudden rush they made for a line of works which seemed extended from the foot of the palisade down the slope between the timber and the open field. Here they made a last stand; with a rush our brave fellows swept up to the works, but so stubborn was the resistance that for a moment it seemed to us that the lines and colors were intermingled and the assailants captured. But the enemy's colors soon broke to the rear, and disappeared in the woods. The clouds settled down over the scene and only desultory firing was kept up. Until night-fall and even after, a few scattering shots were heard on the slope. Then all was still. The audacity of the plan and the suddenness of its execution paralyzed the enemy, and amazed those who witnessed its execution.

# "This was one of the few times in battle that it took a braver man to run than it did to stand."

## PRIVATE JOHN W. SIMMONS

### 27TH MISSISSIPPI INFANTRY, WALTHALL'S BRIGADE

*Low on ammunition and hopelessly outnumbered, Walthall's embattled Mississippians had no choice but to retreat down the eastern face of Lookout Mountain. Eventually they rallied, as the Union pursuit slowed with the onset of darkness. Simmons and his surviving comrades then hunkered down in the gloom, concerned about further attacks and talking of the loss of friends and the destruction of their brigade.*

When the Yanks advanced on us in three lines of battle, we had but one thin line and no reserve, as a good portion of the brigade had been captured early in the morning while on picket duty by Lookout Creek, where the pickets had been carrying on a friendly exchange of papers, tobacco, coffee, etc.

Walthall's Brigade extended from the perpendicular cliffs near the top down the rugged mountain side, north toward the Tennessee River; and as the ground was covered with large rocks we were afforded fair protection, except from the artillery, which played on us incessantly from Moccasin Point across the river.

As the enemy would advance and drive us from one position, we would fall back a short distance, reform, get positions behind the rocks, and give it to them again. Many of our boys were captured that day on account of our line holding its position until the enemy were so near that it was almost certain death to run. This was one of the few times in battle that it took a braver man to run than it did to stand; because those who remained behind the rocks could surrender in safety, and those who ran would draw the fire of the heavy Yankee line.

It was near the noted Craven House that our line was formed, when the blue coats crowded us and came very close before our line gave way. Just as we started to fall back, the color bearer, who had bravely carried our regimental flag through many hot places, fell dead. One of the other boys, seeing this, turned back and grasped the colors when he, too, went down and fell across the former with the color staff under him. By this time the enemy was almost upon the flag, when a gallant youth from south Mississippi turned back and running to within a few steps of the enemy's line, seized the colors, breaking the staff off short, and ran after his regiment, waving the flag and hallooing at the top of his voice. It appeared that the entire Yankee line was shooting at him, but he soon regained his regiment and, with the short flag staff in his hand, mounted a large rock and waved it as high as he could reach, at the same time calling out that old saying so familiar to soldier boys: "Rally 'round the flag, boys!" which they were very prompt to do. The boys loved that old flag better after that than ever before.

That night we were relieved by other troops and the little handful of us that was left was moved down into the valley, and there in the shadow of Lookout Mountain that dim, moonlit night, that little short flag staff was stuck in the ground, and the boys crowded around it with saddened hearts and recounted the eventful and dangerous scenes of the day, some telling where Tom, Jack or Jim had fallen and others had surrendered. Many of them showed where minie balls had cut their hats, coats or blankets. The meeting at that flag was one never to be forgotten, and many of us joined hands around it and pledged that no Yank should ever lay hands on it without passing over our dead bodies, and they never did. Strong men unused to tears, although accustomed to the cruel scenes of war, cried like children.

*Edward Cary Walthall (left) began the war as a first lieutenant but advanced rapidly in rank and by December 1862 was a brigadier general. At Lookout Mountain, Walthall persisted in riding bravely about his disintegrating battle line and encouraging his men to fight, even after he had been hit in the foot by a Union bullet. He recovered from this wound, was elevated to major general, and fought until the Confederacy's collapse.*

## CAPTAIN JAMES W. A. WRIGHT

36th Alabama Infantry, Holtzclaw's Brigade

*The men of Holtzclaw's brigade had passed most of the day near Missionary Ridge, watching, said Wright, "with deep interest and astonishment this evident attack in heavy force along a line deemed so nearly impregnable that earth-works there seemed almost unnecessary." When, in the late afternoon, Bragg ordered the brigade to Lookout Mountain, it was too late for them to have any impact on the battle.*

Late in the afternoon our brigade . . . was marched from its trenches across Chattanooga Creek by the bridge on the road from Rossville to Lookout, and, losing a few men by shells from the Moccasin Point batteries as we were crossing this deep ravine, we relieved Pettus' and Walthall's wearied men about dusk, and together with Moore's brigade held their rocky ramparts till after midnight. The Thirty-sixth Alabama—my regiment—relieved our neighbors of the Twentieth Alabama, our left extending, as theirs had done, to the very base of the palisades. The right of our brigade connected with the left of Stevenson's division. Here we maintained a lively fire with the enemy's advance till after nine o'clock, losing some men even by the random shots in the darkness.

Friends who remained in the valley informed us next day that the rifle-flashes at night along the waving lines of attack and defense, which extended eastward half a mile or more down the mountain slope from the beetling palisades, presented a curious and beautiful sight, not unlike thousands of sparkling fire-flies on a mid-summer's night. We were not, you may well suppose, in a position just then to appreciate such picturesque beauty. . . . For us it was not safe to have fires, although after midnight it was cold, clear, and frosty. Our position would have been revealed by them, and a heavier fire would have been drawn upon us.

The moon was full and was in a partial eclipse at 3 A.M. when, under orders, our troops silently withdrew from the last line of defense on Lookout Mountain. A grim sight, never to be forgotten, greeted the eyes of some of us as we left that rocky ridge in the dead of night. In a small open ravine some of our poor fellows lay stark and cold, one with outstretched arms. Those pallid faces, those staring eyes, upturned to the bright moon, how startingly distinct! No time to bury them; no time for weary men to bear these bodies with them over that rugged, rocky trail. It was all we could do to look after our wounded. How often since has that vivid scene come up in memory unbidden, as a type of utter desolation and loneliness, of death upon the battle-field!

## LIEUTENANT ALFRED PIRTLE

Headquarters Guard, Army of the Cumberland

*Pirtle describes conditions that must have made the night of November 24 a miserable one for the victorious Yankees on Lookout Mountain, trying to coax warming fires out of sodden logs, and an unspeakably dreary one for the Rebels, evacuating their positions on Bragg's collapsing left flank.*

Forming line of battle, the first regiment advanced at double-quick across the field, their colors borne thirty yards before them, and amid the shouts of our army, who saw the gallant deed, took the white house, made good their hold on the enemy's rifle pits, and remained under a heavy fire. A second regiment soon joined them, and the enemy's supports came up too late. The Fortieth and Ninety-ninth Ohio regiments are said to-day to have done this gallant deed, and, whoever they were, they deserve to be remembered well by their country, for it filled all our army with admiration. A tremendous rain and mist soon came down, hiding the fight from us, but the steady rattle of musketry behind the veil showed a stubborn resistance from the enemy. This fire was kept up, dying away at times, again to be renewed and lull again, until about 10 p.m., when it ceased.

The rain was over by dusk, giving way to a most splendid moon about full, and the night turned very cold before day. On Lookout Mountain, over the space newly gained so bravely, gleamed a line of fires, beacons of loyalty, carrying glorious news and encouragement to General Grant's army that lay at the mountain's foot. Early in the night from the east slope of Lookout Mountain, the side where the two lines of foemen lay fighting, bright sparkles of vivid light, quick and bright as lightning, gleamed at each shot, sometimes so frequent as to almost illuminate the spot where the brisk skirmish was going on, kept up by the enemy to enable them to extricate the forces from the summit of Lookout, and hide the rattling of wagons that all night long were hurrying down the big guns and supplies.

## CAPTAIN JOHN WILSON

### 8th Kentucky (U.S.) Infantry, Whitaker's Brigade

*Before dawn on November 25 Wilson led a small detachment to the very summit of Lookout Mountain, where they unfurled their regiment's national flag. As the sun came up over Chattanooga, its rays fell upon the banner, creating a sight that dismayed Confederates and elated Union troops. At right, Wilson's squad reenacts their climb using scaling ladders that had been left behind by the Confederates.*

We were placed in one of the columns on the extreme right that marched around the palisades of Lookout Mountain on the 24th of November. We marched around to the nose or point of the mountain and lay that night above the Craven House. Just before daylight on the 25th, Gen. Whitaker came to our regiment and said:

"Col. Barnes, have you an officer that will volunteer to carry your flag and place it on the top of the mountain?"

I said, "General, I will go."

Turning to the regiment, he said: "How many of you will go with Capt. Wilson? I could order you up there, but will not, for it is a hazardous undertaking; but for the flag that gets there first it will be an honor."

Five men went with me. I handed my sword to my Color-Sergeant to bring up, and I took the flag and started, accompanied by Sergeant James Wood, Company H; Private William Witt, Company A; Sergeant Harris H. Davis, Company E; Sergeant Joseph Wagers, Company B; and Private Joseph Bradley, Company I.

Those who have seen the awe-inspiring precipice at the top of the great mountain can realize what a serious undertaking was before us, not to mention our lack of knowledge concerning the Confederates, who the day before had held Hooker at bay. Dim daylight was dawning. We crept cautiously upward, clutching at rocks and bushes, supporting each other, using sticks and poles and such other aids as we could gather. At every step we expected to be greeted with deadly missiles of some sort from the enemy. But fortune favored us, and before sun-up I, in front, reached the summit and planted the flag on top of Lookout Mountain. It was the highest flag that was planted during the war. Soon other detachments came up and congratulated me and my party, and we were the lions of the day in the Union army.

"Fortune favored us, and before sun-up I, in front, reached the summit and planted the flag on top of Lookout Mountain. It was the highest flag that was planted during the war."

*Captain Wilson poses on one of Lookout Mountain's numerous rock ledges with the five soldiers of the 8th Kentucky (right) who helped him signal victory by carrying the first Union flag to the crest of the mountain. From left to right stand Sergeant Joseph Wagers, Private Joseph Bradley, Sergeant Harris Davis, Private William Witt, and Sergeant James Wood. The bearded, 49-year-old Wilson balances at the edge of the stone outcropping, holding the flag. All of the men were granted 30-day furloughs for their brave and inspiring action. In the photograph at left, Wilson is visible on the uppermost ladder, waving his hat while he grasps the flagstaff in his left hand. Both photographs were taken months after the battle by Royan M. Linn, who established a studio on the peak to cater to the countless Yankee soldiers and civilians trekking to the now famous site to pose for pictures.*

# Missionary Ridge

While multitudes of troops in the valley below broke into wild cheers at the sight of Old Glory flying from Lookout Mountain at dawn on November 25, eight miles to the north at the tip of Missionary Ridge, the outlook for the Federals was anything but cheerful. Although Sherman enjoyed an overwhelming superiority in numbers—an assault force of 26,000 men against 10,000 in the Confederate divisions of Patrick Cleburne and Carter Stevenson—the terrain greatly favored the defenders.

To reach the Rebel line a mile or so away, Sherman's troops would have to descend the hill they had occupied, cross an open valley under fire, and climb another steep slope—Tunnel Hill. The topography made deployment difficult, and it was not until midmorning that Sherman was able to attack. Even then the assaults were piecemeal and poorly coordinated.

The Federals faced a compact line fashioned by Cleburne. Secured on the left by Stevenson's division south of the railroad tunnel, the line ran north for several hundred yards, following the ridge of Tunnel Hill to its summit; then it angled sharply eastward along a spur that descended to South Chickamauga Creek. Cleburne had bolstered the line with artillery on the ridge above the tunnel, in the angle at the summit, and in the north-facing leg of the line. In the crucial center position atop the hill, he placed the Texas brigade of Brigadier General James A. Smith.

Sherman's attack was spearheaded by Brigadier General John A. Corse's brigade, while another brigade under Colonel John M. Loomis advanced along the western slope toward the tunnel. For five hours the two sides fought, often at close quarters with clubbed muskets and bayonets, but the Federals could not secure a lodgement. Finally about 3:00 p.m., after suffering nearly 2,000 casualties, Sherman called a halt. He sent word to Grant that his men could do no more. Grant dispatched a two-word response: "Attack again."

Sherman obeyed, but only nominally, sending in 200 men from Brigadier General Joseph A. J. Lightburn's brigade. Their ranks were badly cut up, and soon the survivors were reeling back. There would be no more attacks on Tunnel Hill.

Grant wanted to turn a Confederate flank on Missionary Ridge before committing Thomas' Army of the Cumberland, in which he had little faith, against the center of Bragg's line on the ridge. Sherman's failure on Bragg's right lent urgency to Hooker's advance against the Rebel left. That morning, Hooker, as ordered, had taken aim for Rossville Gap but had progressed only as far as Chattanooga Creek by 1:30 p.m. And because the Rebels had destroyed the bridge over the creek, it took him several more hours to make repairs and get his troops across.

Sometime after 3:00 p.m., however, Hooker's forces captured Rossville Gap and secured a foothold on the southern slope of Missionary Ridge. The outnumbered Confederates on that flank, commanded by Breckinridge, slowly and grudgingly gave way. The destruction of a Confederate flank that Grant had been looking for was under way, but it was the left flank, not the right, and it was Hooker, not Sherman, who was accomplishing it.

Watching the battle unfold from Orchard Knob, Grant decided to wait no longer and ordered Thomas forward to relieve pressure on Sherman. Grant gave Thomas only a limited objective: Take the Confederate rifle pits at the foot of Missionary Ridge and await further instructions.

Bragg had divided his forces along most of his line, sending half of each regiment into the rifle pits 200 yards in front of the base of the ridge while deploying the rest on its crest. If attacked, the men in the rifle pits were to fire one volley and retreat up the hill.

Thomas formed his ranks with characteristic precision. Brigadier General Absalom Baird's division was on the left, then Thomas Wood's, Philip Sheridan's, and Brigadier General Richard W. Johnson's. When the Army of the Cumberland emerged onto the plain, 20,000 strong, it presented a fearsome sight to the Confederates watching from the mountaintop a mile away.

The great mass surged forward, skirmishers in front. The men burned to refute Grant's low opinion of them, and soon the main body broke into a trot and caught up with the skirmishers. The Confederates in the rifle pits fired a withering volley at 200 yards. Most of them then started heading up the ridge as instructed. But the tactic backfired—it heartened the Federals and dismayed the Rebels higher up on the ridge, who were unaware of Bragg's order and thought their front line was being routed.

The attackers took the rifle pits swiftly but then found themselves exposed to heavy fire from above. Recognizing their predicament, some soldiers started up the hill. More followed, and soon long lines of men began pushing their way up the slope, seemingly heedless of the destruction raining down on them.

Grant, watching the scene through field glasses on Orchard Knob, wheeled in disbelief and barked at Thomas, "Who ordered those men up the ridge?" Grant was watching a commander's nightmare: a battle gone out of control. At one point, he considered calling the men back. Then he decided to wait a few minutes. "It's all right, if it turns out all right," he muttered. "If not, someone will suffer."

Missionary Ridge was now a scene of swarming activity. The Rebels who had abandoned the rifle pits were racing frantically uphill and interfering with the fire of their comrades on the summit. The climbing Federals, although taking heavy artillery and musket fire, advanced undaunted. "Foot by foot and pace by pace," wrote Colonel Charles G. Harker, whose brigade was in the forefront of the assault, "the crest was being reached to the admiration of all who witnessed it, and to the surprise even of those who participated in the perilous undertaking."

In the face of such determination, the resolution of the Confederates crumbled. Men threw down their weapons and fled, and their panic proved contagious. Soon Missionary Ridge became a sea of Yankee regimental banners. A great victory roar arose as the jubilant Federals realized what they had accomplished.

Meanwhile, at the north end of the ridge, Cleburne's soldiers were cheering their own victory over Sherman when their corps commander, General Hardee, rode up with the bad news. Hardee ordered Cleburne to shield the retreat. Reluctantly, Cleburne withdrew from Tunnel Hill and deployed his troops as a rear guard for the broken army.

That night Grant wired news of the triumph to General in Chief Halleck in Washington: "Although the battle lasted from nearly dawn until dark this evening I believe I am not premature in announcing a complete victory over Bragg. Lookout mountain-top, all the rifle pits in Chattanooga Valley, and Missionary Ridge entire, have been carried, and are now held by us. I have no idea of finding Bragg here tomorrow."

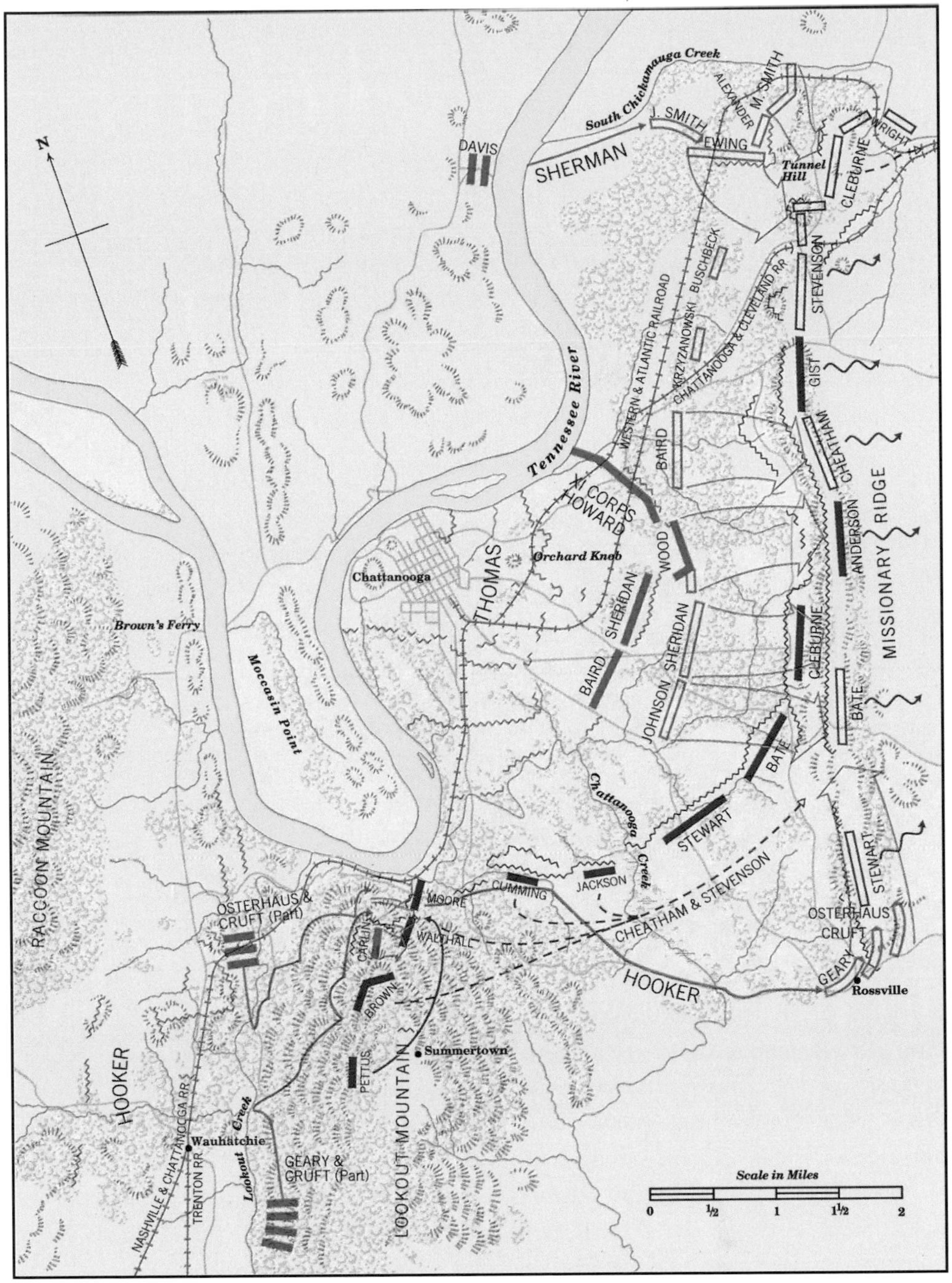


*On the morning of November 25, Sherman's Federals attacked the Rebel right at Tunnel Hill but were stopped by Cleburne's and Stevenson's divisions. That afternoon, however, Thomas' divisions under Johnson, Sheridan, Wood, and Baird advanced up Missionary Ridge and routed the Confederate center, while Hooker pummeled Bragg's left. Bragg's front dissolved, and his army began a retreat into Georgia.*

## CAPTAIN EMORY W. MUENSCHER

30th Ohio Infantry, Lightburn's Brigade

*After passing a cold, sleepless night engaged in the tiring work of digging entrenchments, Muenscher and his fellow Buckeyes were ordered by Sherman to take a small hillock in front of their position on Billy Goat Hill. Though the Ohioans initially pushed back an outgunned skirmish line of the 24th Texas, their attack soon ground to a halt in the face of stiffening enemy resistance. And so began Sherman's balky, uncoordinated, costly, and unsuccessful effort to take Tunnel Hill.*

*As a youth, Joseph A. J. Lightburn (left) lost an appointment to West Point in favor of a neighbor named Thomas J. Jackson—later to win everlasting glory as Stonewall. In the war Lightburn first served as colonel of the 4th West Virginia, then, in March 1863, was promoted to the rank of brigadier general. He survived a close call during the 1864 Atlanta campaign when a bullet glanced off his skull.*

When the morning of the 25th dawned we found that the hill we had taken was not the main ridge, but a large isolated knob separated from the main ridge by a deep and narrow ravine through which ran a wagon track. Soon after daylight Gen. Sherman came up on the knob, and a few minutes later an order came to me and Capt. Warner of Company E to take our companies and carry the point of the main ridge, where the rebels had a line of rifle pits. The men were still digging when the order came, and they threw down their shovels, picked up their guns, formed their line and started. It was the understanding that they were to advance firing, then halt behind trees, load and advance again; but once started this was forgotten and they went on a dead run down one side of the ravine, across the valley and up the other side, driving before them or capturing a few skirmishers in the valley. In less than five minutes they had driven the rebels out of their rifle pits with the bayonet. One man was killed and one wounded in the charge. A Johnny raised his gun to shoot Capt. Warner, who yelled out, "Who the hell are you shooting at?" Either the fellow was a raw recruit or the Captain's voice had a peculiarly persuasive influence over him, for he immediately dropped his gun and surrendered.

I now moved my company forward in skirmishing order about 20 rods and lay down to await further orders. The ridge was very narrow at the point, but widened rapidly and rose with considerable rapidity toward the south. The timber was thin and scattered so that we could plainly see the entertainment which our friends, the enemy, were preparing for us. About 40 rods or less from where we lay they had thrown up a line of log breastworks clear across the ridge, and behind it lay part of Gen. Pat Cleburne's Texas and Arkansas troops, as stubborn fighters as the rebel army contained, and we could count the muzzles of 12 pieces of artillery. While we lay there we could see regiment after regiment coming down the slope at a double-quick and forming behind the works, until they were packed several lines deep. The point that we were threatening was a vital one, for if we succeeded in carrying these works Bragg's retreat would have been cut off, and he was weakening his center to protect his flank.

About 10 o'clock an order came to me to charge the rebel lines. I had been so absorbed in watching them that I had not observed what was going on behind me, and supposed that the order was to us alone. I exclaimed, "Thunder! Do they expect me to take those works with my 40 men?" But orders were orders and we started. Then the infernal regions seemed to break loose. Shell, grape, canister and bullets seemed to fill the air. Fortunately they all went over our heads, but we had advanced only a few rods when bullets began to whistle past our ears from behind.

Looking around to learn what the trouble was, I saw some 10 rods behind us our line of battle advancing and opening fire. The 40th Illinois, 46th Ohio, part of the 30th Ohio, and parts of the 103rd Illinois and 37th Ohio, probably not more than 1,000 men in all, were all that there was room for on the narrow ridge. I hurriedly moved my men by the left flank out of their fire and formed on the left of the line. Gen. John M. Corse led them on gallantly and they made a long and desperate fight against four or five times their number, until the General fell and was carried off the field.

## LIEUTENANT ROBERT M. COLLINS

15TH TEXAS CAVALRY (DISMOUNTED), J. A. SMITH'S BRIGADE

*Fighting on foot, the troopers of Smith's command, supported by the four canister-firing guns of Swett's Mississippi Battery, delivered volleys against the Federals struggling toward the Confederate defenses. The Union troops took shelter where they could and gamely returned fire, knocking General Smith off his horse with two wounded legs, as well as sending Collins' comrade Pat Kane "up" to heaven.*

We could see the city and the valley. Long lines of infantry were moving up in our front. Now they are in range of our batteries, shot and shell were sent into their lines, they waver, but on they come. Cheatham's Tennessee division on a high mountain to our left sally out and drive the enemy in their front. But they rally and on they come in splendid order. Just now Maj.-Gen. Cleburne comes up on foot in rear of our line; he ordered the writer to take one company of the 3d and 5th Confederate and deploy them as skirmishers some forty yards down the mountain and in front of our line, and to remain until driven in by the enemy. We tipped our cap, formed the company and obeyed the command. We were immediately under our own guns, and when the artillery duel opened between the Douglas battery and the Federal battery on the high point just in our front, ours and our company of Irishmen's position was a noisy one, and very dangerous. The writer after getting the company deployed crouched down behind a very friendly chestnut tree. A big burly Irishman a few paces to our right said he was too busy to take a tree, when we reproached him for not protecting himself as much as possible. He was a fine soldier, the balls were flying fast, but he would stand out in a clear place, take deliberate aim and then watch to see the effect of his shot. Like all others of his race he was a wit. We had been there for some time; he finally with a twinkle about his eyes said, "Are you cold, Lieutenant?" We assured him that we were not. "Well," he said, "I didn't know, but thought ye were either cold or domed badly scared, from the way you're trembling and shaking." He was a splendid specimen of manhood. Just before sundown a shot broke his neck and he fell dead not ten feet from where the conversation occurred in the morning. Pat Kane went up from Missionary Ridge. He said during our conversation in the morning that if Jeff Davis would feed him and let him play cards all he wanted to, and furnish him a fight now and then, that he wouldn't care if the war lasted forty years.

*A native of Ireland, Major General Patrick Ronayne Cleburne (left) was one of the ablest combat commanders to fight on either side during the war. His tenacious defense of Tunnel Hill on November 25 was the lone bright spot in the Army of Tennessee's otherwise failed defense of Missionary Ridge. In a little over a year, on November 30, 1864, Cleburne would be shot dead while leading his men in a futile charge at the Battle of Franklin.*

## COLONEL CHARLES C. WALCUTT

46TH OHIO INFANTRY, CORSE'S BRIGADE

*Walcutt, who would later become a brigadier general, first saw action at Shiloh, where a Rebel ball ripped into his left shoulder. Despite being in constant pain from this injury, the Ohioan won plaudits for his service as a regimental commander, proving his mettle in numerous engagements. At Tunnel Hill, Walcutt's men nearly broke through Cleburne's entrenched line before being repulsed.*

At 7 a.m., 25th, General Corse gave orders for the Fortieth Illinois, Major Hall, and Companies A, F, and B, of the One hundred and third Illinois, under Major Willison, to be deployed as skirmishers, with the Forty-sixth Ohio, under my command, in reserve, for the purpose of charging the enemy intrenched on the ridge between us and Tunnel Hill. This charge the general led in person, driving the enemy before him and finally from his works to the protection of his guns on the opposite hill. After the brigade had taken position on this ridge, our eager general gave orders to charge the enemy's battery on Tunnel Hill. Three lines of skirmishers were deployed: Fortieth Illinois, Major Hall; one wing of the One hundered and third Illinois, under Major Willison; one wing of the Forty-sixth Ohio, under Captain Ramsey, with the remainder of the brigade organized as reserve, under my command. This charge, too, was led by our gallant general. The advance was sounded, and the several lines rushed over the brow of the hill under a most terrific fire. Being in easy canister and musket range, it seemed almost impossible for any troops to withstand it, but so eager were the men to take the new position that they charged through it, all with a fearlessness and determination that was astonishing. In this charge, our brave general fell badly wounded. Once only did the line waver, and that was when he was being borne from the field, but they were soon rallied. Every effort was made to reach the enemy's works, and only after repeated efforts had failed did the main portion of the men retire upon the ridge; some of the men yet remained in clusters on the opposite slope during the entire day, doing the enemy much damage; a few even reached the enemy's works, but were killed. Finding it impossible to accomplish the desired result, I ordered the regimental commanders to reorganize their men as fast as they returned under the crest of the hill. About 3 p.m., the enemy having repulsed the troops on our right, after their long and gallant struggle, showed himself in large numbers, both on my right and front, with bayonets fixed, with the evident intention of charging the retreating troops and my little band. Then it was that the Second Brigade did its work. In an instant every man was at his post and poured into the enemy volley after volley, that sent him running to his works. That this firing punished the enemy good is evidenced by the haste in which those coming upon us went back, from the fact that his guns, even his muskets, did not fire a shot for at least thirty minutes after I had given my men the order to "cease firing."

*Five feet eight inches tall and weighing 125 pounds, Brigadier General John A. Corse (left) was known for profane language and love of battle. While driving his men toward a wall of Rebel fire on Tunnel Hill, Corse was hit by a spent ball. The round failed to penetrate the skin, but the injury was very painful, and he had to be carried from the field. Without his leadership, his brigade's attack stalled though only 50 yards from the enemy earthworks.*

## CAPTAIN SAMUEL T. FOSTER

24TH TEXAS CAVALRY (DISMOUNTED), J. A. SMITH'S BRIGADE

*Once behind the fortifications, the hard-bitten soldiers of the 24th helped to smash several Union attacks, although it is doubtful that many of them felt as gleeful as Foster about the killing. After his wounding, Foster received treatment at a dirty, overcrowded field hospital, an experience he claimed made him feel like he was going to be "carved up into soup bones." Nonetheless, he managed to keep his leg, the injury healed, and he returned to his unit in May 1864.*

As soon as it is light enough to see anything one of my men (Theo Cullen) says "Capt. I see one. Can I shoot at him?" I told him wait till it was a little lighter and then blaze away. He fired at him in a few minutes thereafter and in so doing fired the first gun for that day. . . . We keep up a brisk fire until 8 1/2 or 9 o'clock a.m. when the Yanks charge us or rather they advance with their line of battle on our skirmish line. I passed the word down the line "to fall back slowly, but keep firing, from tree to tree as we fall back"—After falling back about 200 yards we come into an open ground; that is no undergrowth; but plenty large trees—so I could see nearly all my men at once—a thing I had not been able to do heretofore, and they are in a very good line—and going back from tree to tree—stop and load and shoot two or three times and go on again. . . . After going this way about 3/4 of a mile, we find the Brigd. behind some temporary works made that morning of logs piled up on each other—I assemble my men, get over the works and take our place in line.

Then the fun commenced in good earnest. . . . In a few minutes the Yank line of blue coats come in sight at about 400 yards and our small arms, and theirs, all open, and they keep coming—but when they get about 100 yds closer they fall back in bad order—in other words they run—all of which I enjoy hugely—we just laugh and hollow.

By going just over the hill 500 yds they are out of sight of us. They reform and come again—and just to see them blue coats fall is glorious. We can see them dropping all along their lines, sometimes great gaps are made, they can't stand it, and away they go to find shelter from our bullets.

In a little while a fresh set comes. They have a flag. I told my men to go in for that flag and down it came, another one picks it up and own he went, then another—until away they all go leaving three dead in trying to carry that flag. They got in nearly 100 yds of us before

# "Still they advance, and still we shoot them down—and still they come. Oh this is fun to lie here and shoot them down and we not get hurt."

*This Alfred R. Waud illustration portrays one of the ill-fated charges made by Corse's brigade against Tunnel Hill. While these soldiers from Iowa, Illinois, Michigan, and Ohio suffered and died on the slopes defended by Cleburne's men, sustaining more than 200 casualties, nearby Federal brigades that could have supported them were busy cooking breakfast. After Corse was wounded, Colonel Walcutt took command of the brigade. He later praised the courage of his troops during the battle, stating, "We had no lurkers; on the contrary, each man endeavored to outdo the other."*

they broke—and there are a great many dead left on the ground, and wounded ones crying for help—One man is helping another to get away and they are both shot down together. Now the fun of all this is that we are behind these logs and are not getting hurt one particle. . . .

There are men bringing us ammunition and the men don't put it in their cartridge boxes but lay it upon the logs in front of them to be convenient—Here they come again for about the sixth time, and they come like they were going to walk right over us—Now we give them fits. See how they do fall, like leaves in the fall of the year. Still they advance, and still we shoot them down—and still they come. Oh this is fun to lie here and shoot them down and we not get hurt.

This is business, we can see what we are doing here, when we kill a man we know it, we see him fall—They are now coming in a run stooping low to the ground but when they get in about 50 yards of us they halt, commence wavering, some keep coming, others hang back, some are killed 20 ft of our works, and finally, without any command our men commenced jumping over the works like sheep and Yelling like only Texans can, and charged into them killing a great many more, and run them back again. I was standing on top of the logs Yelling like an indian, when some poor deluded Yank—not having the fear of Confederates before his eyes, supposed to be a long way off, shot me in the right leg—the ball going cross ways under my knee, and just over the big leader. Several cried out, "Capt. you are hit. The Capt.s hit," and several came to help me down, at first I could not realize that I was shot. It felt like someone had struck my leg with the side of a ramroad or a stick and benumbed it somewhat.

## DRUMMER JOHN S. KOUNTZ

### 37TH OHIO INFANTRY, LIGHTBURN'S BRIGADE

*Detached from their own brigade in order to support Corse's left flank, the Buckeyes of the 37th got into action too late to have a major impact on the outcome of the fighting at Tunnel Hill. Kountz was among the wounded, lying in front of the Rebel works with a leg mangled by a bullet. His rescuer, William Schmidt, a blacksmith from Maumee, Ohio, was, like Kountz, only 17 years old. In 1895 Schmidt was awarded the Medal of Honor for the incident described here.*

Early on the morning of the 25th Sherman made his dispositions for the attack when we passed the valley which lay between us and the next hill, where the enemy had massed the corps of Hardee and other troops, the point of the ridge in our immediate front being held by that gallant Confederate General Cleburne.

General Corse attacked the enemy's position about 80 yards from his main line but it was so strong that but little headway was made, although the contest for an hour was very stubborn. During this time I saw the General carried off the field badly wounded.

While the fighting was going on to our right our brigade was under cover of temporary works, from which the enemy had been driven that morning. It was about 4 o'clock in the afternoon when the order was given to advance. As our men moved upon the enemy's works, I became so enthused that I threw away my drum and went forward with the regiment. The assault lasted but a few minutes, the firing from the enemy's entrenched position being simply terrible—grape, canister, shot and shell rained upon us. The fire was so murderous that it fairly plowed up the leaves and made the very ground seem alive. Twice our forces charged upon the Confederate works, and twice our bleeding lines were compelled to fall back. So strong was General Cleburne's position in our immediate front that 1,000 men could hold it against ten times their number. In this assault my regiment lost thirty percent of its number in killed and wounded.

*Thirty-seven-year-old Captain John Hamm (left) acted as a guardian to Kountz, the drummer boy less than half his age. The dapper officer poses with what may be a company order book in his coat pocket and wears a watch chain attached to his vest. Hamm, also from Maumee, Ohio, was one of nine men in his regiment wounded during heavy skirmishing against the Army of Tennessee near Resaca, Georgia, on May 13, 1864, in the opening stages of the Atlanta campaign.*

During the battle I was hit by a rifle ball just above the knee and the wound bled until the ground under me was covered with blood. I became very thirsty, but fortunately had two canteens of water. At my side lay Weber of Company A, who had been instantly killed. As I was not very far from the enemy's works and our men had fallen back to the point from which the advance was made, my position was not an enviable one as I lay between two fires. Captain John Hamm of Company A, who had always been very kind to me, having been told that I lay wounded in front of our line, walked over to my company and reported that Johnny Kountz lay in front, and asked, "Who will go and get him out?" William Schmidt promptly answered, "I will," and another comrade pointed out the direction in which I lay. Schmidt advanced some distance, then sprang forward and hurriedly placed me upon his back, and although there was much firing we were under cover of the hill to the left of our line.

I was then placed upon a stretcher and carried to the rear where the boys gathered around me expressing their sympathy. My leg was bandaged by Surgeon Billhardt of the 37th and I was carried to a log cabin in the ravine, below the point from which we made the advance. I remained upon the porch with other wounded until dark, when I was placed upon a stretcher and carried some distance over another hill and then put into an ambulance and taken to a point on the Tennessee River, near the mouth of Chickamauga Creek, where I was placed upon a rough table. After examination of my wound the surgeon informed me that my leg was so badly shattered that amputation was necessary, or words to that effect. I objected, but my objection was not heeded. I was then chloroformed and on awakening felt for my leg but it was gone. At this time I was 17 years of age.

## SERGEANT ALBERT JERNIGAN
6th Texas Infantry, J. A. Smith's Brigade

*After repulsing several Federal assaults, Smith's brigade mounted a brief counter-charge to drive back the Yankees. Struck by shell fragments, Jernigan later begged surgeons not to amputate his fractured right forearm—to no avail. Upon waking up from a dose of chloroform, Jernigan was stunned to find a stump where his arm had been. Mournfully he later wrote, "I had departed with the dearest friend of my being. . . . what relative as near or friend so dear, as one's own 'good right arm'?"*

"Now a scene of the wildest disorder and confusion ensues, some fly, others surrender, while others, for a brief space continue to fight."

Now the enemy is massing his forces against our right, a second, third, fourth and fifth lines come in sight. Blue coats seem to rise up out of the ground. They seem to be without number—Tis now past noon—On he comes in force, seemingly irresistible, but we occupy an advantageous position. Like a mighty wave swept on by a furious wind, he rushes to the foot of the ridge. Here he has some protection behind the rocks and uneaven surface of the hill-side. He begins the ascent, which in places is rough and somewhat precipitous. The artillery on both sides now ceases. Ours, because the side of the hill is so steep that the pieces cannot be sufficiently depressed to take effect; the enemy's because they are liable to injure their own men. In many places along the side of the Ridge, the enemy is entirely protected by the boulders and ledges of rock, along over and around which he crawls and clambers until near our line, when he rises and rushes upon us. Now ensues a scene, awfully wild and murderous beyond description. His front rank is mowed down at one fell swoop. Their places are filled immediately as if by the spirits of the lifeless bodies at their feet; these share a similar fate to those who have gone before. But still they come, more, and still more. In many places they are within a few feet of our line. The dead and dying lie heaped upon the ground; while their blood commingles and runs in streams down the steep hill-side. The angel of death seems to spread his dark wings over the two armies, and rejoice in the feast and harvest which he is reaping—At length the enemy begins to waver, seeing which, a charge is ordered upon him; now a scene of the wildest disorder and confusion ensues, some fly, others surrender, while others, for a brief space continue to fight, but they are soon overcome. We persue the flying enemy to the foot, and are then ordered back to our position on the Ridge. The artillery which has for sometime been silent, now opens furiously on both sides—Our army is in confusion, some having outstripped others in the persuit of the enemy, hence the necessity of falling back, that we may occupy our strongest and most protected position while reforming our lines. Some of the more valient of the enemy seeing that they are no longer persued, turn and commence back at us, seeing which, I was torn to leave without giving them a parting salute, I fire at them, load and fire a second shot, and now I find myself alone, my comrades having obeyed the order to fall back—Notwithstanding the enemy have discovered me, and are firing at me direct, and their shot falling thick and close about me. I step behind a pine and concluded to load, and give them one more shot before retiring. While loading, a ball grazed the tree striking my gun and splintering the stock. I am putting on a cap, a shrapnel explodes near me, my right arm falls paralyzed to my side, Am shocked by the concussion, feel a dreadful pain in my elbow, my gun falls to the ground, a momentary dizziness comes over me. I recover, take up my fallen right arm in my left hand to hold it steady and walk back up the Ridge in indescribable anguish, both of body and spirit, for my arm is dreadfully mangled from the wrist to the elbow, waiding through gore, clambering over the bodies of the dead and dying, many of the latter begging in the most piteous tones for help and for water, and expecting every moment to receive further wounds from the shot that are plowing up the ground about me or lodging in the gory bodies which lie thick upon the ground, I find myself at length in rear of our battle line seated by a tree sick and faint from loss of blood for my wound is bleeding profusely.

## LIEUTENANT SAMUEL H. M. BYERS

5th Iowa Infantry, Matthies' Brigade

*In the early afternoon Byers' regiment participated in yet another attempt to overrun the Confederate works on Tunnel Hill. As the Yankees rushed across the open ground toward the ridge, Rebel gunfire devastated them. Before the doomed assault ended, the 5th had lost its colors and 106 soldiers, including 82 men taken prisoner. The palpable terror and confusion of the experience pervades Byers' account.*

We started on a charge, running across the open fields. I had heard the roaring of heavy battle before, but never such a shrieking of cannonballs and bursting of shell as met us on that charge. We could see the enemy working their guns, while in plain view other batteries galloped up, unlimbered, and let loose at us. Behind us our own batteries (forty cannon) were firing at the enemy over our heads, till the storm and roar became horrible. It sounded as if the end of the world had come. Halfway over we had to leap a ditch, perhaps six feet wide and nearly as many deep. Some of our regiment fell into this ditch and could not get out, a few tumbled in intentionally and stayed there. I saw this, and ran back and ordered them to get out, called them cowards, threatened them with my revolver; they did not move. Again I hurried on with the line. All of the officers were screaming at the top of their voices; I, too, screamed, trying to make the men hear. "Steady! steady! bear to the right! keep in line! Don't fire! don't fire!" was yelled till we all were hoarse and till the awful thunder of the cannon made all commands unheard and useless.

In ten minutes, possibly, we were across the field and at the beginning of the ascent of the Ridge. Instantly the blaze of Rebel musketry was in our faces, and we began firing in return. It helped little, the foe was so hidden behind logs and stones and little breastworks. Still we charged, and climbed a fence in front of us and fired and charged again. Then the order was given to lie down and continue firing. That moment someone cried, "Look to the tunnel! They're coming through the tunnel!" Sure enough, through a railway tunnel in the mountain the graycoats were coming by hundreds. They were flanking us completely.

*This photograph looks due east toward Tunnel Hill and the passageway that gave the location its name. On November 25 this area was alive with rifle fire and cannon fire and teeming with soldiers locked in mortal strife. As Byers mentions in the account above, many harried and frightened Union troops thought that Cleburne's graycoats were actually pouring forth from the tunnel. This was a misconception caused by the rugged terrain. The soldiers of the 6th, 10th, and 15th Texas Regiment (consolidated), who mounted the savage counterattack, actually charged down from positions along the steep crest of the hill.*

"Stop them!" cried our colonel to those of us at the right. "Push them back." It was but the work of a few moments for four companies to rise to their feet and run to the tunnel's mouth, firing as they ran. Too late! an enfilading fire was soon cutting them to pieces. "Shall I run over there too?" I said to the colonel. We were both kneeling on the ground close to the regimental flag. He assented. When I rose to my feet and started it seemed as if even the blades of grass were being struck by bullets. As I ran over I passed many of my comrades stretched out in death, and some were screaming in agony. For a few minutes the whole brigade faltered and gave way.

Colonel Matthies, our brigade commander, was sitting against a tree, shot in the head. Instantly it seemed as if a whole Rebel army was concentrated on that single spot. For a few moments I lay down on the grass, hoping the storm would pass over and leave me. Lieutenant Miller, at my side, was screaming in agony. He was shot through the hips. I begged him to try to be still; he could not. Now, as a second line of the enemy was upon us, and the first one was returning, shooting men as they found them, I rose to my feet and surrendered. "Come out of that sword," shrieked a big Georgian, with a terrible oath. Another grabbed at my revolver and bellowed at me "to get up the hill quicker than hell." It was time, for our own batteries were pouring a fearful fire on the very spot where we stood. I took a blanket from a dead comrade near me, and at the point of the bayonet I was hurried up the mountain. We passed lines of infantry in rifle pits and batteries that were pouring a hail of shells into our exposed columns. Once I glanced back, and—glorious sight!—I saw lines of bluecoats at our right and center, storming up the ridge.

*Prussian-born Brigadier General Charles Leopold Matthies (left) had a "sanguine temperament," one of his Iowa boys recalled, and was "on kind and familiar terms with every soldier in his command. . . . The soldiers loved 'Old Dutchie' he was so good and brave." Matthies recovered from his Tunnel Hill wound in time to rejoin his brigade for the Atlanta campaign.*

## PRIVATE NELSON STAUFFER

### 63D ILLINOIS INFANTRY, ALEXANDER'S BRIGADE

*From their reserve position, Stauffer and his compatriots watched as the other brigades of their division took heavy fire. The veteran 20-year-old, however, seemed as worried about the contents of his coffeepot as about a Rebel bullet. Before the opening of the Cracker Line, Stauffer had eaten raw onions "as if they were apples."*

Nov. 25—Fighting began in good earnest about daylight and was kept up constantly until dark. We threw up one line of breast works on the bank of the river, and another about a half mile from it. Then the third line near the top of the ridge. After throwing up one line of works for our Regiment I was detailed to help throw up another to protect battery—making four lines of works in which I took an active part, and there wasn't much fun in it, or if there was I couldn't see it, for two of them were built under fire.

The 80th Ohio charged the rebs several times, but were repulsed each time with considerable loss. At one time they were driven clear back to the valley—and one little fellow I guess went clear to never. He threw his hat one way and his gun another, then walled up his eyes like a scared cat and made a B line for the open space near the battery, and such a gettin up and goen I never did see. He started toward the tennessee River, but where went is hard to tell. As he passed our regiment we gave him the right of way and all the encouragement we could by yelling at him, "Go it little one, they're after ye." The next Regt. took up the theme, and so on as far as we could see him. He seemed willing to take our advice and go.

Just as this little fellow passed out of view and the roar of our encouraging words ceased, and my coffee pot on the fire looked enticeing—the water was just beginning to siz and the coffee grounds blubber—when the rebble reserve came down the hill with a fiendish yell, and gave our men no chance to rally. Just then our colonel yelled out "Attention 63rd, fall in—fall in—forward double quick!" I gave my coffee pot a glancing doleful look as if to say "Fare you well brother Watkins oh." But we saved the battery at our left which the Rebs expected to take, and while they beat a hasty retreat up the hill I beat one toward my coffee pot, and strange to say it was still there.

## "COMAL BLUFF"

10TH TEXAS INFANTRY, J. A. SMITH'S BRIGADE

*Smith's brigade, core of the defense of Tunnel Hill, repeatedly hammered back Yankee attacks. "Comal Bluff"—a pseudonym for a soldier-correspondent in the 10th who had this account published in the Memphis Daily Appeal—reported that the Texans of his brigade had "left their homes and families, and without a murmur remain in the army of Tennessee, facing the foe, to beat him back from Georgia."*

The enemy strengthened their line at the foot of the hill and again threw forward a heavy line of skirmishers—far up the hill. We expected that the main line would soon assault us with their rapidly increasing force from below, but the fight declined between the skirmishers as before, until about 4 o'clock P.M., when Gen Cleburne passed along the lines and ordered the men to charge the enemy, meeting the enemy down the hill. Again rose above the war of arms that wild, hideous yell, which is only heard in battle, when a man regains that natural savagery he seems to have lost by civilization. With fixed bayonets, down the mountain side they rushed, a human avalanche, more terrible than if the crags themselves had been loosened from their steeps. The skirmishers of the enemy had been swept down—trampled under foot—but the flood of the Texans paused not—on it swept, accumulating strength as it advanced, carrying everything before it to the foot of the hill. . . . They piled the ground with the dead foe—some in their haste threw aside their guns as delaying them, and hurled rocks at the retreating enemy. The bayonet did its bloody duty, and the fallen autumn leaves was the death couch of many an invader on the side of that once peaceful ridge. Several stands of colors were captured, and a large number of fire-arms. Our men were, after a short struggle, in complete possession of the ground—the entire line of the enemy being either killed, prisoners, or fugitives across the fields. The enemy were evidently surprised at the charge, and perhaps expected to await until darkness at the foot of the hill and assault us in the night. This closed the fight on the evening of the 25th. As we had full possession of all the ground over which the skirmishing had been during the day, we saw how disastrous to the enemy had been our fire. There dead was on every side. Our men fell back to their position on the top of the hill and there we remained until night—no more firing going on, save from weak skirmishing parties. The men felt that they had done their duty, and knew not of our disasters in other positions until they were ordered at night to leave the post they had defended with such gallantry and success during the day. To sum up—we lost no prisoners, lost no artillery, held our position against five times our numbers; took two hundred prisoners and five stands of colors; repulsed the enemy and charged them twice from our works, driving them from the field.

## CORPORAL HENRY H. ORENDORFF

103D ILLINOIS INFANTRY, CORSE'S BRIGADE

*Orendorff, a member of Company F, does not mention that he was among the 74 men in his regiment who were wounded during the fight for Tunnel Hill—although his injury was relatively slight—in addition to 15 killed. Orendorff remembered "tenderly" burying comrades in a hastily dug trench. The 25-year-old Peoria resident claimed that his comrades who died within reach of the Rebel works were "robbed of their watches and other valuables, as well as their shoes."*

The enemy outnumbering us nearly two to one, and being behind strong works and having two batteries of artillery bearing on the line of our approach, the attempt to take the hill was abandoned. The loss of the brigade had been very great in the two assaults, the 103rd suffering heavily. The three companies A, F and B, being on the skirmish line, of course suffered most. Many of the killed and wounded fell within 50 feet of the Rebel works, and some of them were riddled with canister and musket balls. A member of Company F, Joe S. Walters, getting a little too near, a lean, lank, hungry-looking Johnnie sergeant jumped over the works and demanded of him, "gimme that gun, and come in hur, you damned yankee coward." Joe replied, "Here, take the gun, it ain't worth a cuss anyway." It had been hit with a bullet and was bent and spoiled. At this time a little corporal

"Again rose above the war of arms that wild, hideous yell, which is only heard in battle, when a man regains that natural savagery he seems to have lost by civilization."

sprang over the works and grabbed Joe's other arm and with much bluster and many big oaths, ordered that "you come over here, you yankee coward," but Isaac Harn and another comrade were just at the right and heard the conversation. Harn gave the big sergeant the contents of his gun, bringing him to the ground, and Joe gave the little corporal a blow that brought him to the ground. Turning, he ran down the hill under a shower of bullets, escaping with the loss of one finger. Harn was killed soon afterward.

The three companies were recalled and those who were able formed on the color line, occasionally reminding the Rebs that we were still alive and in business at the old stand. We could hear the battle on our right and the cheers of our troops under Thomas as they drove the enemy from their works that they had left so thinly occupied, in order to strengthen their position on our front.

*Most of the 103d Illinois' casualties at Tunnel Hill were incurred by its three-company skirmish line commanded by Major Asias Willison (left). Deployed in a loose formation that covered much of the front of Corse's brigade, Willison's detachment was engulfed by a "terrific fire" from the enemy entrenchments, stated an officer of the 40th Illinois, that "seemed almost impossible for . . . troops to withstand." In May 1864 Willison was wounded near Resaca, Georgia.*

## BRIGADIER GENERAL THOMAS J. WOOD

### Division Commander, Army of the Cumberland

*On November 25 Wood's division was centered on Orchard Knob, the site of Grant's headquarters. Hoping to draw off Rebel defenders from in front of Sherman, Grant ordered Wood's infantry to participate in a limited assault against Bragg's center. An 1845 graduate of West Point and a decorated veteran of the Mexican War, Wood was shot twice in the left foot during the Civil War and hobbled for life.*

Quite early in the forenoon of the 25th, General Grant, General Thomas and General Granger commanding the Fourth Corps, with their staff officers, took position on Orchard Knob. Mr. Charles A. Dana, the Assistant Secretary of War, General M. C. Meigs, quartermaster-general of the army, and other distinguished officials were also on Orchard Knob. . . .

Every eye on Orchard Knob was turned on General Sherman's operations, keenly watching his movements, and, in profoundest sympathy, ardently desiring success to crown his sturdy efforts. But all in vain! Assault after assault was repulsed. About half past two p.m. it was plainly and painfully evident to every beholder on Orchard Knob that General Sherman's attack, which, according to the plan of battle, was to be the dominant *coup* of the battle, had been hopelessly defeated, and was an irretrievable failure. It was evident that his further progress toward the crest of the Ridge was peremptorily stopped.

It chanced that at the moment of the repulse General Grant was standing near me. He approached and said: "General Sherman seems to be having a hard time."

I replied, "He does seem to be meeting with rough usage."

To this General Grant said, "I think we ought to try to do something to help him."

I said, "I think so too, General, and whatever you order we will try to do."

General Grant continued, "I think if you and Sheridan were to advance your divisions and carry the rifle pits at the base of the Ridge, it would so threaten Bragg's center that he would draw enough troops from the right, to secure his center, to insure the success of General Sherman's attack."

I replied, "Perhaps it might work in that way; and if you order it, we will try it, and I think we can carry the intrenchments at the base of the Ridge."

General Grant walked immediately from me to General Thomas, distant about ten paces. I did not accompany him, though there would have been no impropriety in my doing so. Generals Grant and Thomas were in conversation a very short time, perhaps two or three minutes, when General Thomas called General Granger who stood near to him. After perhaps two minutes conversation between Generals Thomas and Granger, the latter came to me and said: "You and Sheridan are to advance your divisions, carry the intrenchments at the base of the Ridge, if you can, and, if you succeed, to halt there."

He further said, "The movement is to be made at once, so give your orders to your brigade commanders immediately, and the signal to advance will be the rapid, successive discharge of the six guns of this battery."

I immediately sent for my brigade commanders, Hazen, Willich and Beatty, repeated to them the orders received from General Granger (who, on giving them to me, said they were General Grant's orders) and directed them to give the orders to their regimental commanders in person, who, in turn, were to give the orders to their company commanders in person. I was thus careful in having the orders transmitted, because I desired commanders of every grade in the division to fully understand what the movement was to be, and that there might be neither misconception nor confusion.

## SERGEANT CHARLES C. HEMMING

### 3D FLORIDA INFANTRY, FLORIDA BRIGADE

*Hemming's thinly spread regiment held a position in the Rebel center at the point where the Moore road ascended Missionary Ridge. The Floridians were dug in halfway up the slope, Bragg's headquarters behind them on the crest. Hemming was soon to be captured by one of the Federal battle lines he so admired and sent to an Illinois prison camp. In September 1864 he escaped to Canada, where he served as a spy.*

Our regiments, when in battle line, were conspicuous for our evidences of weakness. One file could scarcely touch another, and we discovered almost at once that in order to deceive the enemy, who could plainly see us on the crest of the hill, our commander was marching and countermarching for some time before the battle commenced, a constant stream of men moving toward our right and then circling back and the same men coming along in the rear.

*The artist Thure de Thulstrup painted this scene of Generals Gordon Granger, Ulysses S. Grant (in overcoat), and George H. Thomas observing the attack against Bragg's center on Missionary Ridge from the summit of Orchard Knob. To the left of the commanders, a soldier of the signal corps stands with a flag used for communicating with forward positions. Staff officers and cavalrymen serving as couriers also wait in readiness to deliver dispatches to field officers. In the background, columns of gun smoke rise from the ridge as Rebel soldiers try desperately to slow the determined Yankee onslaught.*

*This unusual photograph, taken in 1864, shows Colonel William Grose's brigade engaged in skirmish drill. The scene is similar to what the Confederates would have seen on November 25 as a dozen Union brigades charged Missionary Ridge. In the foreground a skirmish line and its reserve lie prone to avoid hostile fire. The remainder of the brigade is drawn up in two-ranked regimental battle lines. Artillery pieces, limbers, and caissons occupy the field in the distance at left.*

It was somewhere about one-thirty when we heard the reverberation in the hills around of a tremendous gun, and over our heads screeched the large shells it was sending at us. Then we looked out on the plain, and with the precision of a dress parade their magnificent army came in view. The officers, all superbly dressed, pranced out on their high-mettled chargers; the bands played, and to the music came the most wonderful array of splendidly equipped soldiers I ever saw. The old flag waved beautifully at the head of each regiment and the smaller flags were in their places with the brigade and division commanders. The atmosphere was perfectly still excepting just breath enough to straighten out the banners.

I loved the old flag dearly when I was a boy, and when the Fourth of July came I had my miniature cannon lined up on small entrenchments in our game to cannonade the fort and salute the flag. When I looked upon the old flag at the head of that wonderful army, I confess that it drew my silent admiration, as I suppose it did that of many others of our Confederate soldiers.

However, we had a duty to perform and a new flag to serve; so we lay down on the top of the hill, waiting for the coming foe.

## LIEUTENANT WILLIAM A. MORGAN

23D KENTUCKY (U.S.) INFANTRY, HAZEN'S BRIGADE

*Morgan, an Irish immigrant, stirringly describes the Federal surge up Missionary Ridge. Grant's orders were for the men of the Army of the Cumberland to advance only to the base of the ridge and no farther. Once they had taken Rebel works there, however, the Yankees found themselves exposed to deadly fire from above. Spontaneously, and often without direct orders, they began to claw their way up the precipitous slope to shut off the rain of shot and shell that was tormenting them.*

From the position occupied by my regiment, Orchard Knob was in view and all eyes were leveled in that direction. Suddenly a commotion was discernible on Orchard Knob. Officers were seen mounting their horses and riding towards the several commands. Then every man in the line knew the crucial hour had come. Intense excitement seemed to stir every soldier and officer. Excitement is followed by nervous impatience.

Time moves slowly. Here and there a soldier readjusts his accouterments or relaces his shoes. All know that many will never reach the enemy's works, yet not a countenance shows fear. The delay is becoming unbearable.

At last the first boom of the signal is heard. Men fall in and dress without command. Another gun, and nervous fingers play with gunlocks. Another and another, and each man looks into the eyes of his comrade to ascertain if he can be relied upon. The examination must have been satisfactory, for, just as the report of the fifth gun breaks upon their ears, the line is moving without a word of command from anyone, and when the sixth gun is fired the troops are well on the way, with colors unfurled and guns at "right shoulder shift." All sensations have now given way to enthusiasm. It is a sight never to be forgotten. Fifteen to twenty thousand men in well-aligned formation, with colors waving in the breeze, almost shaking the earth with cadenced tread, involuntarily move to battle.

The troops have scarcely left the rifle-pits when the guns upon the ridge open upon them. Our heavy guns in Fort Wood and the field batteries vigorously respond. We see the enemy in the rifle-pits, at the base of the ridge, looking over the works, with guns in hand, prepared to deliver fire. Why do they hesitate? We are in range. They are evidently waiting so that every shot will tell. From the enemy's lower lines now comes a storm of bullets and the air is filled with every sound of battle. The noise is terrible. Our artillery is exploding shells along the top of the ridge, and a caisson is seen to burst off to the right.

Now all feeling seems to have changed to one of determination. A terrific cheer rolls along the line. Not a rifle has yet been fired by the assaulting column. The quick step has been changed to the "double quick." Another cheer, and the enemy's first line of work at the base of the ridge is ours, together with many of his troops. Shelter is sought on the reverse side of the enemy's works, but the fire from the hilltop makes protection impossible.

. . . The bursting projectiles seem to compress the air and one's head feels as if bound with iron bands. Unable to return the enemy's fire, the delay drives the men to desperation. To remain is to be annihilated; to retreat is as dangerous as to advance. Here and there a man leaps the works and starts towards the hilltop; small squads follow. Then someone gave the command, "Forward!" after a number of men began to advance. Officers catch the inspiration. The mounted officers dismount and stone their horses to the rear. The cry, "Forward!" is repeated along the line, and the apparent impossibility is undertaken.

## CHAPLAIN JOHN J. HIGHT

58TH INDIANA INFANTRY, WAGNER'S BRIGADE

*Hight, who had joined the 58th Indiana in March 1862 while near Nashville, spent the hours after the attack ministering to the wounded. He recalled trying to help one soldier shot by "a grape shot through the back of the head" who was "moving and struggling about, though he was entirely unconscious."*

At length the signal gun was fired from Orchard Knob, and long lines of men rose from the grass and began to advance. In a few minutes the 58th received orders to fix bayonets. . . . When bayonets were fixed there was manifested on the part of nearly all a disposition to go double quick.

"The taking of Missionary Ridge, therefore, was inaugurated not so much by the genius of commanders, or the bravery of soldiers, as by mistake."

First, there was a little belt of woods to pass. Here the men were checked again and again, but their impetuosity knew no bound. They continued to advance, faster and faster; already their shouts filled the woods and fields. The rebels were aroused by the charge, and from many points on the line the shots and shells were flying. Two batteries especially played on Wagner's brigade; one of these was in front of and a little to the right of Orchard Knob, and the other was at Bragg's headquarters. Twenty or twenty-five guns were firing at our brigade as fast as the ingenuity of the gunners would permit, and some of these shots came disagreeably near to where I was standing.

The regiment emerged from the woods in plain view of the enemy at the base of the ridge. As they advanced the speed of the men increased. The line was pretty well maintained until it came to a little water course. Here it was broken, but still it swept on. The 57th Indiana took the works and fell into the front line as it came up. Their line was but poorly defended, as the rebels had to reinforce their right during the day. The men were now in range of the rifles at the top of the ridge and a terrible hail of lead was poured down upon them. The artillery dealt out grape and canister, which seemed to "come in shovelfuls."

A blaze of fire now burst from the Union columns. Greek had met Greek and the tug of war had come. Wagner's brigade was the first of all to advance beyond the rebel works. It was but a moment's work to pass the rebel camps. An enfilading fire was poured upon our columns from right and left, and it was here that many of our brave men fell. The troops on the right and left of us, seeing Wagner's men advancing, also went forward, and thus the whole line was moved. The taking of Missionary Ridge, therefore, was inaugurated not so much by the genius of commanders, or the bravery of soldiers, as by mistake. It was fortunate for us that this mistake was committed, as it would have been very disastrous to have remained long at the foot of the ridge.

## PRIVATE ROBERT WATSON

7TH FLORIDA INFANTRY, FLORIDA BRIGADE

*The men of Watson's regiment tried vainly to resist the Union juggernaut but soon had to flee as Colonel Charles G. Harker's regiments thundered toward them. As the Floridians retreated in confusion up the slope, they obstructed the fire of the infantry and artillery on the crest, giving the Federals precious seconds to reorganize their lines and reload. Though Watson contends that his regiment "poured" lead into the enemy, relatively few of Harker's men were hit at this point in the battle.*

They advanced on us in fine style. We held our fire until they were within about 300 yards of us and then poured a deadly fire into them and made many of them bite the dust but we were very few in number, merely a line of skirmishers in single rank and scattered at that. I judged from the looks of their numbers that there must be all of 100,000 men. We mowed them down until they were within 30 yards of us and then we retreated up the hill and made a

*Three IV Corps officers instrumental in the Missionary Ridge attack were, from left to right, Major General Philip H. Sheridan, corps commander Gordon Granger, and Colonel Charles G. Harker, whose brigade was among the first on the summit. Granger was relieved in April 1864, Sheridan went on to greater glory in the war's eastern theater, and Harker was killed at Kennesaw Mountain in 1864.*

## "A bullet struck my knapsack at the right shoulder and came out at the left shoulder making 23 holes in my blanket."

short stand at the second breastworks, but it was of no use for although we mowed them down yet they advanced on us and we were again forced to retreat and then came the worst part of the fight for the hill was dreadful steep and the enemy kept up a continual fire and threw a continual shower of bullets among us and I only wonder that they did not kill all of us. Many a poor fellow fell exhausted and was taken prisoner. I did not think that I should be able to reach the top for I had on a heavy knapsack and 3 days rations in my haversack and a canteen full of water. I stopped several times and took a shot at the d——d Yankees and at the same time it rested me. The bullets flew around us so thick that it seemed impossible to escape unhurt. I would have thrown away my knapsack but could not get it off and it was lucky for me for a bullet struck my knapsack at the right shoulder and came out at the left shoulder making 23 holes in my blanket. When I reached the top of the ridge I was so much exhausted that I fell down and lay there for several minutes to recover breath. Then I got behind a log and went to work with a will shooting Yankees. They advanced slowly keeping up a continual fire. We mowed them down by scores when unfortunately for us our artillery got out of ammunition and retired but we held the ridge until the enemy were on the top and had their flags on our breastworks. We then retreated down the hill under a shower of lead leaving many a noble son of the South dead and wounded on the ground and many more shared the same fate on the retreat. We retreated in great confusion, men from different companies all mixed up together.

## PRIVATE ASBURY WELSH

15TH OHIO INFANTRY, WILLICH'S BRIGADE

*Tough farmboys like Welsh, a 21-year-old veteran of Shiloh, Corinth, and Murfreesboro, made up the core of the Army of the Cumberland at Chattanooga. As he clambered toward entrenchments held by several Mississippi regiments, a Minié ball struck Welsh in the left forearm, ensuring that Missionary Ridge would be his last engagement. Surgeons removed four inches of shattered bone from the limb; the procedure, called a resection, saved Welsh's arm but left him disabled for life.*

On the afternoon of the 25th Willich's Brigade joined in the assault on the Ridge. Our alignment was not very good after we got on the double-quick, and the farther we got the more room we had. Having been on half rations for the past two months came in good play here, as we had got rid of all surplus fat. This explains why no general officers got across that valley to stop us at the rifle pits at the foot of the ridge; also, Grant's and Thomas's anxiety for us. We just ran away from them. . . .

I would suppose we traveled at least one mile before reaching the works at the foot of Ridge, most of the way on the run, our nerves strung to their highest tension. The Johnnies rained their shot and shell down into the valley, and our own batteries in the rear were hurling their shot over our heads at the Ridge.

We stopped just long enough after taking their first works to catch a breath. Then, without any general orders, commenced to climb the hights, keeping no particular order as we slowly fought our way up.

It is a well-known fact that after leaving the works at the foot of the Ridge we went the balance of the way on our own responsibility and without any orders except from Colonels and Captains. It has been said that when Grant asked Thomas, as they stood on Orchard Knob, who gave the order, Thomas said, "No one; they just seem to be going up themselves."

Soon after the battle, while lying wounded, in hospital in Chattanooga, a complimentary order was laid on my cot, which read about this way:

"Wood's Division may consider themselves under arrest for disobedience to orders, as when ordered to make a diversion on the enemy's first line, they disobeyed and took the Ridge."

*Troops of Granger's IV Corps storm Missionary Ridge (background), while others prepare to advance in support in this Theodore Davis sketch printed in Harper's Weekly. Rebel cannon fire bombards the buildings at center, as Yankee guards (left center) usher to the rear a group of Confederate prisoners, some of the hundreds who surrendered to the Union troops as they surged toward the ridge's crest. Many soldiers in the Army of the Cumberland, elated at having restored their reputation as good fighters, shouted taunts of "Chickamauga! Chickamauga!" at their now humbled adversaries.*

808
HARPER'S WEEKLY.
809
THE ARMY OF THE CUMBERLAND—THE FOURTH CORPS, UNDER GENERAL GORDON GRANGER, STORMING MISSIONARY RIDGE.—SKETCHED FROM THE LEFT OF THE LINE BY MR. THEODORE R. DAVIS.—[SEE PAGE 812.]

## LIEUTENANT COLONEL JOSEPH S. FULLERTON

STAFF, MAJOR GENERAL GORDON GRANGER

*Fullerton witnessed both the sudden rush of the IV Corps up Missionary Ridge and the reaction of various Union commanders. Grant, who saw the battle momentarily slipping beyond his control, was agitated and angry. The fiery Sheridan was energized; he rode behind his division, exhorting his troops onward.*

As soon as this movement was seen from Orchard Knob, Grant quickly turned to Thomas, who stood by his side, and I heard him say angrily: "Thomas, who ordered those men up the ridge?" Thomas replied in his usual slow, quiet manner: "I don't know; I did not." Then, addressing General Gordon Granger, he said: "Did you order them up, Granger?"

"No," said Granger, "they started up without orders. When those fellows get started all hell can't stop them." General Grant said something to the effect that somebody would suffer if it did not turn out well, and then, turning, stoically watched the ridge. He gave no further orders.

As soon as Granger had replied to Thomas he turned to me, his chief of staff, and said: "Ride at once to Wood and then to Sheridan, and ask them if they ordered their men up the ridge, and tell them, if they can take it to push ahead." As I was mounting, Granger added: "It is hot over there and you may not get through. I shall send Captain Avery to Sheridan and other officers after both of you."

As fast as my horse could carry me I rode first to General Wood and delivered the message. "I didn't order them up," said Wood; "they started up on their own account and they are going up too! Tell Granger if we are supported we will take and hold the ridge!"

As soon as I reached General Wood, Captain Avery got to General Sheridan and delivered his message. "I didn't order them up," said Sheridan, "but we are going to take the ridge." He then asked Avery for his flask and waved it at a group of Confederate officers standing just in front of Bragg's headquarters, with the salutation, "Here's at you!" At once two guns—the "Lady Breckinridge" and the "Lady Buckner" —in front of Bragg's headquarters were fired at Sheridan and the group of officers about him. One shell struck so near as to throw dirt over Sheridan and Avery.

"Ah!" said the general, "that is ungenerous; I shall take those guns for that!"

*As the 24th Wisconsin was struggling on Missionary Ridge, one of its officers, Lieutenant Arthur MacArthur Jr. (left), grabbed the regimental flag and rushed up through salvos of canister shouting "On, Wisconsin." The Badgers poured over the crest, and MacArthur, as he later wrote, "had the honor of planting the colors . . . in front of Bragg's old headquarters," for which he later received the Medal of Honor. His son was General Douglas MacArthur.*

## CAPTAIN TILMON D. KYGER

### 73d Illinois Infantry, F. T. Sherman's Brigade

*Before the ascent up Missionary Ridge described by Kyger, Colonel James Jaquess had challenged the regiment to "capture . . . one horse—a good one . . ." to replace the mounts he had lost to Rebel fire at Chickamauga. His request was answered when a soldier brought him a handsome gray. Jaquess learned later that the horse had belonged to a member of Breckinridge's staff and was named for the Rebel general.*

General Sheridan rode up behind the 73d and remarked: "I know you; fix bayonets and go ahead." We were in the front line. We halted at the rifle-pits for a short time to rest and give the short-winded soldiers time to get up. Then we moved to the second line of works; rested again, after driving the rebels and taking many prisoners. Moved again, and under a terrific fire, reached the third line. Many fell. Started again; had to move up a hill at an inclination of about thirty degrees, exposed to bursting shell and a shower of grape, canis-ter and minie-balls. The only shelter that we had was now and then a tree, a log or a stump. The flags moved up gradually; the color-bearers would stop and await the coming up of the men, who were pouring on the enemy a terrible fire; the enemy, having all reached the top of the ridge, except those who had been either killed, wounded or captured.

. . . This was our hardest time; we had to pass a more exposed point. From tree to tree, from stump to stump, and from log to log, we went until we came to a point where the slope was greater, the ascent steeper, perhaps about forty degrees elevation. Here we remained about twenty minutes, to get in readiness to make the final charge. General Sheridan came riding up, when we started and moved steadily on until we reached the top of the ridge. Just before we got there the rebels threw hand grenades and rocks at us. No matter for that, our flags and banners must be planted on top of the ridge. Hasty fell, I took the flag and moved forward, but soon became exhausted and fell. Hasty caught up and we went on together, and planted the colors on top the ridge at five o'clock p.m., about three paces in rear of the 88th Illinois.

Now came a time of rejoicing as those coming up the ridge would reach its crest. Yell after yell went up the whole length of the ridge. But with us this did not last long. We charged down the eastern slope, taking many prisoners and some artillery in the valley. Our losses were not heavy when compared to the work accomplished. The 73d lost three

# "That warm water was the best drink I had ever taken, and I thought perhaps it was my last."

killed and twenty-two wounded. This was a great victory, something that, to look the ground over, would seem impossible to accomplish—charging a distance of two miles, about half the way at an average angle of thirty-five degrees.

## PRIVATE SAMUEL A. MCNEIL

### 31st Ohio Infantry, Turchin's Brigade

*Many of the Union soldiers who helped capture Missionary Ridge called it a soldier's battle, an engagement fought on the initiative of individual soldiers or small groups, with little overall coordination by officers. McNeil, only 19 at the time, describes the nature of the fighting and tells of being wounded. Despite his initial fears, the injury was not serious, and after a three-month convalescence in Nashville the Buckeye returned to duty. He was promoted to sergeant in March 1864.*

We moved rapidly toward the ridge sweeping the confederate skirmishers and their reserves before us like chaff before the wind. Their artillery on the crest of the ridge, five hundred feet above the valley we were crossing, sent a perfect storm of shot and shell into our ranks, but the lines of blue kept steadily on until the rifle-pits at the foot of the ridge was in our possession. I remember we got the impression, somehow, that we were to stop there, but the fireing from the crest of the ridge, above us, was terrific, and as if by impulse, the boys in the ranks began to climb the west side of the ridge, shouting, "Come on boys." and on we went, without any orders, so far as I know, excepting our own. . . .

Farther up and to the right I saw a man waving a United States flag. He was too far away to see his uniform but I believed, at the time, that he was a confederate, tauntingly waving a captured flag at our line. While looking up at the flag, a rebel musket ball, evidently fired from the point to our left, struck me just below the jaw bone passing through my neck. Two streams of blood caused me to believe an artery was opened and that I would soon bleed to death. The first impulse was to get back down the ridge, as far as possible before I should fall from the loss of blood. This I did and reached the rifle-pits at the foot of the ridge. A shower of shot and shell was falling around me as I lay were I really thought was my last resting place while in the flesh.

An awful thirst came over me and in my frantic efforts to get at the canteen strapped under my waist belt, I cut the canteen strap and got the water to my lips. That warm water was the best drink I had ever taken, and I thought perhaps it was my last. There was no fear of eternity, which it seemed to me was very near. The thought of the possible failure of the assault, and that my body would be left within the enemy's lines, was worrying me more than anything else just at that time.

. . . After resting a few minutes I found that the blood was not flowing so freely. In the pocket of my blouse was a silk handkerchief, a present from my mother. By pressing the soft silk into the wounds the flow of blood almost ceased. I was the happiest boy in the army. . . . I started back toward Orchard Knob to find a surgeon, but became dizzy and was resting when a mounted officer came up, making a few remarks about stragglers and cowards. I never had much respect for officers who kept out of a battle for the avowed purpose of stopping stragglers. My Springfield rifle was loaded and bringing it to a "ready" told him to git. Doubtless he then saw the blood on my clothes, for he muttered a sort of an apology and rode away, but not in the direction from which I had come.

During one of the frequent halts for a brief rest I saw the flags of Turchin go over the works along the crest and heard the cheers of my comrades. Off to the south other flags were going over the Confederate works and, "presto change."

The thunder of the enemys guns ceased.

*This Alfred E. Mathews print depicts the fighting on the left flank of the Army of the Cumberland, as soldiers of the 31st Ohio, in Turchin's brigade, assail Missionary Ridge. Despite the fairly even battle line and the smooth topography depicted in this rendering, the commander of the 31st reported that the ground his men moved over was "precipitous and intersected by deep and narrow ravines, [that] utterly precluded an attack in military formation." The regiment took 47 casualties on November 25.*

## SERGEANT ALFRED T. FIELDER

12TH TENNESSEE (C.S.) INFANTRY, VAUGHAN'S BRIGADE

*Fielder and the other Tennesseans of Vaughan's command put up a hard fight against Colonel Edward Phelps' brigade while backing up Missionary Ridge. They delivered "death-dealing missiles . . . thick and fast," according to a Yankee attacker. Phelps himself fell dead in a hail of Rebel lead, but the Federals eventually prevailed, forcing the Tennessee boys down the rugged, trackless eastern slope of the ridge.*

About 3 o'clock the enemy in our front was to be seen moving upon us in three lines of battle (besides their line of pickets) and steadily advanced toward us when at the designated point we fired upon them and fell back as ordered to the top of the Ridge and took our position in line of battle. The sight in the valley below was truly imposing—the enemy like blue clouds by tens of thousands were advancing while our artillery was playing upon them from every available point upon the Ridge and mowing them down by hundreds. Still on they came and when within range of our Enfields, we mowed them down with fearful havoc. But on they came and when within 100 yds. or less of the top of the Ridge, Deas' Brigade immediately on our left gave way and the enemy soon began to show his head on the top of the Ridge. We were ordered to direct our fire at that point and right well the boys obeyed. The enemy faltered, staggered and fell back. There was an effort made to rally Deas' men, which was partially effected, but they again soon ran off in total confusion. The enemy again took courage, and renewing their fire at that point succeeded in gaining the top of the Ridge; hence they had an enfilading fire upon us which is always dangerous, yet we withstood them until our ammunition was greatly exhausted.

Having no support and being greatly outnumbered, we fell back a short distance and again rallied, shortly after which I received the third wound of the battle through the left hip, which disabled me and I was compelled to retire from the field. I had been wounded in the right foot and left knee, though comparatively slight.

## LIEUTENANT ANDREW J. NEAL

MARION (FLORIDA) LIGHT ARTILLERY

*As Baird's Federal ranks crossed the open ground below Missionary Ridge, Neal's four cannons poured down upon them a deadly shellfire that, he said, made the "mountain wilds resound with their awful roar." Even after his Georgia and Mississippi infantry supports had fled before the onrushing Yankees, Neal's fieldpieces continued belching death until the last moment, and he barely escaped with two guns. A Union bullet killed Neal near Atlanta, Georgia, in August 1864.*

I had my guns in position on the extreme left of the Battalion and was giving them fits—had the colors hoisted and waving, when a shower of balls came in upon us from the left. Looking in that direction I observed five heavy columns in a line perpendicular to ours on a hill one hundred yards to our left flank. I had noticed them when I first came up & called attention to it. Major Hoxton, Chief of Artillery on Gen. Hardee's staff, had observed them through his glasses as had several other field officers, but as they had given me no orders, I continued firing on those at our front. Soon as I saw the stars & stripes flashing along the line, I swung my guns around and brought them to bear on the flanking column—but the cannoneer ran the two left pieces too near each other to fire & before I could get the guns apart, Jackson's Brigade came rushing along through our Battalion in utter panic. My men stood steady as veterans, but in vain. The infantry rushed over us pell mell & we could do nothing.

The Battery mounted along side of my guns, seeing the danger, limbered up and ran away. Finding our support gone & that it was impossible to drive back the immense column, I determined to retire fighting. But the mountain ridge was too rough to manage the pieces by hand & I could not get the horses up to the guns, so I ordered the limbers away & retreated together.

I am proud of the conduct of my men, & believe they would have stood with me to the guns until we were bayonetted. I left only when valor was in vain, & of all that wing I brought up the rear. I lost two guns & one limber & had several men wounded & have myself a slight wound. A minie ball struck me on the shoulder cutting a great hole through my coat & shirt & bruising the flesh. It stung me some but did not disable the arm. I am in the field with two guns, which I hope may yet avenge the loss of their comrades.

We lost much property etc. by this mortifying affair. Everybody thinks our infantry did not stand up squarely. This thing never happened to Confederate soldiers before—God grant that it may never happen again.

*This handsome banner, both sides of which are shown here, was given to the Marion Artillery in April 1862 and proudly flown by Lieutenant Andrew Neal and his gunners at Chattanooga. Made from a woman's silk bridal shawl, it was replete with leather numerals, letters, and stars embossed with gold leaf, traces of which remain. In July 1864, a month before his death, Neal sent the flag home to Zebulon, Georgia, for safekeeping. His sister later hid it under her skirt when Federal cavalrymen rode through the town.*

## PRIVATE BENJAMIN T. SMITH

### Staff, Major General Philip H. Sheridan

*Although Smith enlisted in 1861 into the ranks of the 51st Illinois Infantry, he left behind the drudgeries of the foot soldier's life when he became a mounted orderly in September 1862. During the Battle of Missionary Ridge, he was assigned to Sheridan's 2d Division, IV Corps headquarters and witnessed the Union advance on Bragg's center. After Sheridan departed the western theater, Smith remained a divisional aide, one of the lucky privates in the war to enjoy such a privileged position.*

The troops having rested, started to climb the steep sides of the ridge. An aide having been sent to Genl. Granger for further orders, came back with a suggestion that the troops be recalled if it was judged expedient. By this time they were half way up the ridge. Every regiment had lost its organization, and were all massed in a sort of triangle with the point upwards. About every flag of our division was struggling to reach the top first, every man for himself. Now and then a flag would fall, its bearer being shot, but it appeared in an instant held by the next soldier. The General said, "Let them go, they will be over in five minutes," and so it proved. A dozen flags went over the works, the men following. Nothing could stop their rush. The rebels deserted their guns and fled, hundreds of them staying a moment too long were captured.

An old log hut standing just to the left to where our division went over was occupied by Genl. Bragg and his staff. They had barely time to mount and ride away. Some of the rebel guns were turned upon their retreating ranks and shots sent after them. More than fifty guns were captured.

When we reached the top of the ridge my horse was about ready to drop from the unusual hard work he had done. So I took the harness off of a big white horse that had belonged to one of the rebel batteries, and put my saddle on him, turning mine loose to shift for himself. And that was the last I ever saw of my good old friend. But this animal is the tallest piece of horseflesh in four counties. I must look like a fly on a ridge pole, and feel as though I am astride of a small mountain.

Our troops are in full cry after the retreating enemy and it is growing dark.

## CAPTAIN CUTHBERT H. SLOCOMB

### 5th Company, Washington Artillery of New Orleans

*Slocomb, a survivor of a chest wound received at Shiloh, recounts the panic that seized the Rebels as Yankee infantry breasted the summit of Missionary Ridge. All six of his guns were lost, including the four he tried to send to the rear. Despite Slocomb's belief, the rounds that exploded his limbers were most likely fired by Union infantry manning abandoned Rebel cannon.*

Barely had my battery got into position when the cheers and advancing lines of the enemy disclosed their purpose of storming the ridge under cover of the fire of their batteries, which at the same moment had sprung into full play from various and unexpected points in the valley. At the sound of these cheers the pickets in front of my right half-battery retreated up the hill and disappeared in my rear. This unusual timidity in our infantry, and the nature of the slope in my front, which made it apparent that as soon as the foot of the ridge was obtained the enemy would be protected from my fire, induced me to open rapidly upon them as soon as their lines emerged from the woods. I had also hopes thereby to reassure our troops and intimidate if not check the foe. Steadily, however, they advanced, my fire compelling them only to abandon my immediate front and bear off from it to the right and left. This movement exposed their flank to a raking fire from my right half-battery, from which they sought shelter behind a swell in the slope of a hill farther to the right. Under this protection they gained the crest of the ridge, some 200 yards to my right, the infantry at that point abandoning their works without a struggle, leaving in the hands of the enemy two or more pieces of artillery which were afterward turned upon my battery. At this stage of the engagement, considering the defection of the infantry around me, the exhausted state of my limber chests and the difficulty of removing artillery from the ridge, I might have been warranted in withdrawing my battery. But judging the battle as only begun, and firm in my reliance upon our infantry rallying

“We could see our troops charge right up to the mouth of the cannons and take the batteries and turn them on the rebels.”

and retaking the position on my right, I ordered my right half-battery to be turned upon the enemy on the ridge, and I sent for a fresh supply of ammunition. In the meantime myself and officers exerted ourselves in arresting the flight of the infantry, but with little success. Of the ammunition ordered up, but one limber chest reached me, and that only by running the gauntlet of the enemy’s fire, as the only practicable road from my caissons lay between my guns and the position just stormed. Other attempts were made, but the road was soon occupied by the enemy and several of my limbers compelled to retrace their steps.

My fire had been speedily opened and its effect was marked, when a shell from one of the batteries in the valley exploded both the limber chests of the Napoleon guns of my right half-battery, shattering the chests and carriages, killing and disabling most of the horses, and so entangling the remainder as to require cutting them out of the harness to save them. This calamity added to the confusion and panic of the infantry. The supports of my left half-battery caught the contagion and the enemy soon gained the summit of the ridge on my left. I now ordered to the rear the four pieces that could be limbered up. The roads on both of my flanks being in possession of the enemy, this could be accomplished only by plunging down the slope in my immediate rear. It was done, with what success will be shown hereafter. The detachments of the two disabled pieces were retained near the eminence occupied by their guns in hopes that some turn in the line of the battle or the arrival of re-enforcements might enable us to use them again, if not to save them eventually. These hopes for a while seemed realized, as a regiment was seen advancing from our rear. Lieutenant Chalaron, Sergeant Allen, and Corporal Adams, with the colors of my company, placed themselves in advance of it and endeavored to lead it to a charge.

## SERGEANT WILLIAM H. HUNTZINGER

79TH INDIANA INFANTRY, S. BEATTY’S BRIGADE

*Huntzinger’s regiment and the troops of the 86th Indiana led the advance of Brigadier General Samuel Beatty’s brigade up Missionary Ridge. Beatty claimed his soldiers captured 176 prisoners, eight cannons, more than 200 small arms, and two flags in their attack while suffering 161 casualties—including 28 men from the 79th. As Huntzinger implies here, it is probable that soldiers from this brigade were the troops who blasted the Washington Artillery with captured fieldpieces.*

We got to the rebel line of breastworks at the foot of the ridge and rested about three minutes, for we were nearly out of breath, some entirely given out. Some of the boys started on. I heard Col. Knefler say “Forward!” and we all started to charge the ridge. Grape and canister rained all around us. There was a high point just before our regiment and we charged for that point. The battery on that point, a battery to our left and two batteries to our right had a complete cross fire on us. The hill was very steep and rocky, with a few scrubby oaks growing on its side. Our two regiments (86th and 79th) were so far in advance of the other troops that the rebels shelled us from the right and left and from the point in our front. Their shells and the grape and canister plowed up the ground all around us and a good many were killed.

We reached within a few feet of their breastworks on top of the ridge and lay down, being so tired we could go no farther. We looked back and saw lines of troops coming to our support and the troops on our right and left were nearly up as far as our regiment, and being rested up a little we got up to go in their works, for we could see the troops to our right nearly ready to take the different points and the rebel battery. We could see our troops charge right up to the mouth of the cannons and take the batteries and turn them on the rebels, and I know the rebels could not have been very far down the mountain on the other side when our men turned their guns and fired at them as they were retreating.

We charged up and took the little outpost that lay about 50 yards farther than the main straight line. A shell bursted close to James Hague, knocking him down senseless. He rolled down the hill a little ways and lodged against a tree. Someone took him back. I was not allowed to leave the line. I had orders not to shoot but I disobeyed and fired every good opportunity I had.

*The sketch below shows straining Confederate gunners trying to haul their cannon out of the reach of the Union troops—possibly members of Beatty's brigade—sheltering below the lip of Missionary Ridge. After the battle Colonel Frederick Knefler of the 79th Indiana (left) went on leave to move his family to Indiana from Spencer County, Kentucky, which, he claimed, was "infested by robbers and guerrillas." In the spring of 1864 General Beatty resigned, and Knefler took command of his brigade.*

## LIEUTENANT JOSEPH A. CHALARON

5TH COMPANY, WASHINGTON ARTILLERY OF NEW ORLEANS

*Chalaron became an impromptu commander of an infantry attack when he tried to lead the North Carolinians and Virginians of Brigadier General A. W. Reynolds' brigade against the threatening Union lines. The effort failed, forcing Chalaron to destroy his cannon and order his men to flee.*

"Under a pelting fire we spiked the guns and hurled them down the declivity towards the ascending enemy. My men were then told to save themselves."

The Federals never got up in front of our battery. Extending for 250 yards, it was kept clear by a rapid and well-sustained fire, from which the attacking lines diverged to the right and left, seeking shelter in the depressions between the abutments of the ridge, avoiding our direct fire.

My position was overlooking a gap in the ridge, facing Chattanooga, where at first I had two guns which I soon took outside, to the front of the work, that sufficient depression might be obtained to sweep the declivity in my front and to my right. The elevation to my right across the gap was occupied by two guns of Dent's Battery, and this point was the first one on the ridge to be carried by the Federal troops. I had turned my two Napoleons on this point as soon as I noticed its capture, and had fired two shots at the foe on and around the guns, when the limbers of these two Napoleons were exploded by a shell from a gun on Orchard Knob. I have read that Gen. Granger had sighted that shot. If he did so, it was a most opportune hit, for the next discharge of my guns would have played havoc with the small force of Federals that was forming to advance upon me from the point they had captured.

Gen. Bragg sent Reynolds' brigade forward to retake the position. As this brigade reached my guns, coming from my left and rear, I started with a mounted Sergeant and a Corporal afoot, of my company and bearing its flag, to lead the column in a charge across the gap. The troops did not respond.

Failing to clear the only way by which my caissons could send me their limbers, I returned to my guns. The rifled gun that had been out of ammunition about the moment of the explosion of the Napoleons' limbers was ordered off to the hollow in the rear, and Capt. Slocomb and several of the men then ran to the left half-battery some 100 yards off, and returned bearing arms-full of ammunition. This we could not use, for we found ourselves without friction primers.

The close advance of the Federal sharpshooters, creeping up under cover of rocks and trees, and the movement of others to our rear from the gap, admonished us to save our men and what horses we had left. Under a pelting fire we spiked the guns and hurled them down the declivity towards the ascending enemy. My men were then told to save themselves.

*The Washington Artillery was perhaps the most famous gunnery unit in the Confederate army. The 1st through 4th companies served with Lee, and the 5th, whose banner is shown here, fought in the Army of Tennessee.*

## LIEUTENANT COLONEL JAMES J. TURNER

30TH TENNESSEE (C.S.) INFANTRY, TYLER'S BRIGADE

*Turner had been captured at Fort Donelson and imprisoned in Fort Warren, Boston, before being exchanged. At Chickamauga he suffered a bullet wound to the chest. It was still bothering him when he led a stubborn rearguard action to slow the Federal pursuit at Chattanooga.*

The position occupied by my command—the Tenth and Thirtieth regiments—was only a good skirmish line, and as we were heavily assaulted some three battalions and parts of regiments were sent to our assistance. We drove the enemy in our front and wings far down the ridge. I was pressing them when informed that Deas' and Manigault's brigades had broken on our left and right, and I then saw that the Federals occupied the ridge at these points and were turning our own artillery on us. I ordered an immediate retreat to the top of the ridge. I could then see our forces, except our brigade, retreating in great disorder.

. . . As we started to retreat from the ridge Col. Tyler was severely wounded, and I assumed command of the brigade as the senior officer. We fell back about fifteen hundred yards to where there was a considerable ridge, and where Gen. Bragg and staff were attempting to rally the army and make a stand; but he had lost the confidence of the army and officers and men dashed by without heeding his commands or appeals.

Our brigade was in good condition, and on reaching this ridge I halted it and in a few minutes had a line of battle formed across the road. Our division commander directed me to follow on to the pontoon bridge at Chickamauga Creek, the sun then being nearly an hour from setting. Men from Cobb's battery and a number of detached soldiers, numbering some five hundred, came up and fell into our line of battle. As all the generals had left and we were free to act independently, we concluded to stop the Federal forces at this point till darkness should arrest their advance. I directed Major Caswell to deploy his battalion of sharpshooters, consisting of five companies splendidly drilled and armed, and cover our front and feel for the enemy, and if forced to retire to do so slowly and contest every inch of ground. The order was executed to the letter. Soon they were hotly engaged and though compelled by force of superior numbers to retreat, they did so very gradually, holding a large force in check till dark, when they fell back and took position in our line.

As soon as the Federals came in range both sides opened with great spirit. We had the advantage of position and full knowledge of the

ground, but were outnumbered by at least three to one. The Federals had advanced to close range, and the firing was very severe.

In the meantime the brigade was nearly out of ammunition, and it was quite dark, being at least an hour after sunset. At this juncture Gen. Breckinridge and a part of his staff came up from the rear and inquired what command it was and why remaining there. I informed him, and he said his entire command had been broken and were retreating, and that hearing the firing he came to it, but ordered me to retire at once as we were surrounded on all sides except the rear by overwhelming forces. I issued the order for a retreat, yet nothing but the darkness and our knowledge of the roads enabled us to get out.

*Bragg had anchored his left flank on Rossville Gap, a break in Missionary Ridge (below, left). On November 25 Grant ordered Hooker to march from Lookout Mountain and attack the gap in coordination with Sherman's push on the Rebel right at Tunnel Hill. But Hooker was delayed when his troops had to build a bridge over Chattanooga Creek, and he did not engage the Confederates until the late afternoon.*

# "I stood there until every man left me, begging them to come back and fight the enemy."

## LIEUTENANT COLONEL JOHN W. INZER

### 58TH ALABAMA INFANTRY, HOLTZCLAW'S BRIGADE

*About 4:00 p.m., Confederate major general John C. Breckinridge ordered Inzer's Alabamians and four other regiments to engage Hooker's lead division. After about two hours the Yankees overwhelmed the outnumbered Rebels, their attack stopped only by the onset of darkness. Inzer's bravery cost him a slight wound and a trip to the Johnson's Island prison pen, where he spent the remainder of the war.*

*Lieutenant Simeon T. Josselyn of the 13th Illinois captured this flag of the 18th Alabama of Holtzclaw's brigade during the fighting near Rossville Gap. Holtzclaw's regiments lost two more flags and some 700 riflemen to Hooker's flank attack.*

We then commenced the fight in earnest. Before a great while, I discovered the enemy was flanking us on the left. He was coming up a hollow some 100 yards from the left of our regiments, moving by the flank (Capt. Lister first called my attention to the fact). I then attempted to rally my right and move by the left flank across the hollow for the purpose of checking the flanking column of the enemy. After repeated efforts, succeeded only partially in doing what I desired to do. In a few minutes more, the balance of the Bri-gade commenced giving away. Moving up the ridge on the top, *I never worked so hard in my life* as I did at this time to rally my command. They may have heard the command "Retreat" given. I never did hear an order to fall back. I stood there until every man left me, begging them to come back and fight the enemy. I remained here until the men who had been with me were some 100 or 150 yards from me—near where Col. Holtzclaw was sitting on his horse. During this whole time, I saw nothing of Col. Jones or Maj. Thornton, understood they were at the breast-works on the right of the regiment. Seeing my men all gone, I moved up to where Holtzclaw was sitting on his horse. I went to him and begged him to rally the men. I told him most of the men knew him and I believed he could rally them at a point some 200 yards in our rear. Then asked him to send one of his staff. I was on foot. He declined to do so. In a few minutes more he told me the order was to face back in four ranks (column of squads). This was the first order I ever heard to face back. After the above conversation, the Colonel put spurs to his horse and that was the last I ever saw of him.

I then moved back on the ridge in the direction of General Breckinridge's Quarters, some 300 yards. Saw the men filing to the right down the ridge through a field. Here Col. Jones and Maj. Thornton passed me—both on the Colonel's mare. I turned down the hill trying to get the men to my left to follow me. After getting some 100 yards down the ridge, was fired into several times from my left. The hogweeds were so high and thick I could not see anyone. Believing this to be our friends, I hollowed several times to stop the fire, but without effect. Turned—saw several of my officers and men on top of the ridge waving their hats. Thought they were hollowing to the men on my left to stop shooting into us. There being so much noise and confusion, I could not hear what they said. Being so anxious to stop the firing, I went back to where my officers were, but to my sorrow, saw when I got there they had surrendered, surrounded by thousands of the enemy—seeing further resistance useless, I stuck my sword in the ground and became a prisoner. A large number of the officers and men of the 32—36—38 and 58 Ala. regiments were captured at and near said point. This was about sun set. *Surrendered to the Second Ohio.*

## LIEUTENANT JOHN R. BOYLE

111TH PENNSYLVANIA INFANTRY, COBHAM'S BRIGADE

*The 111th had shivered away the nights of November 24 and 25 while bivouacked in captured enemy camps at the base of Lookout Mountain. After being issued 100 rounds of ammunition per man, the weary Pennsylvanians broke camp and moved toward Missionary Ridge with the rest of Hooker's force. Expecting more combat, Boyle and his comrades were undoubtedly relieved to find the enemy defeated and watched happily as Bragg's troops fled in disorder and panic toward Georgia.*

*Colonel George A. Cobham Jr. (above) of the 111th Pennsylvania commanded the 2d Brigade of Geary's division in the Chattanooga campaign. In his campaign report he wrote in praise of his brigade, stating that the soldiers, "though short of food, and without blankets or overcoats, and a majority . . . with but the pretense of shoes upon their feet . . . never murmured, but did their duty faithfully and well." Cobham returned to command the 111th during Sherman's Atlanta campaign and was killed while leading the regiment in a charge during the Battle of Peachtree Creek.*

Hooker, with Geary's, Osterhaus's, and Cruft's divisions had moved from Lookout Mountain, on the right of Palmer, at ten o'clock, without rations, and had pushed toward Rossville Gap. The bridge across Chattanooga Creek was destroyed, and after waiting four hours for its repair, he finally forded the deep stream. Reaching the Gap, Osterhaus and Cruft passed through and charged the Ridge from its western end and rear, and Geary, with Candy's brigade in front and Cobham's in second line, pressed up on the front of the heights and formed a junction with Johnson's division of Palmer's corps just as the latter gained the crest at sunset. Thus, with Sherman near Graysville and Geary behind Rossville, the wings of Grant's army almost encircled the enemy's flanks, while his center, like a lance, had passed completely through its vitals. Bragg's broken and disorganized troops surged like a mob through the narrow line of retreat that remained open toward Ringgold, leaving the roads littered with burning stores and abandoned wagons and arms, and the depot with all its valuable supplies, in ashes.

It was one of the cleanest and most complete victories of the war. Grant had a superiority in numbers, but this was more than compensated by Bragg's great advantage in position. The weather was perfect, and from Orchard Knob at the right center was revealed a stretch of nearly seven miles, within which one hundred and thirteen thousand men were struggling for mastery. The curving, elevated line of the enemy on the Ridge, the intersecting angle of Sherman's line on the extreme left, and the shorter, interior front of Thomas at the base of the hill, all enveloped in smoke and vomiting fire, the quick shifting of roops, the flash of steel, the gallop of staff officers, and the cheering shouts of sixty thousand men breaking upon the terrific thunder of arms, exhibited a thrilling example of war. And the final moment, when the besieging front gave way, and with redoubled huzzas the triumphant Union army swept after the retreating foe, General Grant among them, was an overwhelming climax of human power. Within exactly thirty-three days the man who had reduced Forts Henry and Donelson, won the battle of Pittsburg Landing, and captured Vicksburg had raised the siege of Chattanooga and turned the despair of a great army into the joy of conquest.

# " 'What does all this mean' was the question asked in low tones one of another. I cannot tell, there is some mistake, I thought we had gained a great victory."

## LIEUTENANT ROBERT M. COLLINS

15th Texas Cavalry (Dismounted), J. A. Smith's Brigade

*While Bragg's center and left were crumbling under the pressure of Thomas' and Hooker's attacks, Cleburne's men had remained resolute on the right, staunchly holding Tunnel Hill to the end of the day. Surrounded by the human debris of Sherman's failed assaults, Collins and his fellow Texans were shocked to learn that their comrades to the south had given way. They withdrew under the cover of darkness, heartbroken that their victory had been nullified by a larger defeat.*

Near where we were standing on the line of skirmishers, a wounded Federal was sitting on the ground with his back against a tree, he had been shot through the bowels. He seemed to be a very intelligent young man and spoke of the certainty of having to die very soon in a very quiet, dignified manner. He belonged to the 26th Missouri infantry. Another young man of powerful build, and we suppose from the same regiment, had been seriously wounded in the head; he was some distance higher up the mountain than the one already named. He would rise to his feet and then fall face foremost down the mountain, uttering cries and groans that pierced the hearts of old soldiers. We thought at first that it was a ruse he was playing to get through our line, but upon examination we found he was seriously wounded and was as crazy as a "march hare." But those surroundings were tame to our feelings compared to the effect of the huzza, huzza, huzza, that commenced in the Federal lines to our left, and died away, away down yonder toward the base of Lookout mountain. "What does all this mean" was the question asked in low tones one of another. I cannot tell, there is some mistake, I thought we had gained a great victory. Anyway we have the satisfaction and the glory of mopping up the ground with everything that has come against we Texas and Arkansaw fellows today, we will wait and see what we will see. About 11 o'clock the order was passed down the line in a whisper, from post to post, for us to move out by the left flank, and to be careful as to making any sort of noise, not to allow saber or gun to strike with canteens, and not to tread on any sticks that might break and make a noise. We were old soldiers enough by this time to know what all this meant. We knew that the day had been lost, and in less time than it requires to pen one of these lines, such thoughts as these passed through our minds in rapid succession: if we can't hold such a line as this against those blasted Federals, where is the line or position between here and the coast of Georgia that we can hold? . . . We moved out as quietly as if there had been but one man only. Up, over the mountain and down through a deep gorge, wrapped in deep darkness inside and outside. Not a word being uttered. The writer, along with Capt. Jack Leonard, was marching at the head of the column, and if our memory is not out of joint, the first words spoken was the following little speech made by the writer to Capt. Leonard. "This, Captain, is the death-knell of the Confederacy, for if we cannot cope with those fellows over the way with the advantages we have on this line, there is not a line between here and the Atlantic ocean where we can stop them." He replied by saying, "Hush, Lieutenant, that is treason you are talking." Doubtless such expressions in the presence of the men might have been wrong, but we thought it all right as between officers.

## PRIVATE SAM WATKINS

1st Tennessee (C.S.) Infantry, Maney's Brigade

*As evening fell over Missionary Ridge, Watkins' regiment joined the columns of battle-weary Rebel soldiers clogging the roads leading eastward from the ridge toward Bragg's new line near Chickamauga Station. In a little over a month, Bragg had steered the Army of Tennessee from the euphoria of victory at Chickamauga to the despair and demoralization of defeat at Chattanooga.*

The Yankees were cutting and slashing, and the cannoneers were running in every direction. I saw Day's brigade throw down their guns and break like quarter horses. Bragg was trying to rally them. I heard him say, "Here is your commander," and the soldiers hallooed back, "here is your mule."

The whole army was routed. I ran down on the ridge, and there was our regiment, the First Tennessee, with their guns stacked, and drawing rations as if nothing was going on. Says I, "Colonel Field, what's the matter? The whole army is routed and running; hadn't you better be getting away from here? The Yankees are not a hundred yards from here. Turner's battery has surrendered, Day's brigade has thrown down their arms; and look yonder, that is the Stars and Stripes." He remarked very coolly, "You seem to be demoralized. We've whipped them here. We've captured two thousand prisoners and five stands of colors."

Just at this time General Bragg and staff rode up. Bragg had joined the church at Shelbyville, but he had back-slid at Missionary Ridge. He was cursing like a sailor. Says he, "What's this? Ah, ha, have you stacked your arms for a surrender?" "No, sir," says Field. "Take arms, shoulder arms, by the right flank, file right, march." just as cool and deliberate as if on dress parade. Bragg looked scared. He had put spurs to his horse, and was running like a scared dog before Colonel Field had a chance to answer him. Every word of this is a fact. We at once became the rear guard of the whole army.

I felt sorry for General Bragg. The army was routed, and Bragg looked so scared. Poor fellow, he looked so hacked and whipped and mortified and chagrined at defeat, and all along the line, when Bragg would pass, the soldiers would raise the yell, "Here is your mule"; "Bully for Bragg, he's h——l on retreat."

. . . When we had marched about a mile back in the rear of the battlefield, we were ordered to halt so that all stragglers might pass us, as we were detailed as the rear guard. While resting on the road side we saw Day's brigade pass us. They were gunless, cartridge-boxless, knapsackless, canteenless, and all other military accoutermentsless, and swordless, and officerless, and they all seemed to have the 'possum grins, like Bragg looked, and as they passed our regiment, you never heard such fun made of a parcel of soldiers in your life. Every fellow was yelling at the top of his voice, "Yaller-hammer, Alabama, flicker, flicker, flicker, yaller-hammer, Alabama, flicker, flicker, flicker." I felt sorry for the yellow-hammer Alabamians, they looked so hacked, and answered back never a word. . . .

Our army was a long time crossing the railroad bridge across Chickamauga river. Maney's brigade, of Cheatham's division, and General L. E. Polk's brigade, of Cleburne's division, formed a sort of line of battle, and had to wait until the stragglers had all passed. I remember looking at them, and as they passed I could read the character of every soldier. Some were mad, others cowed, and many were laughing. Some were cursing Bragg, some the Yankees, and some were rejoicing at the defeat. I cannot describe it. It was the first defeat our army had ever suffered, but the prevailing sentiment was anathemas and denunciations hurled against Jeff Davis for ordering Longstreet's corps to Knoxville, and sending off Generals Wheeler's and Forrest's cavalry, while every private soldier in the whole army knew that the enemy was concentrating at Chattanooga.

# *Tennessee in Union Hands*

On the night of November 25, Bragg's demoralized army gathered at Chickamauga Station and made preparations to retreat into northern Georgia aboard trains and on foot. Protected by a rear guard that held off the pursuing Yankees, the Confederates escaped but left behind abundant evidence of their state of disarray. The first Federal soldiers to arrive at the depot the following morning found fires everywhere: Shattered wagons, wrecked artillery pieces, discarded pontoons, and huge piles of grain were all burning in the streets.

For a time Grant pressed the pursuit. Hooker, positioned at Rossville Gap, led the chase. Thomas' and Sherman's armies, starting from farther north, also moved out in pursuit, engaging Rebel rearguard elements at Graysville, just inside the Georgia line. On November 27 Hooker's lead units caught up with Cleburne's rear guard at Ringgold, Georgia, about 15 miles southeast of Chattanooga. Just below Ringgold lay a narrow, heavily timbered mountain pass about a half-mile long and scarcely wide enough to accommodate a stretch of Western & Atlantic Railroad track, a wagon road, and a branch of East Chickamauga Creek. Cleburne placed the greater part of his force in hiding across the middle of this natural trap, while his cavalry lured Hooker into ambush. As the Federals entered the pass, the Confederates suddenly opened up on them with artillery fire and musket fire.

Hooker's troops reeled back, seeking the protection of a railroad embankment. But they recovered quickly, and a fierce engagement ensued. For six hours Cleburne held fast, while the rest of the Army of Tennessee hastened to put itself out of reach of the pursuing Yankees. Finally, when Bragg's main force was at a safe distance, Cleburne slipped away from the fight with Hooker. His heroic action—carried out at a cost of only 221 casualties among his 4,200 men, against the enemy's loss of 442—had saved Bragg's wagon train and artillery, a feat that would earn Cleburne the commander's gratitude and an official resolution of thanks from the Confederate Congress.

On November 28 Grant called off the pursuit. His army was low on rations, and he did

*Color Corporal William C. Montgomery displays the tattered national color of the 76th Ohio. He lost an arm carrying this flag in the futile attack on the Rebel rear guard at Ringgold, Georgia, where the 76th suffered 25 percent casualties.*

not think it could live off the barren country below Chattanooga. He was also concerned about Burnside, whose Army of the Ohio was under siege by James Longstreet at Knoxville. President Lincoln, Secretary of War Stanton, and General in Chief Halleck were all clamoring for the rescue of Burnside.

"Well done," read Lincoln's message of congratulations to Grant. "Many thanks to all. Remember Burnside." Halleck had dealt with the victory at Chattanooga cursorily—"I congratulate you on the success thus far of your plans"—before making the real point of his wire: "I fear that General Burnside is hard-pressed and that any further delay may prove fatal. I know that you will do all in your power to relieve him."

Grant had been told that Burnside had only enough rations left to last until December 3, so he had ordered Thomas to send Major General Gordon Granger's IV Corps north as soon as Bragg was no longer a threat. But when Grant returned to Chattanooga on the night of November 29, he found Granger still there. Granger had "decided for himself" that advancing on Knoxville "was a very bad move to make." Furious, Grant placed Sherman in charge of the mission to relieve Burnside. Sherman's relief force would consist of his Army of the Tennessee plus Granger's corps.

Sherman's men, having marched farther, worked harder, and faced tougher fighting than the rest of Grant's army, were exhausted, undernourished, and short of equipment. Sherman nevertheless took them on a grueling 85-mile forced march to reach beleaguered Knoxville. His cavalry vanguard just made the December 3 deadline, only to discover that Longstreet, after being decisively whipped by Burnside's men at Fort Sanders four days earlier, had gotten wind of the relief force's approach and had withdrawn.

As for Burnside, he and his men seemed in much better shape than had been anticipated. On his arrival Sherman was surprised when he was taken to a local home, where he and Burnside and their staff officers were treated to a roast turkey dinner—a gift of the townspeople. Burnside cheerfully explained that the Tennesseans had been sharing their food with his army and that the Federals had never been in serious danger of starvation—although the rank and file were down to a morsel of salt pork and a little bran bread each day.

Sherman took his Army of the Tennessee on a leisurely march back to Chattanooga, leaving Granger's corps to be added to Burnside's army. Thus reinforced, Burnside briefly pursued Longstreet into the easternmost mountains of Tennessee. Then, much to Grant's annoyance, Burnside and Granger gave up the chase and returned to Knoxville. Longstreet remained at large in Tennessee, but his troops were no longer a threat; they would slip away after a hard winter.

Meanwhile, Bragg had sent a telegraph to Richmond to report on the state of his shattered command. He closed with the words "I deem it due to the cause and to myself to ask for relief from command and an investigation into the causes of the defeat."

Bragg was not prepared to accept any of the blame himself for the loss of Chattanooga. In his official report, he condemned his soldiers for losing Lookout Mountain: "No satisfactory excuse can possibly be given for the shameful conduct of our troops on the left in allowing their line to be penetrated. The position was one which ought to have been held by a line of skirmishers against any assaulting column."

Bragg also castigated his generals, charging that their "warfare against me has been carried on successfully, and the fruits are bitter."

His only moment of self-awareness came when he ruefully admitted to President Jefferson F. Davis: "I fear we both erred in the conclusion for me to retain command here after the clamor raised against me."

On November 30 Davis accepted Bragg's resignation as head of the Army of Tennessee and appointed William J. Hardee to take his place. Bragg was transferred to Richmond, where he became a military adviser to Davis and the Confederate cabinet.

The wrecked Army of Tennessee would convalesce in northern Georgia that winter. But the Confederacy as a whole would never be able to recover from the effects of the fighting around Chattanooga. Confederate railroad communications in the West had been crippled and the gateway to the heart of the Deep South flung open to the Yankees.

Grant's three forces went into winter quarters in Chattanooga. The troops were kept busy repairing and securing the railroad connections between Nashville and Chattanooga in anticipation of a spring campaign.

As the general who had turned a desperate situation into a stunning victory, Ulysses S. Grant was the Union's man of the hour. A few months after the victory at Chattanooga, President Lincoln made Grant the first officer since George Washington to hold the full grade of lieutenant general and called him to Washington to become the head of all the Union armies. Grant's successor as commander of Federal forces in the West would be his trusted subordinate, William Tecumseh Sherman.

Henceforward, the two friends would work in tandem, putting into devastating effect the strategy that Lincoln had been advocating virtually since the outbreak of the war—but always before now without the cooperation of his generals. No longer would the Federal armies in the East and West act "independently and without concert, like a balky team, no two pulling together," in Grant's barnyard metaphor. Instead they would press forward simultaneously, squeezing the Confederacy in a giant pincers.

While Grant moved to destroy Lee's army in Virginia, Sherman would corner and break up the Army of Tennessee in Georgia. Grant did not give his old friend a specific geographical objective. But Sherman judged his immediate target to be Atlanta, the manufacturing and railroad center of the Deep South, some 100 miles to the southeast of Chattanooga. Thus was the stage set for the burning of Atlanta and Sherman's destructive march to the sea.

## CHATTANOOGA CASUALTIES

November 23-27, 1863

### FEDERAL

| | |
|---|---|
| Killed | 753 |
| Wounded | 4,722 |
| Missing | 349 |
| Total | 5,824 |

### CONFEDERATE

| | |
|---|---|
| Killed | 361 |
| Wounded | 2,160 |
| Missing | 4,146 |
| Total | 6,667 |

## SERGEANT MAJOR LEVI A. ROSS

86th Illinois Infantry, D. McCook's Brigade

*Hours after the Yankees had chased the Rebel army off Missionary Ridge, Ross and his mates were rousted from their campfires to lead the pursuit of the fleeing Bragg. Writing in a diary he kept throughout his three-year war service, the 26-year-old Ross recalled the clash with the Confederates when Union forces caught up with them at Chickamauga Station.*

Were called up at midnight and started in pursuit of the skedaddling Bragg, who began his retreat early last evening. We pressed the flying battalions and captured many prisoners. Genl. Sheridan distinguished himself in the pursuit of the enemy by a flank movement so skillfully executed that he gobbled in a large number of prisoners. "Phil" has much dash and skill in action.

Along the road side of the route of Bragg's retreat was scattered cornmeal, flour, salt, ammunition, caissons, broken wagons, exhausted mules and horses, and worn out soldiers as well as many deserters.

On we pushed singing: "We'll rally round the flag boys, down with the traitor and up with the stars," etc. A short time before sun set the enemy was pressed so closely that he had to either lose his train or fight for it. He chose the latter alternative, and accordingly made a stand, and poured upon our advance a volley of rebel lead. Our boys went into the fight with a yell, inspired by our great victory. This cheer ran back along the lines of the advancing columns like the mighty waves of the ocean. Every soldier shouted to the utmost strength he possessed. I

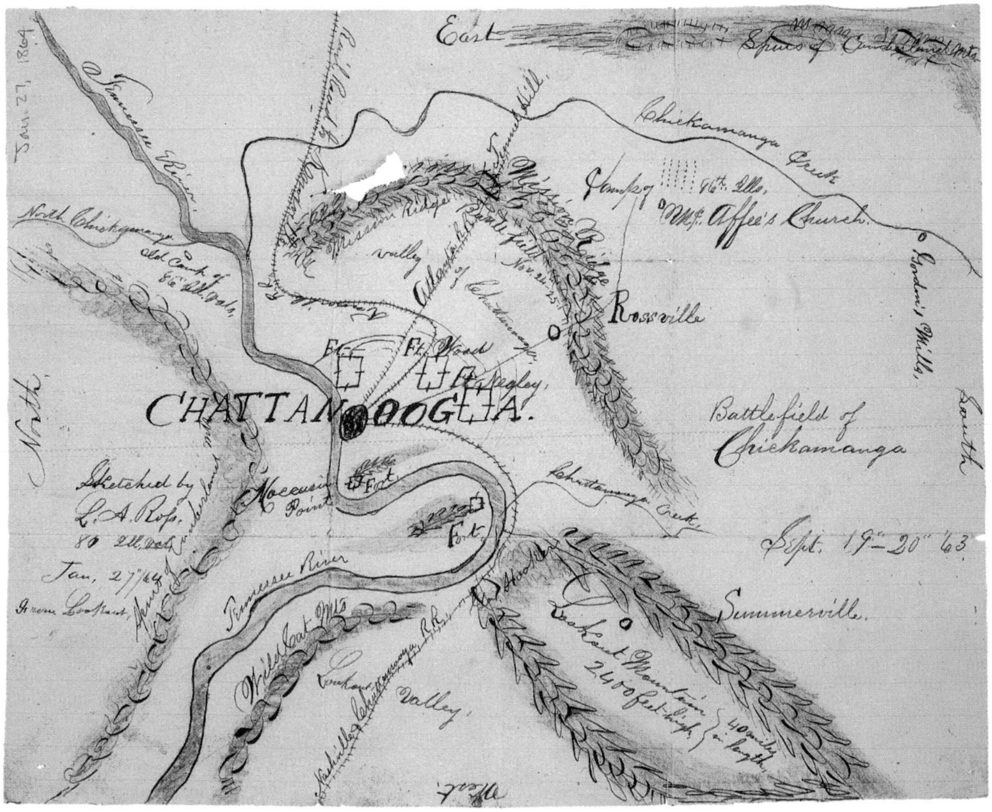


*From a vantage point on Lookout Mountain two months after Union forces drove the Confederates from Tennessee, Sergeant Major Levi Ross sketched this map in his wartime journal. Except for the erroneous fishhook shape he gives to Missionary Ridge, the map presents a reasonably accurate view of Chattanooga and its environs. Ross indicates the former and current locations of his regiment's campsite as well as the battlefield of Chickamauga, where the 86th Illinois also saw action.*

never before heard such cheering. Really it was an appropriate manner for a soldier to spend this national Thanksgiving day.

The 3rd Brigade was brought into line and ordered to fix bayonets. Gen. Davis just then rode along the line and shouted: "Go in boys, with a yell!" It was not necessary to say more to his Prairie boys. We *did* yell with a hearty good will and charged the Johnnies about three fourths of a mile through an open field and a skirt of woods along a small stream which we were obliged to ford. We pushed them through another field and finally they made a stand behind a high fence in the edge of some timber.

Night coming on put a stop to the fighting. The rebels continued their retreat and the Union army rested from its labors around large burning rail piles. A sublime scene today is worthy of note. We were deployed and marched by battalions with companies, right in front, deploying distance. The sun shone brightly upon the burnished guns and the buttons even seemed to partake of the brilliance of the day as the army strode on.

*Nicknamed Marse Frank by his troops and much beloved by them, Major General Benjamin F. Cheatham was said to be "one of the most provident soldiers," always motivated by an abiding concern for his men's welfare.*

## PRIVATE THOMAS J. WALKER

9TH TENNESSEE (C.S.) INFANTRY, HUMES' BRIGADE

*Walker's regiment was ordered to help cover the southward retreat of Cheatham's division on November 26. Desperate to avoid discovery by nearby Yankee pursuers, and having been forced off the Graysville road, which was made impassable by mud and stalled artillery, Walker and his comrades marched overland through the night under terrible conditions. Wounded in early 1864, the Tennessee native surrendered on April 26 at Greensboro, North Carolina, and was paroled five days later.*

I will never forget that night retreat. It was bitter cold way along in the night [when] our columns were halted. Pickets were thrown out on our right and orders came from Gen. Cheatham that when the march again commenced that we must march with as little noise as possible. As the enemy had cut us off from the rest of the Army, we had to make a detour and cross Chickamauga Creek lower down at a ford unbeknown to the enemy.

We marched pretty well all night over the roughest mountain road I have ever travelled. Just before day, the head of the column reached the ford. All the while, the enemy was passing parallel to our line of march on the main pike. General Cheatham stood on the bank and as each file passed going down the bank, he would say, "Boys, keep quiet! If you make the least noise, we are lost."

File after file plunged into that icy flood four feet deep, struggling to reach the opposite shore. The men held their guns and accoutrements on top of their heads. With bated breath and chattering teeth they waded waist deep in that ice cold water. Oh, how I dreaded my turn! As my file reached the edge of the water, we plunged in with clenched teeth for fear our breath would come out in such force that it would end in a scream. It proved to be too severe an ordeal for one of my file who was a great big fellow. As we stepped into the icy water to our waists, he hollered out at the top of his voice, "Jesus Christ! God Almighty!" However, with few exceptions, we passed over very quietly and struck the mountain trail and were soon on its top. We struck the main road with the enemy in our rear. Safe from capture at last!

We reached a safe place to camp about sunrise with our clothes frozen stiff upon us, after one of the most trying night marches I experienced during the war.

"He was making his best speed across that open field when another yank blazed away at him which helped Granger along a good deal & enabled him to increase his speed by about double."

## SERGEANT MAJOR JOHN W. GREEN

9TH KENTUCKY (C.S.) INFANTRY, LEWIS' BRIGADE

*Green's wartime journal is full of humorous accounts like the one below. But the jocular tone in his writings hid a darker side to Green's character: Angered at not receiving an officer's commission by war's end, for example, Green threw away his sword. And despite having later achieved success and stature as a financier, Green, after a period of severe illness in 1920, committed suicide.*

We are still operating with Cleyburn's brigade, covering the retreat. We camped at Chicamauga station last night. The roads are very heavy & the wagon trains are falling back very slowly. Great quantities of commisary stores are being abandoned at this place [and] the boys are filling their haversacks with sugar & hard tack. We had a sharp skirmish with the yanks here. We had to keep them back until the wagon train got out of the way. We were deployed in line of battle on a wooded ridge & the yanks advanced across a wide field about one mile away. Our artillery opened on them & though they outnumber us ten to one we deterred them from advancing for an hour or more; finally they advanced against us in force & we, having delayed them as long as we could, fell back through an open field.

We had first to climb a high staked & rider fence. George Granger, a fat short leged boy in Co. H who was a good deal handicapped by a big supply of sugar & hard tack which he had just gotten at the station, was pressed pretty hard & had a close shave when he had to climb the fence. Before he had gotten well over a mr. yank fired at him but missed him. He was making his best speed across that open field when another yank blazed away at him which helped Granger along a good deal & enabled him to increase his speed by about double. When a second yank fired & missed him he yelled at him, "Run you scoundrel of a rebel!"

Granger called back at him, "You blamed fool you, dont you see I am doing my best."

## LIEUTENANT COLONEL DANIEL F. GRIFFIN

38TH INDIANA INFANTRY, CARLIN'S BRIGADE

*Griffin and his Hoosiers bagged some 300 Rebels on Missionary Ridge, then joined the Federal advance on Graysville. The New Albany, Indiana, native resigned his commission in November 1864, citing pressing family business and a fall from his horse that exacerbated an old hip fracture.*

Joined our Brigade on the Ridge about 9 A.M. having four days rations on hand, and ready for anything. Remained but a short time on the Ridge, when off started our Div. for Graysville and Ringgold, or at least in that direction; our Brigade in advance, the 38th in advance of the Brig.; with 2 companies as skirmishers, another as support, while the remaining 7 moved in line of battle. We advanced to Chickamauga River, picking up in that distance, say six miles, 1 Rebel Capt. and 27 stragglers, all of whom had their "rights" or were fast getting them. Here we found the bridge burned, and two hours time consumed in effecting a crossing, when we were relieved of the advance by the 42nd Indiana and took position in the column.

Advanced very cautiously, now growing dusk, meeting but a few of the enemy's Cavalry, and about 9 P.M. quietly formed line of battle within a few hundred yards of the crossing of the Lafayette and Ringgold roads. The line formed, we could plainly hear the drivers and teamsters "cussing," yelling and making a noise generally, apparently with trains in the mud. Much time was consumed in preparation, as we had some ugly little streams to cross; and Hooker was at the same time to operate on the right. At last all was ready and through the woods we advanced on my first night attack, not knowing what we might run against.

But on we swept; then came a few hurried shots, a yell, a charge, and four pieces of artillery and quite a number of prisoners were ours. Our Div. then changing direction to the left, swept down upon Graysville on the banks of the east Chickamauga, capturing many of the unwary as they lay around their comfortable camp fires, on their beds or as they essayed an escape over the hills. Meantime, Hooker pressed on a few miles toward Ringgold, and we bivouacked at midnight in and around Graysville, appropriating without much ceremony the Rebel fires but not their beds, as we cared but little for the capture of that breed of "grayback."

## PRIVATE JOHN W. DYER

1st Kentucky (C.S.) Cavalry, Grigsby's Brigade

*In a brush with the Federals at Chickamauga Station, Dyer and his mates came within 200 yards of the Yankees and were astonished by their vast numbers. Of that encounter Dyer recalled, "We made a gradual circuit to the left instead of turning square back in order to make them think we wasn't scared." Still unable to shake the Yankees at Graysville, the Kentuckians engaged their pursuers in some sharp fighting. This second encounter, as Dyer relates, left him bruised but intact.*

Our next stand after Chickamauga station was at Graysville, a station a few miles to the south. In forming the line our brigade was on the left of a division of Tennessee infantry and occupied some breastworks that had been thrown up some time before. The Yankees charged our front and we repulsed them. For an hour or more there was no more fighting done, when suddenly a courier dashed up with information that the enemy was flanking us on the right and orders for us to mount our horses and go check the movement. We passed some fifty or sixty yards in the rear of the infantry on our right and just when we were exactly behind them the Yankees charged them, and for about forty minutes there was the hottest of hot times and we could not take a hand. We had to stand and take it. We could see everything that happened. Our infantry tumbling over like ten-pins, the minie balls flying thick among us, shells bursting all about us, limbs of trees falling on us and a general pandemonium reigned. After the scrap was over our brigade was marched back to its old position which it held till next morning.

We had several men and horses wounded, and it seems wonderful that the casualties were not greater as we sat on our horses in good range with nothing to shield us. John T. Quarles (known as "T") and I were beside each other when we were both struck. "T," with a groan, clapped his hand to his head and reeled over towards me. Supposing that he was shot through the brain, I caught and pulled him over in front of me and carried him down the hill to our field hospital where he was laid on the ground for dead. He began to show signs of life when an examination showed that the ball had entered the calf of his leg and ranged down the bone to his ankle where it was afterward cut out.

I did not know that I too had been hit till I got off my horse when I discovered that my foot and leg were asleep. An examination showed that a ball had hit me on the instep, but was glanced off by the hard rawhide shoe I was wearing. These shoes would soften and stretch in wet weather and draw up and get as hard as iron when they got dry. To one of these shoes, in the latter condition, I am indebted for the possession of two feet today.

*Labeled "Battle of Ringgold, Ga." by Alfred R. Waud, this sketch of Taylor's Ridge and Ringgold Gap was never finished. Waud did not cover the western theater, but 25 years later he traveled on the Western & Atlantic Railroad visiting battle sites and making drawings from which engravings were later produced. It was during this extended sketching trip that Waud succumbed to heart disease. He is buried in Marietta, Georgia, far from his South Orange, New Jersey, home.*

## PRIVATE PHILIP D. STEPHENSON

13TH ARKANSAS INFANTRY, GOVAN'S BRIGADE

*Descended from a Virginia family, 16-year-old Stephenson and his brother, Hammett, left their Missouri home to join the Rebel side. He was later disabled by typhoid; rejoining his unit in September 1863, he was not given a gun at Chattanooga. The future Presbyterian minister, positioned for an ambush at Ringgold Gap, watched weaponless as the action unfolded.*

There we stopped. "Ould Pat," our division general, was tired of running—and we were too! Cooler, more willing men never turned to face a foe. There was no fuss, no cheering or anything of that sort. Silence reigned, for Cleburne wanted to lay a trap. We stopped, filed right and left, and quietly occupied that ridge on either side of the gap and also the gap itself. Both gap and ridge were heavily wooded, and we lay down, concealed, and watched the foe coming toward us. Not a skirmisher was thrown out, the valley lay open before us with the little village in the middle.

Our regiment was in the gap, and our company *exactly* in the gap, its left wing resting on the railroad. Two guns were there also of Goldthwaite's Battery just a little beyond our line and "masked" (that is, with branches of trees and leaves piled before them), and the cannoneers lying down concealed. We too, were masked. We were in a gully that seared the slope of the ridge towards the ravine and in a direction just right for our line. There we lay, just behind the guns, waiting!

Ah! That waiting just before a battle. Men never get over it, the

"'Now then, boys, give it to 'em, boys,' suddenly sang out Cleburne in his Irish brogue, jumping up in the air, and clapping his feet together."

thrill of it and tension of it, no matter how many battles they have been in. The *solemnity* of it may pass away, for men get hardened, but the tax on patience and nerves remains. . . .

And the keeping silent and holding our fire! Everything in the little valley was plain before our sight, the railroad running like an arrow from our feet straight through it, and to and through the village in the background. . . . General Cleburne and an aide or so, were hidden behind us, Cleburne behind a tree, standing with field glasses watching. We were not to fire until he said so. As I lay in the gully, I took a look at him now and then. I was looking at him when he gave the order to fire!

He had allowed the head of the enemy's column to come within 100 feet or so of us! Indeed it did not look more than that. On they came! Down the railroad track carelessly, not in line of battle but in marching column, no skirmishers thrown out, no sign of seeing us or suspecting our presence!

What a sight that was! What a moment!

"*Now* then, boys, *give* it to 'em, boys," suddenly sang out Cleburne in his Irish brogue, jumping up in the air, and clapping his feet together. Forth from that ravine and from the ridge went a roar and a flame and a torrent of deadly solid shot and canister and bullets full in the face of those men! They melted away like mist before the sun. The slaughter was fearful. We kept it up until the column disappeared entirely, and all that could be seen were the men lying along the tracks and individuals scattered over the plain and flying for the shelter of the village houses.

## BRIGADIER GENERAL MARK P. LOWREY

Brigade Commander, Army of Tennessee

*Lowrey was a brickmason who at age 24 became a Baptist minister. In 1861 he was commissioned colonel of the 4th Mississippi, and a year later he raised a new regiment, the 32d Mississippi. In an 1867 autobiography this future founder of a women's college recalled with satisfaction his role in the fighting at Ringgold Gap.*

At Ringgold, or Taylor's Ridge, my brigade was at first held in reserve in the gap; and General Polk, having been sent over behind the right hand hill, had sent the First Arkansas regiment upon the hill to watch the movements of the enemy. When General Clebourne saw heavy columns of the enemy moving rapidly to his right he gave me a verbal order, I think in these words: "Go upon that hill and see that the enemy don't turn my right." I moved by the right flank and, with much difficulty, climbed the rugged hill. I got my horse up the hill with much difficulty, but my field-officers all left their horses and went up on foot. On reaching the top of the hill, I heard firing on the right about a quarter of a mile ahead of me. I left a staff-officer to close up the command in haste, and hurry them on, and I went in full speed to see what the firing meant. On reaching the place, I found the First Arkansas standing alone against a large force of the enemy, who had already reached the summit. They felt that they were overpowered, and were just about to give way, but I dashed up to them and encouraged them, by assuring them that my brigade was just at hand. They gathered courage and held their ground. I dashed back in full speed, and knowing that the position would be entirely lost if I waited to bring my whole command at once, as the line had to be changed, I threw forward a regiment at a time, leading each regiment in person, and by a dash drove the enemy from the top of the hill. As I brought up my last regiment, I discovered that Brigadier-General Polk had hastily formed his brigade still further to the right, and was hotly engaged. A staff-officer came from him in full speed asking me for help, saying that the enemy were charging in massed column on the position then held by the First Arkansas, which, having been so long engaged, were out of amunition. I took the Forty-fifth Alabama, which I was just then bringing into position, and went in double-quick, threw them in rear of the First Arkansas, and moved them up in time to repulse the enemy. The victory was ours, and the enemy was gone down the hill in perfect confusion. A deafening shout of triumph went down our line, and General Polk, as if enwrapped in the glory of our success, dashed up to me, and seizing me by the hand exclaimed, "Just in time to save us, General!" The men, observing the rapture of their brigade commanders, again pierced the heavens with their shouts of triumph, greatly to the annoyance, no doubt, of the discomfited columns of the enemy. This was the most glorious triumph I ever witnessed on a battlefield. And there is nothing more certain than that tardy movements would have resulted in not only loss of that position, but the defeat of the entire division, and the loss of the trains and artillery of the army.

## CAPTAIN CHARLES H. KIBLER
### Staff, Brigadier General C. R. Woods

*Kibler was a 33-year-old sawyer when he joined the 76th Ohio as a lieutenant in October 1861. Two months later he was a captain but resigned because of illness in May 1862. Rejoining his brigade in August, Kibler served as a recruiter until named assistant adjutant general a year later. In this account of the slaughter on Taylor's Ridge, Kibler's harsh words were meant for Hooker, who had ordered the attack.*

The order to advance up the ridge was a grave error, following the graver error of an attack in front upon the enemy who occupied the natural stronghold. It was evident that the enemy occupied in force the top and a greater part of the sides of that ridge. In fact, the ridges on each side of the gap, and the gap itself, were held by the division of Gen. Patrick R. Cleburne, one of the best fighting divisions, east or west, of the rebel armies. This fact ought to have been known

*Major Willard Warner (left) led his 76th Ohio troops into a maelstrom of Confederate musketry in attempting to scale Taylor's Ridge on the Union left. "No better fighting was ever done . . . under more hopeless circumstances," recalled an Iowa colonel who witnessed the 76th's advance. "Major Warner did all that a brave and efficient officer could do—at one time seizing the colors from the fallen color bearer, going to the front and cheering the men forward."*

*Private James Beeson (left) and his comrades in the 1st Arkansas rushed to the Confederate right on Taylor's Ridge as Union skirmishers attempted a flanking movement there. Thirty minutes of the regiment's blistering gunfire drove the Yankees back. Led by Colonel John W. Colquitt, the Arkansans captured the regimental flag of the 76th Ohio, nine of whose officers and men were killed or wounded while carrying the banner before it was lost to the Rebels.*

by the General in command of that part of the Union Army which was in pursuit on that highway. To send a small regiment up the ridge, no general advance being intended, was to invite disaster. It is true that after the advance of the 76th Ohio began, the 4th Iowa was ordered to follow and support the 76th, and some time afterward two regiments of the Second Brigade of the Division advanced a part of the way up the ridge, at a point further south and nearer the gap. By an unfortunate *contratemps* they did not reach the crest of the ridge. Only the 4th Iowa supported the 76th Ohio.

At about 9 o'clock a.m. the Regiment, in line of battle, commenced the ascent. The side of the ridge, often called a mountain, was rugged and steep, and covered for a great part with small, loose stones, or shale, which made the ascent slow and exceedingly toilsome. But it moved slowly up, meeting with little opposition until it was near the crest. There it encountered the enemy in great force, but notwithstanding, it pressed forward to the crest and halted. The view from the top of the ridge disclosed a large force of the enemy in front and others hurrying to oppose the 76th Ohio. Here the 4th Iowa, Lieut. Colonel George Burton in command, joined the 76th, and the two regiments thenceforth acted together. One account estimates the force of the enemy opposing the two regiments at a brigade. This force not only covered the front of the two regiments, but also both flanks, so that their flanks were bent back to oppose the enemy. The two regiments met a hot front and enfilading fire. They held this line for about ten minutes. . . .

Seeing that the line at the crest could not be held against the superior force of the enemy on the front and flanks, or that the consequence of holding it longer would be annihilation or capture, Major Warner gave the order to retire down the hill to a more defensible position. This order was to retire slowly and fighting. It was an order full of peril. Would the men be firm, or would they interpret the order as a rout and give way to confusion and flight? They did not so interpret it. In line of battle, fighting, and in as good order as the conformation of the ground permitted, the regiment backed down about 150 feet and re-formed upon a line where the flanks were not endangered. They renewed the fight there under better auspices, and remained undislodged until the enemy retired. There is no record of more than a single act of poltroonery or skulking.

Pity it is that this splendid valor and endurance were in vain. It was not the fault of the regiment or its commanding officer. They were ordered into this dangerous place, and being there, stood as a rock against the assaults of an overpowering enemy.

## LIEUTENANT JOHN R. BOYLE

111TH PENNSYLVANIA INFANTRY, COBHAM'S BRIGADE

*Positioned west of the railroad depot at Ringgold, Boyle watched as Confederate musketry tore into Creighton's brigade. Shortly before 10:00 a.m., Boyle's regiment was sent into the fray, the first serious Federal move against the Rebel left. The Philadelphia-born printer later recalled what it was like to face the withering fire from cannon in the gap and troops on the heights.*

The troops had passed into Georgia, above Graysville, and just below Ringgold they were confronted by a steep and high eminence, more rugged than Missionary Ridge, which lay directly across their path. A little beyond the village the railroad passes through a gap in this hill, which was known as Taylor's Ridge. Upon its crest Cleburne's division of Hardee's corps was posted, Bragg's whole army having gone through the gap during the previous afternoon and night. Osterhaus was already assaulting the Ridge as Geary's men crossed the creek by a toll bridge that had fortunately escaped destruction, and hastened through the town under a brisk musketry fire. He was ordered in on the left of Osterhaus. Creighton's First Brigade came into line under severe fire three fourths of a mile from the gap, and gallantly charged up the precipitous and wooded hillside. For a half hour the brigade advanced from rock and tree toward the crest, fighting at every step. The One Hundred and Forty-seventh Pennsylvania was on the extreme left, and Creighton's own regiment, the Seventh Ohio, was next. This latter battalion was familiarly known as the "Roosters," because of its battle cry, which imitated the crowing of a cock. As it neared the top of the hill, giving its peculiar cry, it entered a ravine, from the sides of which it received a smothering enfilading fire that almost annihilated it. But it pressed on until it was within twenty-five yards of the crest, when, with nearly one half of its men and well-nigh all of its officers struck down, it was retired. The One Hundred and Fifty-seventh Pennsylvania, Colonel Pardee, gained the summit, but its position was found untenable, and it also fell halfway down the hill, and re-formed on the Seventh Ohio. The remaining regiments of the brigade, the Twenty-eighth Pennsylvania and the Sixty-sixth Ohio, held their advance forty yards below the crest, and in this position the brigade fought on for more than two hours. But the splendid Seventh Ohio was almost destroyed. All its officers but one, including its colonel and lieutenant colonel, were killed or wounded, and the regiment stacked less than forty muskets that night and was under command of a first lieutenant.

As soon as Creighton's brigade had begun its movement to the left Cobham's command was brought up and massed in a cornfield behind the stone depot on the outskirts of the town near Taylor's Ridge. It had scarcely taken this position before some of Osterhaus's regiments were pushed back on the right. Cobham moved at a double-quick, under fire, and formed line on a mound on the left of the railroad and the Gap in support of the weakened point. Ireland was four hundred yards to the rear in the main street of the village. The advance of the enemy was checked, but our right was in danger of being flanked. Ireland was hurried to the right in double time, while an intensified fire of grape, canister, and musketry was concentrated on the whole line. He crossed a swamp nearly a half mile in diameter, and, forming along Catoosa Creek, helped to turn Osterhaus's defense into an aggressive battle, which forced the enemy back upon the ridge. Major Reynolds, chief of artillery, opportunely arrived with his batteries, at this time, and at one o'clock Osterhaus charged and held the Ridge, and Ireland pushed his skirmishers through the Gap. The fighting had continued five hours. The One Hundred and Eleventh Pennsylvania was posted in the Gap, and the Union troops held all the field.

JANUARY 9, 1864.]
HARPER'S WEEKLY.
21
CHARGE OF COLONEL CREIGHTON'S BRIGADE AT THE BATTLE OF RINGGOLD.—SKETCHED BY MR. THEODORE R. DAVIS.—[SEE PAGE 23.]


*This Harper's Weekly engraving of a sketch by Theodore Davis shows the Union brigade of Colonel William Creighton ascending Taylor's Ridge. In command of the brigade for only three days, Creighton addressed the men of his old regiment—the 7th Ohio—whose battle cry mimicked the rooster's crow: "We are ordered to take those heights, and I expect to see you roosters walk right over them!" Creighton was mortally wounded in the ill-fated attack, and with his last breath was heard to say, "Tell my wife I died at the head of my command."*

## CAPTAIN ERNST J. KRIEGER

7TH OHIO INFANTRY, CREIGHTON'S BRIGADE

*Of all the units engaged on either side at Ringgold Gap, Krieger's regiment was hardest hit—12 of its 13 officers were killed or wounded climbing Taylor's Ridge. Within an hour, command fell to the German-born machinist, who had himself been wounded at Antietam. Krieger praised his men for their valor in the face of overwhelming fire.*

When the first line reached the foot of the hill they halted to return fire. The rear line continued its march, passed through the first line, and commenced ascending the hill. The Seventh ascended a ravine, which enabled the enemy to direct an effective fire on us from the front and both flanks, making us lose severely all along the line. The steepness of the ascent necessarily made our progress very slow, but the regiment persevered in its advance, not stopping to return the fire. The regiment nearly gained the crest of the hill, within a few yards of the rebel breastworks, when their fire became too heavy and effective for flesh and blood to withstand. Here Lieut. Col. O. J. Crane fell . . . and as a mere handful only remained, and as there was no hope of carrying the hill, Colonel Creighton, commanding the brigade, ordered us to fall back to the foot of the hill, which we did, carrying as many of our wounded with us as possible.

On reaching the foot of the hill, finding that I was the only officer of the regiment not disabled, I took command, rallied the men and rejoined the brigade. Soon after reaching the foot of the hill, Colonel Creighton received his mortal wound, and soon after died from its effects.

The number of enlisted men who were in line at the commencement of the battle was 206 of whom 13 were killed, 48 were wounded, none missing. Most of the wounds are severe ones.

We were repulsed, but not disgraced; humbled, but not humiliated. All that men could do against superior numbers and the advantageous position of the enemy was done. We retired, upon orders from General Geary, from the hill with the consciousness that we had not dishonored our flag.

*Seen here wearing the 7th Ohio's unique insignia, Lieutenant Colonel Orrin J. Crane was killed at Ringgold Gap. The rooster pin at right belonged to Captain Samuel McClelland, who was wounded in the regiment's charge. Weeks later, McClelland inventoried Crane's effects, which were shipped home with his body.*

## PRIVATE SAM WATKINS

1ST TENNESSEE (C.S.) INFANTRY, MANEY'S BRIGADE

*Following four days of hard fighting and marching, Watkins succumbed to exhaustion late on November 26. Awake long enough to know that Cleburne was making ready for a stand against the Yankees, Watkins, by his own account, seems to have slept through the entire battle on November 27. In the account below, he eloquently characterizes the damage the retreating Rebels inflicted on their pursuers.*

Before I got to this fire . . . a gentleman whom I never saw in my life . . . handed me a letter from the old folks at home, and a good suit of clothes. . . . if he ever sees these lines, I wish to say to him, "God bless you, old boy." I had lost every blanket and vestige of clothing, except those I had on, at Missionary Ridge. I laid down by the fire and went to sleep, but how long I had slept I knew not, when I felt a rough hand grab me and give me a shake, and the fellow said, "Are you going to sleep here, and let the Yankees cut your throat?" I opened my eyes, and asked, "Who are you?" He politely and pleasantly, yet profanely, told me that he was General Walker (the poor fellow was killed the 22nd of July, at Atlanta), and that I had better get further. . . .

I went a little further and laid down again and went to sleep. How long I had lain there, and what was passing over me, I know nothing about, but when I awoke, here is what I saw: I saw a long line of blue coats marching down the railroad track. The first thought I had was, well, I'm gone up now, sure; but on second sight, I discovered that they were prisoners. Cleburne had had the doggondest fight of the war. The ground was piled with dead Yankees; they were piled in heaps. The scene looked unlike any battlefield I ever saw. From the foot to the top of the hill was covered with their slain, all lying on their faces. It had the appearance of the roof of a house shingled with dead Yankees. They were flushed with victory and success, and had determined to push forward and capture the whole of the Rebel army, and set up their triumphant standard at Atlanta—then exit Southern Confederacy. But their dead were so piled in their path at Ringgold Gap that they could not pass them. The Spartans gained a name at Thermopylë, in which Leonidas and the whole Spartan army were slain while defending the pass. Cleburne's division gained a name at Ringgold Gap, in which they not only slew the victorious army, but captured five thousand prisoners besides. That brilliant victory of Cleburne's made him not only the best general of the army of Tennessee, and covered his men with glory and honor of heroes, but checked the advance of Grant's whole army.

## LAETITIA LAFON ASHMORE NUTT

CIVILIAN IN RINGGOLD

*Laetitia Nutt was a 27-year-old mother of three girls when her husband, LeRoy Moncure Nutt, organized the Red River Rangers, a company in the Louisiana Cavalry, in 1862. With daughters in tow she followed him on his campaigns and was in Ringgold during Bragg's retreat from Chattanooga. An entry in her wartime journal reveals the Kentucky-born woman's contempt for the Yankees.*

I soon learned . . . that our army was *falling back* in obedience to Gen. Bragg's orders, and not *retreating* before the Yankees. Col. and Capt. Warfield took supper with us, and Mr. Nutt and they left about two hours before the "detestable Blue Coats" came in. Our house was filled with them in a few moments, but they had not completed the search when we heard the most alarming notes of distress from the pig sty, hen house and goose pen. I had just said to Mary that I must get up before daylight and have all the fowls killed, to keep the Yanks from getting them, but with their natural canine instinct they had scented the fowls, made a night attack, outgeneralled me, and left not even a cock to crow in the morning.

Gen. Von Somebody made this his headquarters, placed a guard around the house and assured Mr. Page that nothing should be disturbed. They were here two days. In that time, they killed two oxen, five cows, several calves, several hogs, seven geese, as many ducks, thirty or forty chickens, ten or fifteen goats and dozens of pigeons and squab. Stole a horse and several colts, five hundred pounds of corned beef, quantities of flour and wheat from the mill, then burned the mill, machine shop, office and several other buildings belonging to Mr. Gray, and the general sealed his Yankee faith by taking off a pair of blankets, the only cover that Mr. Page had. The last of them left here Sunday morning, they seemed to be a good deal excited and hurried.

## GENERAL BRAXTON BRAGG
COMMANDER, ARMY OF TENNESSEE

*Bragg's defeat in Tennessee cost the Rebels a rich supply source and a staging area for offensive operations, forcing the Confederacy to take a defensive stance in the West for the rest of the war. It also marked the end of the North Carolina native's active career as a field commander; long a favorite of Jefferson Davis, he subsequently served as the president's military adviser. Bragg accompanied Davis on his flight from Richmond; he was captured in Georgia on May 9, 1865, and paroled.*

Our advance last night was at Tunnel Hill, the enemy just this side of Ringgold. We hope to maintain this position. Our inferiority in numbers, heavy loss in artillery, small-arms, organization, and morale, renders an earlier halt impossible; and should the enemy press on promptly we may have to cross Oostenaula. I have tried to communicate with Longstreet; by prompt movement he can be saved. Burnside's force is far inferior to him. If necessary, he can go on and join Jones' forces. Communication may be opened with him by the East Tennessee route. My first estimate of our disaster was not too large, and time only can restore order and morale. All possible aid should be pushed on to Resaca, and I deem it due to the cause and to myself to ask for relief from command and an investigation into the causes of the defeat.

*Lieutenant General William J. Hardee (left) succeeded Bragg as head of the Army of Tennessee. At his own request, Hardee held the position only briefly, resuming command of a corps when General Joseph E. Johnston was appointed in his place in late 1863. In 1864 the Georgia-born and French-trained cavalryman was sent to command the troops at Savannah. Hardee and his men were among the Rebel forces to surrender in North Carolina in April 1865.*

## MAJOR GENERAL WILLIAM T. SHERMAN
COMMANDER, ARMY OF THE TENNESSEE

*Grant sent Sherman to relieve Burnside's forces at Knoxville. Marching hard over sloppy roads and through numbing cold, Sherman's men were ill-shod, -clothed, and -provisioned by the time they arrived at their destination a week later. Below, Sherman recalls his shock upon discovering the actual situation in Burnside's camp. His help not needed, he took his troops back to Chattanooga, where they made camp for the winter in preparation for their momentous march through Georgia.*

With the head of my infantry column I reached Marysville, about fifteen miles short of Knoxville, on the 5th of December, when I received official notice from Burnside that Longstreet had raised the siege, and had started in retreat up the valley toward Virginia. Halting all the army . . . with General Granger and some of my staff I rode into Knoxville. Approaching from the south and west, we crossed the Holston on a pontoon-bridge, and in a large pen on the Knoxville side I saw a fine lot of cattle, which did not look much like starvation. I found General Burnside and staff domiciled in a large, fine mansion, looking very comfortable, and in a few words he described to me the leading events of the previous few days, and said he had already given orders looking to the pursuit of Longstreet. . . .

Returning to Burnside's quarters, we all sat down to a good dinner, embracing roast-turkey. There was a regular dining-table, with clean table-cloth, dishes, knives, forks, spoons, etc., etc. I had seen nothing of this kind in my field experience, and could not help exclaiming that I thought "they were starving," etc.; but Burnside explained that Longstreet had at no time completely invested the place, and that he had kept open communication with the country on the south side of the river Holston, more especially with the French Broad settlements, from whose Union inhabitants he had received a good supply of beef, bacon, and corn-meal. Had I known of this, I should not have hurried my men so fast; but until I reached Knoxville I thought our troops there were actually in danger of starvation.

"Loyal people of the north were inspirited and encouraged to renewed effort and sacrifice, while the Confederacy was correspondingly weakened if not depressed."

*In this fanciful watercolor, artist Adolph Metzner depicts the Army of the Tennessee leaving Chattanooga in the spring of 1864. A white signal flag and a cannon blast start the Federals across the Tennessee River in a driving rain and then over Raccoon Mountain southeast into Georgia. On May 7, 1864, Sherman, now commanding a Federal juggernaut of some 113,000 troops, moved to strike against the Gateway to the South: the city of Atlanta.*

## PRIVATE CHARLES A. WILLISON

76TH OHIO INFANTRY, C. R. WOODS' BRIGADE

*Armed with a consent form signed by his father, the 16-year-old Willison enlisted in 1862. The Massillon, Ohio, youth came unscathed through the fighting at Ringgold Gap, where his unit took a terrible battering. Willison reconstructed his wartime experiences from letters he kept, and in this excerpt from his memoir he reflects upon the impact the Union victory in Tennessee had on the war.*

This Ringold affair terminated the Chattanooga campaign and left that important point thereafter in undisputed possession of the Union forces. We were given another breathing spell. Grant's troops were drawn back for the winter and distributed in various camps, while plans were discussed and matured and means accumulated for next spring's campaigns. From December 5 to 20 we lay at Bridgeport, Alabama. Results of the last half of 1863 brought about a great change in the spirit and aspect of the war. At Gettysburg, Vicksburg, and Chattanooga had been wrought decisive victories for the cause of the Union. Loyal people of the north were inspirited and encouraged to renewed effort and sacrifice, while the Confederacy was correspondingly weakened if not depressed. So on the part of the north they took up the struggle with renewed heart and grip. Grant was made commander-in-chief, under the president, of all the Union armies, and Sherman given command of the Departments of Ohio, Tennessee, the Cumberland, and Arkansas, with their armies. Inspired by more hopeful prospects and by means of liberal inducements in the way of bounties, the depleted ranks were filled with new recruits and affairs put in trim for a final grapple to suppress the rebellion.

# GLOSSARY

*abatis*—A defensive barrier of fallen trees, with branches pointed toward the enemy.
*bastion*—A projecting portion of a fort's rampart into which artillery is placed, or any fortified place.
*battery*—The basic unit of artillery, consisting of four to six guns.
*bench road*—A road running along a terrace on the side of a mountain.
*bivouac*—A temporary encampment, or to camp out for the night.
*Boanerges*—Greek for "sons of thunder." Jesus used it for his disciples James and John, who wanted to call "fire to come down from heaven" to consume the Samaritans.
*bombproof*—A shelter from mortar or artillery attack, usually made with walls and a roof of logs and packed earth.
*breastwork*—A temporary fortification, usually of earth and about chest high, over which a soldier could fire.
*caisson*—A cart with large chests for carrying artillery ammunition; connected to a horse-drawn limber when moved.
*canister*—A tin can containing lead or iron balls that scattered when fired from a cannon.
*change front*—To alter the direction troops face to deliver or defend against an attack.
*clubbed musket*—A musket swung like a club in hand-to-hand combat.
*counterscarp*—The exterior wall of a defensive ditch built around a fort.
*double-quick*—A trotting pace.
*double-shotted artillery*—Artillery charged with two projectiles rather than the normal one.
*Dutchman*—A term, often pejorative, for a Union soldier of German descent.
*echelon*—A staggered or stairsteplike formation of parallel units of troops.
*embrasure*—An opening in a fort wall through which a cannon was fired.
*Enfield rifle*—The Enfield rifle musket was adopted by the British in 1853, and the North and South imported nearly one million to augment their own production. Firing a .577-caliber projectile similar to the Minié ball, it was fairly accurate at 1,100 yards.
*enfilade*—Gunfire that rakes an enemy line lengthwise, or the position allowing such firing.
*flank*—The right or left end of a military formation. To flank is to attack or go around the enemy's position on one end or the other.
*forage cap*—The standard-issue soft woolen cap, having a short leather bill and a round, high, flat-topped crown.
*friction primer*—A tube containing combustible material that ignited when a wire coated with a friction-sensitive igniter was withdrawn by pulling the lanyard. The device was inserted into the vent of a cannon to discharge the piece.
*grapeshot*—Iron balls (usually nine) bound together and fired from a cannon. Resembling a cluster of grapes, the balls broke apart and scattered on impact. Although references to grape or grapeshot are numerous in the literature, some experts claim that it was not used on Civil War battlefields.
*hardtack*—A durable cracker, or biscuit, made of plain flour and water and normally about three inches square and a half-inch thick.
*haversack*—A shoulder bag, usually strapped over the right shoulder to rest on the left hip, for carrying personal items and rations.
*howitzer*—A short-barreled artillery piece that fired its projectile in a relatively high trajectory.
*lanyard*—An artillerist's cord with a handle on one end and a clip connector for a friction primer on the other. The friction primer was inserted into the touchhole on an artillery piece. When the gunner jerked the lanyard, friction in the touchhole ignited powder in the breech, firing the weapon.
*limber*—A two-wheeled, horse-drawn vehicle to which a gun carriage or a caisson was attached.
*masked battery*—Any concealed or camouflaged battery of artillery.
*Minié ball*—The standard bullet-shaped projectile fired from the rifled muskets of the time. Designed by French army officers Henri-Gustave Delvigne and Claude-Étienne Minié, the bullet had a hollow base that expanded, forcing its sides into the grooves, or rifling, of the barrel. This caused it to spiral in flight, giving it greater range and accuracy. Appears as minie, minnie, and minni.
*mudsill*—A derisive term for a Yankee, coined by Senator J. H. Hammond of South Carolina in 1858 to label a member of the working class.
*musket*—A smoothbore, muzzleloading shoulder arm.
*muster*—To assemble. To be mustered in is to be enlisted or enrolled in service. To be mustered out is to be discharged from service, usually on expiration of a set time.
*Napoleon*—A smoothbore, muzzleloading artillery piece developed under the direction of Napoleon III. It fired a 12-pound projectile (and therefore was sometimes called a 12-pounder). Napoleons were originally cast in bronze; when that material became scarce in the South, iron was used.
*oblique*—At an angle.
*orderly*—A soldier assigned to a superior officer

for various duties, such as carrying messages.
*parapet*—A defensive elevation raised above a fort's main wall, or rampart.
*parole*—The pledge of a soldier released after being captured by the enemy that he would not take up arms again until properly exchanged.
*picket*—One or more soldiers on guard to protect the larger unit from surprise attack.
*pioneer*—Construction engineer.
*rampart*—The main wall of a fort, usually a mound of earth with a flattened top.
*ration*—A specified allotment of food for one person (or animal) per day. The amounts and nature of rations varied by time and place throughout the war. *Rations* may also refer simply to any food provided by the army.
*redoubt*—An enclosed, defensive stronghold.
*rifle*—Any weapon with spiral grooves cut into the bore to give spin to the projectile, adding range and accuracy. Usually applied to cannon or shoulder-fired weapons.
*rifle pit*—A hole or shallow trench dug in the ground from which soldiers could fire weapons and avoid enemy fire. Foxhole.
*salient*—Part of a fortress, line of defense, or trench system that juts out toward the enemy position.
*section of artillery*—Part of an artillery battery consisting of two guns, the soldiers who manned them, and their supporting horses and equipment.
*shrapnel*—An artillery projectile in the form of a hollow sphere filled with metal balls packed around an explosive charge. Developed by British general Henry Shrapnel during the Napoleonic Wars, it was used as an antipersonnel weapon. Also called spherical case.
*skirmisher*—A soldier sent in advance of the main body of troops to scout out and probe the enemy's position. Also, one who participated in a skirmish, a small fight usually incidental to the main action.
*small arms*—Any hand-held weapon, usually a firearm.
*solid shot*—A solid artillery projectile, oblong for rifled pieces and spherical for smoothbores.
*spike*—To render a piece of artillery unserviceable by driving a metal spike into the vent.
*Springfield rifle*—The standard infantry shoulder arm of both sides; it was named for the U.S. arsenal at Springfield, Massachusetts, which produced it in 1861, 1863, and 1864 models. The term eventually referred to any similar weapon regardless of where it was made.
*stack arms*—To set aside weapons, usually three or more in a pyramid, interlocking at the end of the barrel with the butts on the ground.
*sutler*—A peddler with a permit to remain with troops in camp or in the field and sell food, drink, and other supplies.
*tête de pont*—French for "bridgehead."
*traverse*—A trench or other defensive barrier that runs obliquely to the enemy's guns to protect against enfilading fire.
*vedette*—A sentry on horseback (often spelled vidette).
*Whitworth rifle*—A very long range English weapon especially effective for sharpshooting. In early 1863 the Confederacy imported 12; six were sent to each theater, where they were issued to the best marksmen.
*worm*—A long-handled artillerist's tool with a corkscrewlike tip on one end used to extract cloth and other debris from the barrel of a cannon.
*worm fence*—Also known as a snake fence, in which split rails were stacked alternately and at an angle, producing a zigzagging line.

## ACKNOWLEDGMENTS

The editors wish to thank the following for their valuable assistance in the preparation of this volume:

E. Burns Apfeld, Oshkosh, Wis.; Joe Blunt, Fort Oglethorpe, Ga.; Keith Bohannon, East Ridge, Tenn.; Mike Bub, Chattanooga; Dr. Jefferson Chapman, Frank H. McClurg Museum, University of Tennessee, Knoxville; Frank Colburn, Lincoln Memorial University Museum, Harrogate, Tenn.; John M. Coski, Museum of the Confederacy, Richmond; Steven Cox, Tennessee State Museum, Nashville; John Culp, Nashville; Greg Daimwood, Columbia, Tenn.; Donald G. Enders, Harrisburg, Pa.; Peggy Fox, Confederate Research Center, Hill College, Hillsboro, Tex.; Cyndy Gilley, Do You Graphics, Woodbine, Md.; Randy W. Hackenburg, U.S. Army Military History Institute, Carlisle Barracks, Pa.; Robert F. Hanckock, Museum of the Confederacy, Richmond; Mary Alice Harper, Humanities Research Center, University of Texas, Austin; Terri Hudgins, Museum of the Confederacy, Richmond; Kenny Irvin, O'Fallon, Mo.; Mary Ison and Staff, Library of Congress, Washington, D.C., Anne Lipscomb, Mississippi Department of Archives and History, Jackson; Joseph R. Loehle, New Windsor, N.Y.; Karina McDaniel, Tennessee State Library and Archives, Nashville; Scott McKay, Roswell, Ga.; Mary Michaels, Illinois State Historical Library, Springfield; Alden Monroe, Alabama Department of Archives and History, Montgomery; Janie C. Morris,

Duke University, Durham, N.C.; Louis Netherland, Rogersville, Tenn.; Roseanne O'Canas, High Impact, Baltimore; James Ogden III, Chickamauga/Chattanooga National Military Park, Fort Oglethorpe, Ga.; Dorothy Olsen, Georgia State Capitol Museum, Atlanta; James Tracy Power, Columbia, S.C.; AnnMarie Price, Virginia Historical Society, Richmond; Patricia Ricci, Confederate Museum, New Orleans; Laurie Risch, Behringer-Crawford Museum, Covington, Ky.; Matthew Robb, Humanities Research Center, University of Texas, Austin; Dr. Richard A. Sauers, White Oak, Pa.; Sean Seley, Kansas City, Mo.; Neil Sexton, Lewisville, N.C.; John R. Sickles, Merrillville, Ind.; Ruth Silliker, Saco, Maine; Kevin Stewart, St. Charles, Mo.; Kim Timmerman, Fredericksburg, Va.; Ken Turner, Ellwood City, Pa.; Lee White, Summerville, Ga.; Michael J. Winey, U.S. Army Military History Institute, Carlisle Barracks, Pa.; Mary Winter, Kentucky Historical Society, Frankfort; Casey Scot Wohlfeil, Cincinnati.

## PICTURE CREDITS

*The sources for the illustrations are listed below. Credits from left to right are separated by semicolons, from top to bottom by dashes.*

Dust jacket: front, courtesy T. Scott Sanders; rear, Ray Zielin Collection, copied by Richard Baumgartner.

All calligraphy by Mary Lou O'Brian/Inkwell, Inc.

6, 7: Map by Paul Salmon. 8: Massachusetts Commandery of the Military Order of the Loyal Legion and the U.S. Army Military History Institute (MASS-MOLLUS/ USAMHI), copied by Richard Baumgartner. 14: Map by Peter McGinn. 16: From *A Carolinian Goes to War: The Civil War Narrative of Arthur Middleton Manigault, Brigadier General, C.S.A.*, edited by R. Lockwood Tower, University of South Carolina Press, Columbia, 1983, copied by Richard Baumgartner. 17: Courtesy E. Burns Apfeld, photographed by Bill Krueger. 18: Courtesy T. Scott Sanders, photographed by Henry Mintz. 19: Courtesy Craig Dunn, copied by Richard Baumgartner. 20: Frank and Marie-Thérèse Wood Print Collections, Alexandria, Va. 21: Blue Acorn Press, Huntington, W.Va. 22: Frank and Marie-Thérèse Wood Print Collections, Alexandria, Va. 23: From *Cleburne and His Command*, by Irving A. Buck, Walter Neale, New York, 1908, reprinted by Morningside House Inc., Dayton, 1982, copied by Philip Brandt George. 24: Blue Acorn Press, Huntington, W.Va., copied by Richard Baumgartner. 25: Orphan Brigade Kinfolk Collection at the U.S. Army Military History Institute (USAMHI), copied by A. Pierce Bounds. 26: Courtesy E. Burns Apfeld, photographed by Bill Krueger. 27: Frank and Marie-Thérèse Wood Print Collections, Alexandria, Va. 28: From the collection of the Behringer-Crawford Museum, Covington, Ky. 29: Chicago Historical Society. 31: Frank and Marie-Thérèse Wood Print Collections, Alexandria, Va. 32: From *The Photographic History of the Civil War*, Vol. 1, edited by Francis Trevelyan Miller, Review of Reviews, New York, 1912—MASS-MOLLUS/USAMHI, copied by A. Pierce Bounds. 33: L. M. Strayer Collection, copied by Richard Baumgartner. 34: Albert G. Shaw Collection, Virginia Historical Society, Richmond. 35: Smithsonian Institution, Washington, D.C. 37: From *The War between the Union and the Confederacy*, by William C. Oates, published by The Neale Publishing Co., New York, 1905. 38: Frank and Marie-Thérèse Wood Print Collections, Alexandria, Va. 39: MASS-MOLLUS/USAMHI, copied by A. Pierce Bounds. 40: From *Soldiers True*, by John Richards Boyle, Eaton & Mains, New York, 1903, copied by Philip Brandt George. 41: MASS-MOLLUS/USAMHI, copied by Richard Baumgartner. 42: Blue Acorn Press, Huntington, W.Va., copied by Richard Baumgartner; MASS-MOLLUS/USAMHI, copied by A. Pierce Bounds. 43: Smithsonian Institution, Washington, D.C. 44: Frank and Marie-Thérèse Wood Print Collections, Alexandria, Va.; courtesy Karl Sundstrom, copied by Richard Baumgartner. 46: Courtesy Ron Chojnacki, copied by Richard Baumgartner. 47: Robert O. Sweeny, photo, Minnesota Historical Society, St. Paul; from *The Photographic History of the Civil War*, Vol. 2, by Henry W. Elson, Review of Reviews, New York, 1912. 48: Library of Congress, Neg. No. LC-B818-8533. 51: Frank and Marie-Thérèse Wood Print Collections, Alexandria, Va. 52: Frank and Marie-Thérèse Wood Print Collections, Alexandria, Va.; National Archives, Neg. No. 111-B-6262. 53: Courtesy Ellen Allran and Victoria Guthrie; Library of Congress, copied by Philip Brandt George. 54: MASS-MOLLUS/ USAMHI, copied by A. Pierce Bounds. 55: Frank and Marie-Thérèse Wood Print Collections, Alexandria, Va. 56, 57: Alabama Department of Archives and History, Montgomery —National Archives, Neg. No. 77-HT-72A-3; National Archives, Neg. No. 77-HT-72A-4. 58: Museum of the Confederacy, Richmond. 59: Rare Book, Manuscript, and Special Collections Library, Duke University, Durham, N.C. 60: Courtesy collection of William A. Turner—MASS-MOLLUS/USAMHI, copied by A. Pierce Bounds. 61: Frank and Marie-Thérèse Wood Print Collections, Alexandria, Va. 62: A. E. M. Adams via South Carolina Confederate Relic Room and Museum, Columbia; Library of Congress (2). 64: From *Battles and Leaders of the Civil War*, edited by Robert Underwood Johnson and Clarence Clough Buel, Century, New York, 1887. 65: Courtesy Barbara and Robert Brezek. 66: Georgia Capitol Museum in Office of Secretary of State. 68: Collection of New-York Historical Society. 69: Courtesy Frank H. McClung Museum, University of Tennessee, Knoxville, photographed by W. Miles Wright. 70: H. H. Bennett Studio Foundation, Inc., Wisconsin Dells, Wis. 73: Frank and Marie-Thérèse Wood Print Collections, Alexandria, Va. 74: Courtesy Francis H. Evans, Tupelo, Miss., copied by Philip Brandt George. 76: Courtesy Rensselaer County Historical Society, Troy, N.Y.—from *The Photographic History of the Civil War*, Vol. 4, edited by Theo. F. Rodenbough, Review of Reviews, New York, 1912, copied by Philip Brandt George. 77: L. M. Strayer Collection. 78: MASS-MOLLUS/ USAMHI, copied by A. Pierce Bounds. 79: Courtesy Ken Turner Collection, photographed by Chet Buquo (2)—courtesy Michael W. Waskul, copied by L. M. Strayer. 80: Library of Congress, Neg. No. LC-USZ62-77938. 81: Frank and Marie-Thérèse Wood Print Collections, Alexandria, Va. 82: Courtesy Gary Delscamp, Dayton. 83: From *The Campaigns of the 124th Regiment, Ohio Volunteer Infantry*, by G. W. Lewis, Werner, Akron, 1894, copied by Philip Brandt George. 84, 85: MASS-MOLLUS/USAMHI, copied by A. Pierce Bounds. 86: James C. Frasca Collections, photographed by Andy Cifranic. 87: Blue Acorn Press, Huntington, W.Va., copied by Richard Baumgartner. 89: Frank and Marie-Thérèse Wood Print Collections, Alexandria, Va. 90: L. M. Strayer Collection, copied by Richard Baumgartner. 91: MASS-MOLLUS/ USAMHI, copied by A. Pierce Bounds. 92, 93: Blue Acorn Press, Huntington, W.Va.; Library of Congress, Waud #121. 94: Frederick H. Meserve Historical Portraits, courtesy New York State Library. 95: From *Battles and Leaders of the Civil War*, edited by Robert Underwood Johnson and Clarence Clough Buel, Century, New York, 1887. 96: MASS-MOLLUS/USAMHI, copied by Robert Walch. 97: From *Soldiers True*, by John Richards Boyle, Eaton & Mains, New York, 1903, copied by Philip Brandt George. 98: Alabama Department of Archives and History, Montgomery. 99: Courtesy T. Scott Sanders, photographed by Henry Mintz. 101: Frank and Marie-Thérèse Wood Print Collections, Alexandria, Va. 102: Western Reserve Historical Society, Cleveland. 103: From *The Rough Side of War*, edited with biographical sketch by Arnold Gates, Basin, Garden City, N.Y., 1987. 104: N. S. Meyer Collection, photographed by Al Freni—collection of New-York Historical Society. 106: Marshall County Historical Museum, Holly Springs, Miss. 107: L. M. Strayer Collection. 108: L. M. Strayer Collection, copied by Richard Baumgartner. 109: Courtesy T. Scott Sanders. 111: Map by R. R. Donnelley & Sons Co., Cartographic Services, overlay by Time-Life Books. 112: From *Generals in Blue: Lives of Union Commanders*, by Ezra J. Warner, Louisiana State University Press, Baton Rouge, 1964, copied by Philip Brandt George. 113: Alabama Department of Archives and History, Montgomery. 114: L. M. Strayer Collection, copied by Richard Baumgartner. 115: Library of Congress, Waud #230. 116: L. M. Strayer Collection. 118: MASS-MOLLUS/ USAMHI, copied by A. Pierce Bounds. 119: Ray Zielin Collection, copied by Richard Baumgartner—Roger Davis Collection, copied by Richard Baumgartner. 121: Courtesy Illinois State Historical Library, Springfield, copied by Richard Baumgartner. 122, 123: MASS-MOLLUS/USAMHI, copied by A. Pierce Bounds. 124: John Sickles Collection at the USAMHI, copied by A. Pierce Bounds. 125: Ross County Historical Society, Chillicothe, Ohio, copied by L. M . Strayer. 127: Frank and Marie-Thérèse Wood Print Collections, Alexandria, Va.—Donald G. Enders Collection at the USAMHI, copied by A. Pierce Bounds. 128: State Historical Society of Wisconsin, Madison. 130: Rare Book, Manuscript, and Special Collections Library, Duke University, Durham, N.C. 131: Museum of the Confederacy, Richmond, photographed by Katherine Wetzel. 132: Courtesy George C. Esker III, copied by Richard Baumgartner. 134: L. M. Strayer Collection—Frank and Marie-Thérèse Wood Print Collections, Alexandria, Va. 135: From *Confederate Veteran*, Vol. XI, No. 10, October 1903, copied by Philip Brandt George; Confederate Memorial Hall, photographed by Larry Sherer. 136, 137: From *Confederate Veteran*, Vol. X, January 1902, copied by Richard Baumgartner; MASS-MOLLUS/ USAMHI, copied by A. Pierce Bounds (2). 138: Alabama Department of Archives and History, Montgomery. 139: From *Soldiers True*, by John Richards Boyle, Eaton & Mains, New York, 1903, copied by Philip Brandt George. 141: American Documentaries, Walpole, N.H. 142: Courtesy Richard F. Carlile. 146: Courtesy Illinois State Historical Library, Springfield—Levi A. Ross Papers, Illinois State Historical Library, Springfield. 147: National Archives, Neg. No. 111-BA-90. 148: MASS-MOLLUS/ USAMHI, copied by Richard Baumgartner. 150: Library of Congress, Waud #80—P. D. Stephenson Papers, Louisiana and Lower Mississippi Valley Collections, LSU Libraries, Louisiana State University, Baton Rouge. 151: Museum of the Confederacy, Richmond. 152: Courtesy Brad Pruden, copied by Richard Baumgartner; Blue Acorn Press, Huntington, W.Va., copied by Richard Baumgartner. 154: Frank and Marie-Thérèse Wood Print Collections, Alexandria, Va. 155: Blue Acorn Press, Huntington, W.Va., copied by Richard Baumgartner; courtesy Richard F. Carlile; courtesy Ken Turner Collection, photographed by Chet Buquo. 156: From *Courageous Journey: The Civil War Journal of Laetitia Lafon Ashmore Nutt*, edited by Florence Ashmore Cowles Hamlett Martin, E. A. Seemann, Miami, Fla., 1975, copied by Philip Brandt George. 157: Blue Acorn Press, Huntington, W.Va., copied by Richard Baumgartner. 158,159: Courtesy E. Burns Apfeld, photographed by Bill Krueger.

# BIBLIOGRAPHY

## BOOKS


Alexander, E. P. *Military Memoirs of a Confederate*. Dayton: Morningside Bookshop, 1977 (reprint of 1907 ed.).

*Arms and Equipment of the Confederacy* (Echoes of Glory series). Alexandria, Va.: Time-Life Books, 1991.

*Arms and Equipment of the Union* (Echoes of Glory series). Alexandria, Va.: Time-Life Books, 1991.

Baumgartner, Richard A., and Larry M. Strayer. *Echoes of Battle: The Struggle for Chattanooga*. Huntington, W.Va.: Blue Acorn Press, 1996.

Boyle, John Richards. *Soldiers True: The Story of the One Hundred and Eleventh Regiment Pennsylvania Veteran Volunteers, and of Its Campaigns in the War for the Union, 1861-1865*. New York: Eaton & Mains, 1903.

Buck, Irving A. *Cleburne and His Command*. Dayton: Morningside House, 1982.

Bull, Rice C. *Soldiering: The Civil War Diary of Rice C. Bull, 123rd New York Volunteer Infantry*. Ed. by K. Jack Bauer. San Rafael, Calif.: Presidio Press, 1977.

Byers, S. H. M. *With Fire and Sword*. New York: Neale, 1911.

Coggins, Jack. *Arms and Equipment of the Civil War*. New York: Fairfax Press, 1983.

Coles, Robert T. *From Huntsville to Appomattox: R. T. Coles's History of 4th Regiment, Alabama Volunteer Infantry, C.S.A., Army of Northern Virginia*. Ed. by Jeffrey D. Stocker. Knoxville: University of Tennessee Press, 1996.

Collins, R. M. *Chapters from the Unwritten History of the War between the States*. Dayton: Morningside Bookshop, 1988.

Cozzens, Peter:

*The Battles for Chattanooga* (Civil War series). Conshohocken, Pa.: Eastern National Park & Monument Association, 1996.

*The Shipwreck of Their Hopes: The Battles for Chattanooga*. Urbana: University of Illinois Press, 1994.

Davis, William C., ed. *The Confederate General*, Vols. 1-6. Harrisburg, Pa.: National Historical Society, 1991.

Dawson, Francis W. *Reminiscences of Confederate Service: 1861-1865*. Ed. by Bell Irvin Wiley. Baton Rouge: Louisiana State University Press, 1980.

Downey, Fairfax. *Storming of the Gateway: Chattanooga, 1863*. New York: David McKay, 1960.

Grant, Ulysses S. *Personal Memoirs of U. S. Grant*. New York: AMS Press, 1972 (reprint of 1894 ed.).

Green, John W. *Johnny Green of the Orphan Brigade: The Journal of a Confederate Soldier*. Ed. by A. D. Kirwan. Lexington: University of Kentucky Press, 1956.

Greene, Albert R. "From Bridgeport to Ringgold by Way of Lookout Mountain." In *Personal Narratives of Events in the War of the Rebellion: Being Papers Read before the Rhode Island Soldiers and Sailors Historical Society*, Vol. 6. Wilmington, N.C.: Broadfoot, 1993 (reprint of 1890 ed.).

Hannaford, E. *The Story of a Regiment: A History of the Campaigns, and Associations in the Field, of the Sixth Regiment, Ohio Volunteer Infantry*. Cincinnati: private printing, 1868.

High, Edwin W. *History of the Sixty-Eighth Regiment, Indiana Volunteer Infantry, 1862-1865*. Metamora, Ind.: Sixty-Eighth Indiana Infantry Association, 1902.

House, Ellen Renshaw. *A Very Violent Rebel: The Civil War Diary of Ellen Renshaw House*. Ed. by Daniel E. Sutherland. Knoxville: University of Tennessee Press, 1996.

*Illustrated Atlas of the Civil War* (Echoes of Glory series). Alexandria, Va.: Time-Life Books, 1991.

Inzer, John Washington. *The Diary of a Confederate Soldier: John Washington Inzer, 1834-1928*. Ed. by Mattie Lou Teague Crow. Huntsville, Ala.: Strode Publishers, 1977.

Johnson, Clifton, comp. *Battleground Adventures.* Boston: Houghton Mifflin, 1915.
Jones, Jenkin Lloyd. *An Artilleryman's Diary.* Madison: Wisconsin History Commission, 1914.
Korn, Jerry, and the Editors of Time-Life Books. *The Fight for Chattanooga: Chickamauga to Missionary Ridge* (The Civil War series). Alexandria, Va.: Time-Life Books, 1985.
Lewis, G. W. *The Campaigns of the 124th Regiment, Ohio Volunteer Infantry, with Roster and Roll of Honor.* Akron: Werner, 1894.
Long, E. B. *The Civil War Day by Day: An Almanac, 1861–1865.* Garden City, N.Y.: Doubleday, 1971.
Longstreet, James. *From Manassas to Appomattox: Memoirs of the Civil War in America.* Ed. by James I. Robertson Jr. Millwood, N.Y.: Kraus Reprint, 1981.
McClendon, William A. *Recollections of War Times.* Montgomery, Ala.: Paragon Press, 1909.
McDonough, James Lee. *Chattanooga: A Death Grip on the Confederacy.* Knoxville: University of Tennessee Press, 1984.
McNeil, Samuel A. *Personal Recollections of Service in the Army of the Cumberland and Sherman's Army: From August 17, 1861 to July 20, 1865.* Richwood, Ohio: private printing, 1909.
Manigault, Arthur Middleton. *A Carolinian Goes to War: The Civil War Narrative of Arthur Middleton Manigault, Brigadier General, C.S.A.* Ed. by R. Lockwood Tower. Columbia: University of South Carolina Press, 1983.
Morgan, William A.:
"Brown's Ferry." In *War Talks in Kansas: A Series of Papers Read before the Kansas Commandery of the Military Order of the Loyal Legion of the United States.* Wilmington, N.C.: Broadfoot, 1992 (reprint of 1906 ed.).
"Hazen's Brigade at Missionary Ridge." In *War Talks in Kansas: A Series of Papers Read before the Kansas Commandery of the Military Order of the Loyal Legion of the United States.* Wilmington, N.C.: Broadfoot, 1992 (reprint of 1906 ed.).
Mosman, Chesley A. *The Rough Side of War: The Civil War Journal of Chesley A. Mosman, 1st Lieutenant, Company D, 59th Illinois Volunteer Infantry Regiment.* Ed. by Arnold Gates. Garden City, N.Y.: Basin, 1987.
National Gallery of Art. *The Civil War: A Centennial Exhibition of Eyewitness Drawings.* Washington, D.C.: Smithsonian Institution, 1961.
Nutt, Laetitia Lafon Ashmore. *Courageous Journey: The Civil War Journal of Laetitia Lafon Ashmore Nutt.* Ed. by Florence Ashmore Cowles Hamlett Martin. Miami, Fla.: E. A. Seemann, 1975.
Pirtle, Alfred. "Three Memorable Days—A Letter from Chattanooga, November, 1863." In *Sketches of War History: 1861–1865,* Vol. 6. Ed. by Theodore F. Allen, Edward S. McKee, and J. Gordon Taylor. Wilmington, N.C.: Broadfoot, 1992 (reprint of 1908 ed.).
Polley, Joseph B. *Hood's Texas Brigade: Its Marches, Its Battles, Its Achievements.* New York: Neale, 1910.
Seymour, Digby Gordon. *Divided Loyalties: Fort Sanders and the Civil War in East Tennessee.* Knoxville: University of Tennessee Press, 1963.
Shellenberger, John K. "With Sheridan's Division at Missionary Ridge." In *Sketches of War History: 1861–1865,* Vol. 4. Ed. by W. H. Chamberlin. Wilmington, N.C.: Broadfoot, 1991 (reprint of 1896 ed.).
Sherman, William Tecumseh. *Memoirs of General William T. Sherman: By Himself.* Bloomington: Indiana University Press, 1957.
Sorrel, G. Moxley. *Recollections of a Confederate Staff Officer.* Dayton: Morningside Bookshop, 1978.
Stephenson, Philip Daingerfield. *The Civil War Memoir of Philip Daingerfield Stephenson, D. D.* Ed. by Nathaniel Cheairs Hughes Jr. Conway, Ark.: UCA Press, 1995.
Sword, Wiley. *Mountains Touched with Fire: Chattanooga Besieged, 1863.* New York: St. Martin's Press, 1995 (reprint of 1863 ed.).
Todd, William. *The Seventy-Ninth Highlanders, New York Volunteers, in the War of Rebellion, 1861–1865.* Albany, N.Y.: Press of Brandow, Barton & Co., 1886.
Tourgée, Albion W. *The Story of a Thousand.* Buffalo: S. McGerald & Son, 1896.
Underwood, Adin B. *The Three Years' Service of the Thirty-Third Mass. Infantry Regiment, 1862–1865.* Boston: A. Williams, 1881.
United States War Department. *The War of the Rebellion: A Compilation of the Official Records of the Union and Confederate Armies.* Series 1, Vol. 31, Parts 1-3. Washington, D.C.: Government Printing Office, 1890.
Warner, Ezra J.:
*Generals in Blue: Lives of the Union Commanders.* Baton Rouge: Louisiana State University Press, 1964.
*Generals in Gray: Lives of the Confederate Commanders.* Baton Rouge: Louisiana State University Press, 1959.
Watkins, Sam R. *"Co. Aytch": A Side Show of the Big Show.* New York: Collier Books, 1962.
Willison, Charles A. *Reminiscences of a Boy's Service with the 76th Ohio.* Huntington, W.Va.: Blue Acorn Press, 1995 (reprint of 1908 ed.).
Wood, Thomas J. "The Battle of Missionary Ridge." In *Sketches of War History, 1861–1865: Papers Prepared for the Ohio Commandery of the Military Order of the Loyal Legion of the United States, 1890–1896,* Vol. 4. Ed. by W. H. Chamberlin. Wilmington, N.C.: Broadfoot, 1991 (reprint of 1896 ed.).
Woodward, Philip Grenville. "The Siege of Knoxville." In *Glimpses of the Nation's Struggle.* Wilmington, N.C.: Broadfoot, 1992 (reprint of 1903 ed.).

## PERIODICALS

"B. L. T." "With the Wagon Train: Reminiscences of the Chattanooga Campaign." *National Tribune* (Washington, D.C.), December 27, 1900.
"Comal Bluff." "The Battle on the Extreme Right." *Memphis Daily Appeal,* December 8, 1863.
Dines, Philip. "The Cracker Line." *National Tribune* (Washington, D.C.), April 30, 1885.
Jarman, Robert A. "The History of Company K, 27th Mississippi Infantry." *Aberdeen Examiner,* March 7, 1890.
Johnson, Wiley G. "Charge on Fort Sanders at Knoxville." *Confederate Veteran,* Vol. 11, November 1893.
Kephart, William G. "The Recent Battles of Chattanooga." *The Hawk-eye* (Burlington, Iowa), December 8, 1863.
Mansur, John H. Letter to the Editor. *National Tribune* (Washington, D.C.), April 8, 1866.
Walton, Charles W. "Siege of Knoxville." *National Tribune* (Washington, D.C.), April 17, 1884.
Welsh, Asbury. "Up the Ridge." *National Tribune* (Washington, D.C.), June 28, 1900.
Wright, James W. A. "Bragg's Campaign around Chattanooga." *Southern Bivouac,* January 1887.

## OTHER SOURCES

Bolton, William J. Journal, n.d. Philadelphia: Civil War Library and Museum.
Jernigan, Albert J. Letter, n.d., from the Jernigan Papers. Austin: University of Texas, American History Research Center.
Lowrey, Mark P. Autobiography, n.d. Carlisle Barracks, Pa.: U.S. Army Military History Institute.
Metcalf, George Perry. Reminiscences, n.d. Columbus: Ohio Historical Society.
Myers, Robert Pooler. Diary, n.d., from Robert Pooler Myers Papers. Richmond: Museum of the Confederacy.
Neal, Andrew Jackson. Letters, November 25, 26, 1863. Kennesaw, Ga.: Kennesaw Mountain National Battlefield Park.
Wagner, Levi. "Recollections of an Enlistee, 1861-1864." Unpublished manuscript, from *Civil War Times Illustrated* collection. Carlisle Barracks, Pa.: U.S. Army Military History Institute.
Watson, Robert. Letter, n.d. Fort Oglethorpe, Ga.: Chickamauga and Chattanooga National Military Park.
Werts, Andrew Alexander. Memoirs, n.d., from the Ann Ella Mitchell Adams Family Papers. Orangeburg, S.C.

# INDEX

*Numerals in italics indicate an illustration of the subject mentioned.*


## A

Alexander, E. Porter: *60;* account by, 60-61
Anderson road: *22*
Anderson's Crossroads, Tennessee: 10
Anonymous accounts: Confederate defense at Tunnel Hill, 120; Confederate retreat from Smith's Hill, 46; Union supply trains, 25-26
Army of Tennessee: dissension of general officers in, 12, 23, 24, 49, 73; drum, *69;* fraternization, 13, 19, 74; low rations in, 74; morale in, 25; order of battle, 15; reorganization of, 12; sharpshooters, 27, 100
Army of the Cumberland: camp life (18th Ohio), *33;* forage cap (105th Ohio), *86;* fraternization, 13, 19; morale in, 71, 72, 77, 87, 127; order of battle, 15; regimental insignia pin, *155;* skirmish drill, *123*
Army of the Ohio: 13
Army of the Potomac: corps badges, 78, *79*
Army of the Tennessee: corps badges, 78, *79;* Grant's confidence in, 71; irregular appearance of, 76; order of battle, 15
Atlanta, Georgia: 145, 159

## B

B. L. T.: account by, 25-26
Babcock, Orville E.: *60*
Baird, Absalom: 110, 111, 131
Barnard, George N.: 85
Battle above the Clouds: 89, 104. *See also* Lookout Mountain, Battle of
Beatty, John: 12
Beatty, Samuel: 122, 133, 134
Beaumont, Esau: account by, 22
Beeson, James: *152*
Berry, James: *65*
Billy Goat Hill: 88, 89, 91, 112
Bolton, William J.: *54,* 65; account by, 54-55
Bowen, Rodney: 77
Boyle, John R.: *97;* account by, 97, 139, 153-154
Bradley, Joseph: 108, *109*
Bragg, Braxton: 9, 10, 11, 12, 14, 23, 24, 25, 30, 39, 49, 50, 51, 68, 69, 71, 72, 73, 85, 88, 89, 94, 107, 110, 111, 132, 135, 136, 137, 139, 140, 141, 143, 144, 145, 146, 156; report by, 157
Brandley, Arnold: account by, 35-36
Bratton, John: 31, 41, 42
Breckinridge, John C.: 12, 88, 110, 137, 138
Bridgeport, Alabama: 10, 29, 30, 46, 71, 72, 76, 159; railroad bridge at, *78*
Brown's Ferry: *map* 6-7, 30, *map* 31, 32, 33, 39, 43, 71, 72, 73; Federal seizure of, 34-*35,* 36-38, 46; pontoon boats at, *35;* pontoon bridge at, *38,* 72
Buck, Irving A.: *23;* account by, 23
Buckner, Simon Bolivar: 12, 23, 49, 53, 72
Bull, Rice C.: *76;* account by, 76
Burnside, Ambrose E.: 9, 13, 14, 49, 50, 51, 52, 53, 55, 59, 68, 73, 144, 157
Byers, Samuel H. M.: account by, 118-119

## C

Cameron, James: 58
Campbell's Station: action at, 50, 54-55, 56
Cedar Hill: 83
Chalaron, Joseph A.: 133, *135;* account by, 135
Chalmers, James R.: 74, 75, *76*
*Chattanooga* (steamer): *47*
Chattanooga, Tennessee: *panoramic map* 6-7, *8, map* 14, 50, 71, 99, 144, *map* 146; Army of the Tennessee leaving for 1864 spring offensive, *158-159;* battleground at, *map* 73; civilians in, 11; Federal offensive moves in, 71-72, 77; picket lines at, *20;* siege raised, 139; strategic importance of, 9, 11, 145, 157, 159; supply lines for, 10, 13, 21, *22,* 25-26, *27,* 29, 30-31, 32, 46-47, 74, 78; under siege, 10-13, 16, 17-22, 28, 49, 73; Union armies establish winter quarters in, 145, 157, 159; Union camps at, *26*
Chattanooga & Cleveland Railroad: 93
Chattanooga campaign: *map* 14; casualties, 145; chronology, 13; Confederate retreat, 139, 140, 141, 143, 146-150
Chattanooga Creek: 110, 137, 139
Chattanooga Valley: 72, 88
Cheatham, Benjamin F.: 12, 23, *147*
Chickamauga, Battle of: 9-10, 11, 71, 146
Chickamauga Station: 72, 73, 88, 141, 143, 146, 148, 149
Cleburne, Patrick R.: 23, 72, 73, 88, 93, 94, 110, 111, *113,* 115, 116, 118, 120, 140, 143, 150, 151, 152, 156
Cobham, George A., Jr.: 97, *139*
Coles, Robert T.: *56;* account by, 27, 56-57
Collins, Robert M.: account by, 20, 94, 113, 140
Colquitt, John W.: 152
"Comal Bluff": account by, 120
Corput, Max Van Den: account by, 101-102
Corse, John A.: 110, 112, 113, *114,* 116, 121
Cracker Line: 13, 29, 30-31, 32, 46, 47, 71, 74, 119
Crane, Orrin J.: *155*
Cravens house: 89, 97, 98, 99, 100, *102;* fighting at, *101,* 102, 103, 105, 106
Creighton, William: 153, 154, 155
Crittenden, Thomas L.: 11
Cruft, Charles: 88, 139
Cumberland Gap: 14, 50, 51

## D

Dana, Charles A.: 11, 121
Davis, Frederick: corps badge of, *79*
Davis, Harris: 108, *109*
Davis, Jefferson: 12, 23, 24, 49, 50, 145, 157
Davis, Jefferson C.: 72
Davis, Theodore: 127, 154
Dawson, Francis W.: *59;* account by, 59, 68
Dean, Henry S.: *79;* account by, 79
Deas, Zachariah C.: 130, 136
Dines, Philip: account by, 33-34
Dinkins, James: account by, 75-76
Dodge, Grenville M.: 71
Dowd, William F.: account by, 98
Dunne, James: 65
Dyer, John W.: account by, 149

## E

East Chickamauga Creek: 143
East Tennessee & Georgia Railroad: 49-50
Emancipation Proclamation: 11
Ewing, Charles: 75

## F

Fielder, Alfred T.: account by, 130
Flags: 18th Alabama Infantry, *138;* 16th Georgia Infantry, *66;* Marion (Florida) Light Artillery, *131;* 76th Ohio Infantry, *142;* Washington Artillery (5th Co.), *135*
Forrest, Nathan Bedford: 9, 10, 74, 76
Fort Sanders: *48, map* 51, 57, 58, 59, *60,* 144; attack on, 50, 60-*61,* 62-63, *64,* 65-67, *68*
Foster, Samuel T.: account by, 114-115
Fullerton, Joseph S.: 85, *127;* account by, 127-128

## G

Galloway, John D.: 22
Geary, Edward: *42*
Geary, John W.: 30, 31, 39, 40, 41, *42,* 88, 89, 94, 95, 101, 139, 155
Gettysburg, Battle of, 9, 11
Gist, William M.: *58*
Granger, Gordon: 121, *122, 125,* 127, 132, 144, 157
Grant, Ulysses S.: 13, 14, 28, *29,* 30, 31, 49, 50, 69, 71, 72, 73, 74, 80, 86, 88, 110, 111, 124, 126, 127, 137, 139, 143-144, 145, 157, 159; account by, 29
Graysville, Georgia: 148; action at, 143, 149
Green, John W.: *25;* account by, 25, 148

Greene, Albert R.: account by, 41, 103-105
Greene, George S.: *41*
Griffin, Daniel F.: *148;* account by, 148
Grose, William: 123

# H

Halleck, Henry W.: 71, 111, 144
Hamm, John: *116*
Hardee, William J.: 12, 88, 111, 116, 145, *157*
Harker, Charles G.: 111, *125*
*Harper's Weekly:* 44, 81, 127, 154; page from, *52*
Hart, Albert G.: account by, 37-38
Hazen, William B.: 30, *32*, 33, 36, 80, 82, 122; account by, 32
Hemming, Charles C.: account by, 122
Hight, John J.: *124;* account by, 124-125
Hill, Daniel Harvey: 12, 23
Hindman, Thomas C.: 12
Holston River: *56-57*
Holtzclaw, James T.: 107, 138
Hooker, Joseph: 11, 14, 18, 30, 39, 42, 43, 46, 71, 72, 73, 88, 89, 94, 95, *96, 104,* 105, 110, 111, 137, 138, 139, 140, 143, 152
Horrall, Spillard F.: *19;* account by, 19
House, Ellen Renshaw: *53;* account by, 53
Howard, Oliver O.: 11, 30, 31, 72
Humphreys, Benjamin G.: *62,* 63
Huntzinger, William H.: account by, 133

# I

Inzer, John W.: account by, 138

# J

Jackson, John: 98, 131
Jaquess, James: 128
Jarman, Robert A.: *74,* 103; account by, 74
Jenkins, Micah: 31, 49, 55, 56
Jenney, William L.: account by, 74-75
Jernigan, Albert: account by, 117
Johnson, Richard W.: 110, 111
Johnson, Wiley G.: account by, 63-64
Johnston, Joseph E.: 12, 157
Jones, Jenkin L.: *92;* account by, 92
Jordan, William C.: account by, 34-35
Josselyn, Simeon T.: 138

# K

Kane, Pat: 113
Kelley's Ferry: *map* 6-7, 30, 31; Federal supply steamer at, *47*
Kennedy, James B.: account by, 63
Kephart, William G.: account by, 91
Kershaw, Joseph B.: 62
Kibler, Charles H.: account by, 152-153
Knefler, Frederick: 133, *134*
Knoxville, Tennessee: 9, 11, 14, 49, 50, 54, *56-57,* 72, 73, 144, 157; Federal fortifications at, *48, map* 51, *56-57, 60;* Federal occupation of, *52,* 53; Federal withdrawal to, *55;* pro-Union sentiment in, 50, 51, *52*
Kountz, John S.: *90:* account by, 90, 116
Krieger, Ernst J.: *155;* account by, 155
Kyger, Tilmon D.: account by, 128-129

# L

Law, Evander M.: 27, 31, *34,* 35, 43
LeDuc, William G.: *46;* account by, 46-47
Lee, Robert E.: 9, 145
Lenoir's Station: action at, 50, 54, 56
Lewis, George W.: *83;* account by, 83
Lewis, Richard: account by, 39-40
Lightburn, Joseph A. J.: 90, 110, *112*
Lincoln, Abraham: 9, 11, 12, 13, 14, 144, 145
Linn, Royan M.: 109
Logan, John: 78
Longstreet, James: 9, 10, 11, 12, 23, 27, 30, 31, *39,* 49, 50, 51, 53, 55, 56, 61, 62, 66, 67, 68, 69, 71, 73, 88, 144; account by, 39
Lookout Creek: 37, 88, *map* 89, 94, 100: Federal troops preparing bridge at, *95*
Lookout Mountain: *map* 6-7, *8,* 10, *17, 26,* 30, 33, *35,* 36, 37, *38,* 39, 71, 72, *map* 73, 74, 77, 87, 90, *102,* 139; Bench road, *99,* 100, *101;* Confederate fortifications at, *18;* Union flag raised at, *108, 109*
Lookout Mountain, Battle of: 88-89, *map* 89, 94-100, *101,* 102-103, *104,* 105-107; Hooker and staff at, *96, 104*
Lookout Valley: 32, 72, 99, 100
Loomis, John M.: 110
Louisville, Kentucky: 13
Lowrey, Mark P.: *151;* account by, 151-152
Lucas, Elisha C.: account by, 100

# M

MacArthur, Arthur, Jr.: *128*
McClelland, Samuel: insignia pin of, *155*
McClendon, William A.: account by, 36-37, 66-67
McCook, Alexander M.: 11
Mackall, William W.: *24;* account by, 24
McLaws, Lafayette: 49, 50, 55, 56
McNeil, Samuel A.: account by, 129
Manigault, Arthur M.: *16,* 136; account by, 16, 77, 83-85
Mansur, John H.: account by, 57-58
Mathews, Alfred E.: 130
Matthies, Charles Leopold: 92, 93, *119*
Medals of Honor: 116, 128
Meigs, M. C.: 121
Memphis & Charleston Railroad: 10, 11, 71
*Memphis Daily Appeal:* 120
Metcalf, George P.: account by, 45-46, 86
Metzner, Adolph: 17, 159
Military Division of the Mississippi: 13; order of battle, 15
Missionary Ridge: *map* 6-7, 10, *17,* 72, *map* 73, 77, 79, 87, 88, 89, 148
Missionary Ridge, Battle of: 69, *70,* 81, 110-111, *map* 111, *122,* 123-126, *127,* 128-129, *130,* 131-133, *134,* 135-141
Moccasin Point: *map* 6-7, *8,* 17, 30, 33, *35,* 77, 99, 100, 102, 106, 107; batteries at, 106, 107
Monat, David: account by, 42, 95-96
Montgomery, William C.: *142*
Moore, John C.: 89, *98;* account by, 98-100
Morgan, William A.: account by, 124
Mosman, Chesley A.: *103;* account by, 103
Muenscher, Emory W.: account by, 112
Myers, Robert P.: account by, 68-69

# N

Nashville, Tennessee: 10, 129, 145
Nashville & Chattanooga Railroad: 10, 42, 78
Nast, Thomas: 68
Neal, Andrew J.: account by, 131
*New York Herald:* 11
North Chickamauga Creek: 88, 90
Nutt, Laetitia Lafon Ashmore: *156;* account by, 156
Nutt, LeRoy Moncure: 156

# O

Oates, William C.: 30, *37*
Orchard Knob: *map* 6-7, *84-85,* 87, 110, 124; Grant and general officers at, 121, *122*
Orchard Knob, Battle of: 72-73, 80, *81,* 82-86
Orendorff, Henry H.: account by, 120-121
Osterhaus, Peter J.: 72, 88, 89, 139

# P

Patton, Joseph T.: *82;* account by, 82
Pettus, Edmund W.: 89
Phelps, Edward: 130
Pirtle, Alfred: *107;* account by, 107
Poe, Orlando M.: *60*
Polk, Leonidas: 12, 23
Polk, Lucius E.: 151, 152

Polley, Joseph B.: account by, 69
Powell, Eugene: *94;* account by, 94-95

## R

Raccoon Mountain: *map* 6-7, 10, 27, 30, 31, *158-159*
Reeks, Austin J.: 59
Reynolds, A. W.: 135
Rickards, William: 42
Ringgold, Georgia: 143, 150, 151, 153, 156
Ringgold Gap: *150:* rearguard action at, 143, 150-153, *154,* 155, 156, 159
Robertson, Jerome B.: 31, 43
Rosecrans, William S.: 9, 10, 11-12, 13, 14, 28, 32
Ross, Levi A.: *146;* account by, 146-147; map sketched by, *146*
Rossville Gap: *map* 6-7, 72, 88, 110, *136-137,* 138, 139, 143

## S

Sanders, William P.: 50, 58
Schmidt, William: 116
Schurz, Carl: 30
Sequatchie Valley: 10
Shanks, W. F. G.: 11
Shellenberger, John K.: *87;* account by, 87
Sheridan, Philip H.: 71, 72, 87, 110, 111, *125,* 127, 128, 132, 146
Sherman, William Tecumseh: 11, 14, 31, 49, 71, 72, 73, 74, 75, 76, *77,* 79, 88, 89, 90, 91, 92, 93, 96, 110, 111, 112, 116, 140, 143, 144, 145, 159; account by, 77-78, 157
Sherman, Willy: 77
Simmons, John W.: account by, 106
Slocomb, Cuthbert H.: *132,* 135; account by, 132-133
Slocum, Henry W.: 11
Smith, Benjamin T.: account by, 132
Smith, James A.: 94, 110, 113, 117, 120
Smith, Miles: 46
Smith, Orlando: *44*
Smith, William F.: 29, 30, 31, *32,* 72, 77, 92
Smith's Hill: action at, 43-*44,* 45-46
Sorrel, G. Moxley: *53;* account by, 53-54
South Chickamauga Creek: 88, 90, 110
Stanton, Edwin M.: 11, 13, 144
Stauffer, Nelson: *119;* account by, 119-120
Steinwehr, Adolph von: 30, 45
Stephenson, Philip D.: *150:* account by, 150
Stevenson, Alabama: 10; Federal supply dump at, *28*
Stevenson, Carter L.: 88-89, 110, 111
Sturgis, H. Howard: account by, 43
Sweetwater, Tennessee: 50, 53, 54

## T

Taylor's Ridge: *150,* 152; fighting at, 153-*154,* 155. *See also* Ringgold Gap
Tennessee River: *map* 6-7, *8,* 9, 10, 11, 17, *27,* 30, *map* 31, 71, *map* 73, 88, *map* 89, *99, 158-159;* Federal supply steamers on, *47;* Federal troop movements across, 32-34, *35,* 36-38, 91, 92, *158-159;* pontoon bridges on, *38,* 79, 88, 92; railroad bridge at Bridgeport, *78*
Thain, Alexander R.: account by, 17-18
Thomas, George H.: 10, 13, 14, 28, 72, 73, 77, 79, 105, 110, 111, 121, *122,* 126, 127, 140, 143, 144
Thulstrup, Thure de: 122
Todd, George T.: account by, 18-19
Todd, William: account by, 58, 65
Tourgée, Albion W.: *21,* 86; account by, 21, 85-86, 105
Travis, William D. T.: 35, 43
Tunnel Hill: *map* 6-7, *91,* 94, 111, 140; action at, 88, 110, *map* 111, 112-114, *115,* 116-121; railroad tunnel at, *93, 118*
Turchin, John B.: 30, 33, 35, 130
Turner, James J.: *136;* account by, 136-137

## U

Underwood, Adin B.: account by, 28, 44-45

## V

Vaughan, Alfred: 130
Vaughan, Turner: 27
Vicksburg, Battle of: 9, 11

## W

Wagers, Joseph: 108, *109*
Walcutt, Charles C.: 115; account by, 113-114
Walden's Ridge: 10, *22,* 30
Walker, Thomas J.: account by, 147
Walker, William H. T.: 73, 156
Walthall, Edward C.: 89, 95, 98, 99, 100, *106*
Walton, Charles W.: account by, 67
Warner, Willard: *152,* 153
Washington, D.C.: 60
Watkins, Sam: *141;* account by, 141, 156
Watson, Robert: account by, 125-126
Waud, Alfred R.: 93, 115, 150
Wauhatchie, Battle of: 31, 39-*40,* 41-42, *43,* 73
Wauhatchie, Tennessee: 30, 31, 43, 88
Welsh, Asbury: account by, 126
Werts, Andrew A.: *62;* account by, 62
Western & Atlantic Railroad: 143, 150
Wheeler, Joseph: 10-11, 49
Whitaker, Walter C.: 88, 108
Wiley, Aquila: 37
Willich, August: *26,* 80, 82, 122, 126
Willison, Asias: *121*
Willison, Charles A.: account by, 159
Wilson, John: *108, 109;* account by, 108-109
Witt, William: 108, *109*
Wofford, William T.: *62*
Wood, James: 108, *109*
Wood, Thomas J.: 10, 72, *80,* 86, 110, 111, 128; account by, 80, 121-122
Woodson, Henry: 98
Woodward, Philip G.: account by, 59-60
Wright, James W. A.: account by, 107

## Y

Young, James: 75

TIME® LIFE BOOKS Time-Life Books is a division of Time Life Inc.

TIME LIFE INC.
PRESIDENT and CEO: George Artandi

TIME-LIFE BOOKS
PRESIDENT: Stephen R. Frary
PUBLISHER/MANAGING EDITOR: Neil Kagan

VOICES OF THE CIVIL WAR

DIRECTOR OF MARKETING: Pamela R. Farrell

# CHATTANOOGA

EDITOR: Paul Mathless
*Deputy Editors:* Philip Brandt George (principal), Harris J. Andrews, Kirk Denkler
*Design Director:* Barbara M. Sheppard
*Art Director:* Ellen L. Pattisall
*Associate Editor/Research and Writing:* Gemma Slack
*Senior Copyeditor:* Judith Klein
*Picture Coordinator:* Lisa Groseclose
*Editorial Assistant:* Christine Higgins

*Initial Series Design:* Studio A

*Special Contributors:* John Newton, Dana B. Shoaf (text); Connie Contreras, Charles F. Cooney, Robert Lee Hodge, Susan V. Kelly, Beth Levin, Henry Mintz, Dana B. Shoaf (research); Roy Nanovic (index).

*Correspondent:* Christina Lieberman (New York).

*Director of Finance:* Christopher Hearing
*Directors of Book Production:* Marjann Caldwell, Patricia Pascale
*Director of Publishing Technology:* Betsi McGrath
*Director of Photography and Research:* John Conrad Weiser
*Director of Editorial Administration:* Barbara Levitt
*Production Manager:* Marlene Zack
*Quality Assurance Manager:* James King
*Chief Librarian:* Louise D. Forstall

*Consultants*
Richard A. Baumgartner, a former newspaper and magazine editor, has written, edited, or published 16 books dealing with Civil War and World War I history, including *Blue Lightning: Wilder's Mounted Infantry Brigade in the Battle of Chickamauga.* A longtime student of the Civil War's western theater, he served as editor of *Blood & Sacrifice: The Civil War Journal of a Confederate Soldier* and coedited *Yankee Tigers* and two volumes in the award-winning Echoes of Battle series: *The Atlanta Campaign* and *The Struggle for Chattanooga.* He has written numerous articles focusing on the experiences of the common soldier for several military-history journals.

Larry M. Strayer, an editor with Blue Acorn Press, has written or contributed to more than a dozen titles on the war's western theater, including *Yankee Tigers* and the award-winning Echoes of Battle volumes on the Atlanta and Chattanooga campaigns. Well known in living-history circles, he currently serves as adviser for Accuracy Historical Productions. His next publication will photographically chronicle Ohio's involvement in the Civil War, focusing on the common soldier.


First printing. Printed in U.S.A.
School and library distribution by Time-Life Education, P.O. Box 85026, Richmond, Virginia 23285-5026.



Library of Congress Cataloging-in-Publication Data
Chattanooga / by the editors of Time-Life Books.
p. cm.—(Voices of the Civil War)
Includes bibliographical references and index.
ISBN 0-7835-4716-1
1. Chattanooga (Tenn.), Battle of, 1863.
I. Time-Life Books. II. Series.
E475.97.C48 1998
973.7'359—dc21 97-43712
CIP